BUILDING NEW DEMOCRACIES:
ECONOMIC AND SOCIAL REFORM
IN BRAZIL, CHILE, AND MEXICO

In *Building New Democracies* Michel Duquette analyses the main public policies of Brazil, Chile, and Mexico to explore examples of how countries make
the transition from an authoritarian regime to a democratic society.

The main objective of the book is to follow the process of policy formation in
very young democracies. Duquette isolates the specific problems that surround
decision-making in a transitional government, showing how legislating structural change does not guarantee democratic success. He offers a general model
of domestic and international policy-making as a response to the problems of
achieving fundamental political reform. The effectiveness of public policies is
dependent on many factors, including competing ideologies, inexperienced
political leaders, rising political organizations, rule by coalition parties, and the
influence of local politicians and technocrats. It is with the alliance of grassroots organizations and autonomous institutions, Duquette believes, that social
and economic exclusion will be overcome on a national level. *Building New
Democracies* is primarily theoretical in its analysis, but integrates many recent
empirical findings from a wide body of international and Latin American
research, including the author's own field work.

The methodology Duquette employs is genuinely comparative and not
merely a juxtaposition of case studies. His approach and conclusions can be
applied to a number of disciplines, including political science, economics,
sociology, and Latin American studies.

(Studies in Comparative Political Economy and Public Policy)

MICHEL DUQUETTE is an associate professor in the Department of Political
Science, University of Montreal.

Studies in Comparative Political Economy and Public Policy

Editors: MICHAEL HOWLETT, DAVID LAYCOCK, STEPHEN MCBRIDE, Simon Fraser University

Studies in Comparative Political Economy and Public Policy is designed to showcase innovative approaches to political economy and public policy from a comparative perspective. While originating in Canada, the series will provide attractive offerings to a wide international audience, featuring studies with local, sub-national, cross-national, and international empirical bases and theoretical frameworks.

MICHEL DUQUETTE

Building New Democracies: Economic and Social Reform in Brazil, Chile, and Mexico

UNIVERSITY OF TORONTO PRESS
Toronto Buffalo London

© University of Toronto Press Incorporated 1999
Toronto Buffalo London
Printed in Canada

ISBN 0-8020-4402-6 (cloth)
ISBN 0-8020-8209-2 (paper)

∞

Printed on acid-free paper

Canadian Cataloguing in Publication Data

Duquette, Michel, 1947–
    Building new democracies : economic and social reform in Brazil, Chile,
    and Mexico

    (Studies in comparative political economy and public policy)
    Includes bibliographical references and index.
    ISBN 0-8020-4402-6 (bound)   ISBN 0-8020-8209-2 (pbk.)

    1. Brazil – Economic policy.   2. Brazil – Social policy.   3. Chile – Economic
    policy.   4. Chile – Social policy.   5. Mexico – Economic policy – 1970–1994.
    6. Mexico – Social policy.   7. Democracy – Brazil.   8. Democracy – Chile.
    9. Democracy – Mexico.   I. Title.   II. Series.

    HC187.D868 1998   338.981   C98-932367-6

This book has been published with the help of a grant from the Humanities and Social
Sciences Federation of Canada, using funds provided by the Social Sciences and
Humanities Research Council of Canada.

University of Toronto Press acknowledges the financial assistance to its publishing
program of the Canada Council for the Arts and the Ontario Arts Council.

To the beloved memory of Rose-Irène, my mother

Contents

Part III Determinants of Social Reforms

Preface

In undertaking the lengthy research project that served as the keystone to this book, I had first to overcome the perception that nothing significant could be added to the study of adjustment reforms in Latin America. In recent times, comparativists have made numerous valuable contributions to such a study. Adam Przeworski, Carlos Bresser Pereira, and Jorge Maravall have raised issues that I found particularly inspiring. I extend to them my sincere admiration, and hope that they show leniency towards this modest contribution. It seemed to me, however, that the area of study still held some interesting challenges. My conviction was that one could cover, in more depth and up to the present day, individual case countries, while enlarging the scope of comparative analysis to include analytical categories widely adopted by scholars throughout the discipline, yet not fully scrutinized. In the endeavour to merge the study of economic and social reforms into a framework that would give a defining role equally to domestic and to international actors and phenomena, I gathered data on two sets of factors usually treated in isolation from each other. I was supported in this work by many acquaintances and friends, in particular my colleagues and students from Université de Montréal. Among my colleagues, Professors Graciela Ducatenzeiler's and Philippe Faucher's extensive knowledge of the field made me understand how challenging it would be to break new ground in the study of the political economy of the Southern Cone. A close friend and collaborator, Professor Diane Éthier, shared many of my preoccupations and helped me in widening my knowledge of current theories. Our work together as a research team, sponsored by the Social Sciences and Humanities Research Council of Canada and le Fonds pour la Formation de Chercheurs et l'Aide à la Recherche (Fonds FCAR) between 1991 and 1995, was lively and stimulating. We exchanged ideas that sometimes came to challenge accepted views, even each other's. In all likelihood, this book would not have been possible without her support, as well as that of Professor Robert Packenham, of Stanford University, and of Professor Karen Remmer, of the University of New Mexico, who at one time or another, on panels of the American Political Science Association's annual meetings, became acquainted with my work. Professor Peter Evans, of the University of California, Berkeley, made insightful comments on a shorter, earlier version of this work that expounded my main hypotheses. His vast experience of research and close knowledge of the field had, without question, a profound impact on my own way of searching, thinking, and writing. Finally, to my colleague and friend Professor Jane Jenson, who showed much interest in my work and made it possible for me to reach its conclusion, I wish to express my sincere appreciation.

Research assistants gather around us to tackle intellectual challenges and then go on to pursue their own professional goals, but they are never forgotten. Sylvain Turcotte, Carlos Soldevila, and Marcos Ancelovici were present at the outset of this project and did more than collect data; they brought life, intuitions, and talent to this team. Later on, Emmanuelle Abescat, Daniel Charron, and Simon-Félix Laflamme either gathered statistical data or helped to update the material in this book. My special thanks go to Yannick Delancey Morin for her careful and competent work in translating Part Two of this work and, elsewhere in the text, turning my mediocre English into acceptable prose. What I count among the most important moments of my professional life is the privilege of having had many a close and rewarding encounter with a number of collaborators who contributed so much to make this project possible.

In addition, I am most grateful to Virgil Duff, Executive Editor, and Margaret Williams, Assistant Editor, at University of Toronto Press, and to the copyeditor, for their kind assistance in the final preparation of the manuscript.

Montreal, 17 June 1998

BUILDING NEW DEMOCRACIES

Introduction

From Dictatorship to Democracy and Liberalism

This essay joins the intense current debate issuing from a growing concern about the viability of new democracies, even as clouds gather in their skies. Whether in Russia or Peru, the use of force on the part of presidents of praetorian democracies brings to mind the methods of Bonapartism. Wily politicians such as the Russian nationalist Vladimir Zhirinovsky are strategically preying upon the frustration, resentment, and exhaustion of the majority. Ordinary people are disgusted by a tide of economic reforms which have benefited the few while deepening the daily hardship of the many. In President Carlos Carlos Menem's Argentina, constitutional manipulation is an open secret. Corruption as a general mode of government has undermined the credibility of political executives in Brazil, Venezuela, and even Spain, much on the Italian pattern. Social unrest and popular mobilization in Bolivia and Central America threaten to engulf the process of liberalization there. Some claim that the current program of economic reform in Mexico is the root cause of the aboriginal uprisings seen in rural Chiapas since early 1994. New democracies, especially in Latin America and eastern Europe, are surprisingly timid in terms of social reforms. Many analysts view the policies of these new democracies as barely distinguishable from those of their authoritarian predecessors. It is difficult to determine whether new democracies, faced with so many challenges at once, can ever lurch forward with a consistent reform agenda.

While most observers acknowledge that, in the previous fifteen years, liberal reforms have been undertaken by both authoritarian regimes and new democracies throughout Latin America, and that such reforms point to a general process of structural change, the question remains whether democracies can be distinguished from dictatorships in the way they commit themselves to the principle of reform. Are they eager to create the socio-economic conditions through which they can consolidate? If we look closely at the overall features of the environment in which reforms take place, is the process of structural change sufficiently profound in Latin America to put this commitment into perspective? Do new democracies fully extricate themselves from the influence of the political forces representative of the traditional order? Are they acting on their own when confronted with specific challenges? Finally, can we view the new conditions they create as sound enough to point towards a plausible process of democratic consolidation? If not, can we measure the progress of incipient regimes in the tightly related political, institutional, and social arenas?

Latin American authoritarian regimes have left peculiar memories in their wake. Some were patriotic and fixated on quantitative, sometimes lavish, expressions of development, with a clear preference for 'development in the name of national security' over human rights. Others were moralist and displayed strong ideological preferences. They were obsessed by ethical values of their own, which included the restoration of intangible, quasi-religious principles over what they believed were petty politics, of organic order over the confusion of democratic debate, of hierarchy over social mobility. In all cases, the authoritarian model cautiously avoided the representation of interests. As a large body of literature has shown, some preferred to rely on a coveted network of influence involving state bureaucrats and oligopolies. The Chilean regime was reluctant even to enter into arrangements of this type; a narrow team of visionaries, acting behind closed doors, designed and implemented all of Chilean public policy.

Sometimes, the authoritarian state was interventionist, although not in the Keynesian sense, acting as a planning agency for megaprojects and as a provider of subsidies and legal support to a broad clientele of entrepreneurs engaged in infrastructure projects. In Brazil, it yielded to economic nationalism, devoting itself to protectionism and screening foreign investment. It created local conditions which ensured the profitability of a local oligopolist industry possessed of a captive market. In Chile, autocracy went the other way, embracing liberal orthodoxy while displaying little interest in free-trade agreements and regional integration, and eventually creating the conditions for its withdrawal, in 1976, from the Pacto Andino.

In the case of Mexico and Brazil, a long-term industrial strategy was put forward in a manner consistent with nationalistic principles, and pursued with some success. In Argentina and Chile, however, no such strategy was even thought of, at least in the first years of the military regime, and this led to uncontrolled market exposure, ensuing partial deindustrialization, and economic stagnation. In all cases, economic development was an exclusive affair, and failed to tackle the growing number of social problems. Income-distribution patterns featured increasing distortions, which in turn stirred social unrest, cynicism, and mounting violence. The fabric of society was torn apart; individualism and corruption set in. Another feature common to these authoritarian regimes was that the allocation of power and resources was never a rational process involving open and continuing bargaining between the state apparatus and the representatives of social and economic groups. Authoritarianism invariably channelled influence and financial resources into the economy under an ideological tenet that favoured the presumed winners and despised the losers.

In this fashion, authoritarian governments create an illusion of continuity, naïvely interpreted as political stability. Most often they succumb to the temptation of using economic-policy instruments to achieve political ends, especially when faced with fundamental challenges to their rule. Many aging dictatorships managed to politicize otherwise credible development agencies and banks. They resorted increasingly to extensive executive interference in policy, disorganizing the state bureaucracy ever further. The PROALCOOL program in Brazil is highly illustrative of this tendency (Duquette, 1989), and contributed to a legacy of political and economic disorganization which slowed down structural adjustment efforts for many subsequent years (Haggard and Kaufman, 1992: 34).

Authoritarian regimes can be compared to authoritarian personalities; they thrive in narrow environments. Modern psychology has demonstrated that Hitler, Mussolini, and Franco, as individuals, were personal achievers who grew up in a grim period of military defeat, social disarray, political corruption, and national instability. The experiences of a life plagued with deprivation and personal frustration led them to project these sentiments onto the national level, giving rise to a world-view that found resonance among their impoverished countrymen. They constructed a personalist philosophy which advocated more discipline, more social cohesiveness, more political stability. They resorted to symbolic rituals of collective purification, persecuting specific categories of *personae non gratae*: Jews, Gypsies, Communists, and, naturally, democrats. The reason such individuals could seize power, and their regimes thrive, was that the conservative order from which they issued was itself in full decline, while the minimal conditions necessary for a democratic alternative were not yet in place. Dictators expected their authoritarian rule to save what could be saved of a waning grandeur. As we now know, this type of transitional rule was nothing but a palliative. It added only more frustration, social disarray, individualism, and political corruption to an already decadent order. On many occasions, it has also meant war and massive destruction of individuals and economic capacity. Specific conditions (Whitehead is quite eloquent on this point) made Latin America the last refuge of a much-diminished traditional order which disappeared almost fifty years ago from central Europe, and twenty years ago from the Iberian Peninsula (Whitehead, 1993: 1379ff).

To quote Maravall: 'new democracies usually inherit states that are too interventionist in the economy and too weak in social policies. Thus, paraphrasing a well-known political maxim, the state has to be transformed until it becomes as small as possible and as large as necessary' (Maravall, 1993: 78). Democracy in Latin America has to build its own house from decaying materials in the context of a discredited state. It must learn to run a society with very inexperienced new leaders. In the early period, it is bound to rely on illegitimate institutions, whose traditional features were elitist, clientelist, and socially insensitive. New democratic leaders have to convince local oligopolies that times have changed and that the state is their funding agency no more; the wealthy, that they ought to pay income tax; and unionized workers, that business is more than just a locus for a harsh class struggle against an all-mighty bourgeoisie, that a minimal level of agreement is achievable through institutions devoted to mediating conflict and forging compromises. Thus democracy has to rebuild hope, confidence, and proper behaviour from scraps. Then, and only then, can significant work be undertaken in the struggle against poverty, urban violence, and environmental abuse.

Public policies are not spontaneously generated. Political actors design them, and manifest preferences in relation to specific social, economic, and political philosophies. Policies can be designed behind closed doors, in the context of authoritarianism, or even by the self-proclaimed leaders of praetorian democracies; they can also be the outcome of open negotiations and institutionalized bargaining processes among politicians, technocrats, entrepreneurs, and organized labour. We do mean *bargaining*, and not consensus. If, in the first case, they are likely to reflect the particular interests or the ideological preferences of a tight network of decision makers or modern 'enlightened despots,' in the second, they will likely reveal a broad spectrum of opinions which, under favourable political conditions and presented with realistic compromises, will eventually coalesce.

Game theory, with its models of interaction between particular vested interests, can make a useful contribution to comparative analysis. Game theory is quite successful, for instance, in explaining how politicians can eventually counteract the influence of technocrats and of so-called technocratic rationality. It attempts to explain how reformers eventually succeed in imposing their own views over those of the conservatives, within the process of democratic transition; how entrepreneurs change their mind over what they can expect from state intervention and market opportunities; how an alliance of conservatives and the military meets its end, thus opening the path to a formal democracy; and how, consequently, new democratic coalitions can enjoy a measure of autonomy from the military and from the conservatives in defining new kinds of relationships between social groups (technocracy, entrepreneurs, labour organizations, and the poor), giving rise, in turn, to a new political environment which then contributes to strengthening their rule. Because they are the imprints of such phenomena, public policies are indicators of a changing political scene, where actors shift their respective positions in government as their influence gradually rises or declines. Democracy is clearly distinct from authoritarianism in this respect, because the former welcomes such moves, whereas the latter forbids them. Unlike authoritarianism, democracy proposes an accepted game, more cooperative than antagonistic, involving numerous players. The problem is that the rules are unclear, and not familiar to the majority. Furthermore, public-resource allocation is likely to follow the same unfamiliar pattern. Therefore, linkages among public representation, political pressures, and resource allocation seem paramount to the understanding of public action.

Institutional analysis focuses on the general framework which defines the rules of protest and the basis of the electoral process and, consequently, the changing behaviour of collective actors in transitional democracies. An impressive amount of comparative data gathered in the field of institutional research substantiates the view that collective action and community politics are closely related to the study of democratization. Since new actors ask for political and constitutional reforms, founding principles upon which the overall reshaping of society can take place must be stated, and public action must reflect those principles. Therefore, economic and social reforms and their sometimes idealistic definitions are hardly intelligible until translated and implemented into the field of public policy. Even under democratic conditions, there exists a distance between political representation in the daily exercise of citizenship and the allocation of resources by the state. In Przeworski's (1991) words, there is a distance between the blueprint of a policy and the same policy once fully implemented. Such is the case because transitional governments tend to preserve, for a time, the concentrated forms of executive power inherited from the authoritarian regime. Newly elected presidents retain substantial discretionary authority (Haggard, 1990). This corresponds to the meaning O'Donnell (1994) attributes to the term 'delegative democracy.' Once elected, the executive acts upon its own, mainly short-term, political interests, turning its back on promises made during the electoral campaign. Under such conditions, many groups remain incapable of exercising their rights and obligations (Przeworski, 1995: 34). As an alternative to delegative democracy, O'Donnell (1994) insists that citizenship can be exercised only when all individuals enjoy some social and economic prerequisites that will be reflected in their political participation. Only an effective state can generate the conditions that ensure the genuine practice of citizenship. Therefore, public policies, once implemented by democratic leaders, should offer interesting insights into the process of translating an inclusive political discourse into concrete action.

In contrast to the congenial institutionalist perspective predicated upon the universal practice of citizenship, interest-group analysis envisions public policy as a battlefield where diverging groups struggle around and within the state apparatus to shape different political-reform models, in accordance with their own particular interests. Resources allocated to given groups are necessarily withdrawn from others. Miles Kahler (1992: 89ff) opens an interesting debate here, suggesting intrinsic limitations to this approach. Interest groups, he argues, do not always identify where their interests lie in a particular political context, nor which policies are likely to match what they believe to be such interests. Subjectivism therefore weakens the relationship of policy choices to particular goals. What we can take as sure, however, is that the state apparatus (decision-making circles, technocrats) will seek support for this or that policy among other interest groups, as is clearly the case with privatization. But the relationship is not one-way, from the private to the public; it is bound to act both ways.

The main intention of this book is to examine economic reforms that bear social consequences. These reforms, in our view, are the indicators of the way in which minimal principles of democracy have been translated into practice. We may discover that many of these principles came into open conflict with others that retain some features of public policies and ruling practices pursued under the previous authoritarian regime. These also will be accounted for here, as a comparative basis for the understanding of democratic policies, from which, at first glance, they may not differ drastically. Hence, our basic ethical hypothesis is: if its policies are the same, how can a new political regime claim to be different from the previous one? We refuse to believe that, in the long term, two such different types of regimes will advocate and conduct identical policies.

Regimes do not necessarily differ in the goals they try to pursue: democratic reformers and authoritarian bureaucrats may, for instance, adhere to a common diagnosis of their country's economic situation: a growing and unbearable state deficit, an oversized public sector, institutionalized corruption, and a lack of industrial competitiveness. They may agree that these problems deserve special attention in the form of a strict budgetary policy, the privatization of deficit-producing public firms, public sanctions against corruption, market-friendly measures, and so on. Through diplomacy and through daily 'special' relationships with international agencies such as the International Monetary Fund (IMF) and the International Bank for Reconstruction and Development (IBRD; the World Bank), they receive constant advice from international actors, over whom they exert little influence. At times, such leverage can prove overwhelming.

While they may agree on a diagnosis, and perhaps even on appropriate solutions, reformers and autocrats nonetheless diverge in the way they design and implement these policies. As far as the representation of particular interests and a broad access to power are concerned, they belong to radically different political traditions. Democracies tend to build upon the recent past, gradually integrating concerns of their own which flow from a new and highly vocal system of representation. We acknowledge that, under these conditions, policy formation can be either swift and largely improvised, or a very gradual process. Either way, it will probably not mean generalized change from previous practices.

New democratic regimes are often made up of broad and poorly defined coalitions. Their leaders are supported by social groups which were shut out during the previous government, and all of these are calling for social justice and a decisive shift in public policy. New democracies, however, have very little room to manoeuvre. If they seek help and understanding from the Northern liberal democracies, they are frequently disappointed. South American leaders belong to an entirely different political culture from their North American counterparts. Generally speaking, international organizations and leaders of the developed countries display little knowledge of Latin American conditions. Presidents Reagan and Bush laid down conditions for bilateral aid which were based on their understanding of the intangible power of the state and the role of the market in consolidated democracies such as the United States, the United Kingdom, Germany, and France. These fully developed countries, at least by present-day standards, allow the market plenty of freedom to act as a creator of jobs and opportunities. In a fully developed market, the state is only one player among many. This is not quite the case with Latin America, where the market is poorly connected to an anaemic local demand, and state intervention is modest in scope, and therefore highly selective.

International funding agencies have usually advocated orthodox structural adjustment for Latin America. In time, the IMF came to see itself as a truly reformist institution, although we have strong doubts it was committed to social change anywhere, in the broader sense we attribute to the concept. The IMF began to engage in political activism; it astutely used the lever of debt to impose its will over the most indebted countries, because it expected to use Third World countries' experiments as a proof of its influence over international economic policy, to exhibit such experiments as precedents to be followed by reluctant First World countries facing public deficits, such as the United States,

Canada, and Sweden. In the 1980s, developing countries, especially those of Latin America, were to become the laboratory for the testing of genuine and often improvised reformist measures not pursued anywhere else. Along the same lines, Whitehead (1993: 1380–1) makes it plain that international factors were less than favourable to new Latin American democracies, whose priorities were, first, to survive the debt crisis; second, to respond to pressing social demands; and third, to act on their own as reformers of the economy and society – and to meet all of these challenges under very tight schedules.

It is becoming clear that, throughout this crucial period, the International Monetary Fund, along with other multinational agencies such as the World Bank, were playing sorcerer's apprentice. First, the IMF engineered 'monetary stabilization' packages while the World Bank supported long-term 'structural adjustment' plans; their rationale and theoretical justification came *ex post facto*, in a process of 'learning by doing.' Many authors, such as Helleiner (1986), go so far as to conclude that there exists no theoretical-analysis model of the transition from an import-substitution model to liberalism premised upon market equilibrium, particularly when that process includes determining an appropriate sequencing of structural reforms with regard to domestic conditions. Let us keep in mind that the extant economic literature does not offer an accepted model of structural change, only tentative propositions.

In that respect, the more stimulating hypotheses raised by Remmer (1990), Nelson (1990), Haggard and Kaufman (1992; 1995), and Bresser Pereira, Maravall, and Przeworski (1993) address the economics of democratic transition in Latin America on the basis of totally different assumptions. So do those of Thorp and Whitehead (1987), and Przeworski (1991), who offer, from a political-economy perspective, unconventional theoretical insights into the complex processes of democratic transition. In terms of economic theory, we are also using the valuable research conducted by the Chilean academics Foxley (1983) and Ramos (1986). These authors, who, interestingly enough, come from distinct intellectual traditions, offer a provocative basis for discussion. Whitehead and Przeworski were directly inspired by the works of the Woodrow Wilson Center's team project, in the mid-1980s, which focused on transitions from authoritarian rule in southern Europe and Latin America. This team, which included such respected academics as O'Donnell, Schmitter, Maravall, and Santamaria, among others, delivered an outstanding comparative theoretical model based upon the experience of a full set of transitions to democracy. This team's work has served as a keystone to subsequent contributions to the field.

Latin American researchers were at first reluctant to engage in the study of adjustment dynamics. The founding contributions came from Chile. Both

Foxley and Ramos are Latin American economists from the Santiago-based CIEPLAN (Centro de Investigaciones Económicas y de Planificación) who have made a valuable contribution to the study of liberal reforms. Although the two streams of scholarship they represent converge in a common interest in democracy, the progress of citizenship, and structural change, their respective methodologies for achieving progress clearly diverge. Foxley's vision is neo-classical, although unconventional and moderate in its conclusions. It points at liberalism as an enduring feature of most Latin American economies in the last fifty years. Liberalism rises and retreats in short-term cycles, but in the long run it endures. Brazil, for instance, was a liberal country in the late 1940s under the military president Eurico Gaspar Dutra (1945–51); in the late 1950s under the civil government of Juscelino Kubitschek (1956–60); and again in the late 1960s and early 1970s under the military regimes of Humberto de Alencar Castelo Branco (1964–7), Artur da Costa e Silva (1967–9), and Emílio Garrastazu Médici (1969–74). There is no question that Chile favoured liberalism long before (as well as after) the Unidad Popular regime. Structuralist alternatives to orthodoxy lost much ground in the aftermath of the Chilean coup, as did the whole import-substitution model based upon state intervention.

Foxley admits that the 1980s have seen a form of radical liberalism that began in Chile and spread elsewhere, whose philosophical background is to be traced back to the larger industrialized countries such as the United Kingdom, Germany, and the United States, as well as to the prescriptions of the IMF and other such world agencies. Liberalism has strong roots in Latin America, going back to the time of Edwin Kemmerer in the 1930s (Drake, 1989). More than anything else, as they modernized and industrialized, Latin American countries were becoming liberal in the sense that they increasingly opened up their respective markets to international trade and came nearer to accepting the principle of regional integration. This slow yet significant trend would eventually introduce the challenge of supranationality, in opposition to the traditional tenet of the national model of development, so paradigmatic in dependency studies of the 1970s. Acting between 1990 and 1993 as finance minister of the democratic *concertación* regime in Chile, Foxley was in an ideal, although awkward, position to confront the Aristotelian dilemma of putting political theory into daily practice.

Taking a different standpoint, Ramos draws a clear line between the 1970s and the 1980s. He suggests that the emergence of policies based on liberal premises was a new phenomenon, in almost total contrast to the previous state-interventionist model of development, which bore some resemblance to the Keynesian policies of the industrialized countries such as Mexico, Brazil, and Argentina. A very large body of literature has focused on industrialization by import substitution as a general strategy for most Latin American countries prior to the late 1970s. There is no point in establishing or refuting its validity here. Ramos's main argument is that most Latin American countries shifted away at once from the previous model, in a general competition for the honour of being the 'best student in the Southern liberal class.'

We gather from this debate among liberal economists that the nature and classification of economic measures, as a set of policies, still pose a problem of identification for these scholars. What is a liberal policy and what is not? What is the difference between the traditional model of state support to oligopolies and traditional market regulation through the use of a protectionist screen? The difficulty arises from the simple fact that authoritarian regimes – whether orthodox, such as Chile's, or state-interventionist, such as Brazil's and Mexico's – feature many elements displayed in the liberal catechism, quite independently from Hayek's (1943) theoretical teachings. Another difficulty comes from our limited capacity as researchers to draw a consistent picture of a process that is not fully coherent in itself. Research has to assess the outcome of a whole array of policies and programs undertaken, in a relatively short period, in a variety of countries of different structural and cultural backgrounds.

Stabilization, Economic Adjustment, and Beyond

Adjustment programs comprise closely interlinked public actions or steps, in a sequence that may vary from case to case, according to circumstances. Establishing a network of relationships between the outcome of a given policy and the launching of another in some sort of logical hierarchy that we might label 'proper sequencing' becomes possible only after a selection of comparable categories of public interventions has been made. We may therefore compare clusters of related policies to one another, across frontiers, and offer comparative explanations. There are obvious limits to the efficacy of using as models experiments occurring more or less simultaneously in distinct countries whose only available documentation is provided in the rather sibylline economic literature concerning structural reforms. In our view there is no doubt that it is Nelson, Haggard, and Kaufman, in their close linking of political and economic variables, who are currently offering the most accomplished and useful conceptual apparatus with which to view reforms.

Joan M. Nelson, in her introductory chapter to her extensive edited collection of research, talks of two distinct sets of policies: narrow, short-term policy packages focused on stabilization, as opposed to a broader set of measures to encourage structural change (Nelson, 1990: 17 ff). Short-term and long-term policies may differ, and not only in scope and content; far from being complementary (a conventional orthodox belief), they may well be contradictory in their goals as well.

Thus, public-policy choices may result in conflicting messages to corporate players and to civil society. Their outcome in the domestic arena cannot always be foreseen. On the one hand, a restrictive monetary policy (higher interest rates coupled with currency devaluation) may temporarily curb inflation. On the other hand, market liberalization, the phasing-out of tariffs on industrial imports, and the end of state subsidies to either emerging or declining industries will deeply affect the competitive rules for local entrepreneurs. With the decline in domestic demand resulting from the monetary policy, the impacts of these phenomena may well be simultaneous. A shrunken market for local products combined with mounting worldwide competition is likely to drive many Latin American businessmen out of the international market, and even out of the domestic market. Local consumers will be affected inevitably: while the upper middle class is likely to benefit from lower prices for sophisticated imported goods, the lower middle class will suffer from higher prices imposed on basic goods produced locally, and unemployment will soar.

The reduction of state intervention and the opening up of a traditionally protected market are anything but stabilizing measures. There is no question that structural adjustment policies weaken an already shaken domestic economy; they shift the balance of power from old to new economic sectors, from state interventionism to private initiatives, from technocrats to entrepreneurs. Among entrepreneurs themselves, they will likely discriminate against traditional industries in favour of export-oriented activities. As they mature, they will eventually raise new concerns related to work-qualification, social, and educational policies, under the banner of a renewed 'national competitiveness.' Therefore, a new democracy faces the challenge of changing economic structures rather than stabilizing them. Furthermore, democracy, as a continuous process, is in itself a process of reform. It participates in the general trend of liberalization and broader political representation. We cannot envision democracy as acting independently from and externally to economic policy. It feeds on the rewards obtained from economic policy, and will consolidate itself as far as all private interests, corporate and labour alike, comply with its new rules and practices.

Most authors establish a clear distinction between stabilization measures, on the one hand, and structural adjustment policies, on the other. Nelson makes it clear that they constitute two closely but mutually independent cycles of reform. Stabilization measures come first: they are intended to reduce, in the short term, the disequilibrium between public spending and the balance of payments. Their instrument is a monetary policy whose objective is to curb long-term inflationary tendencies. Structural adjustment policies come second; they are broader in range because they tackle many interrelated structural problems, such as the public-sector deficit, a defective pricing system, low industrial productivity, and agricultural backwardness, all of which contribute to the poor integration of a local market into the international economy. They therefore engage in a process of re-evaluation of the government's role as owner or manager of enterprises; deregulate prices; suppress protection, controls, or subsidies to producers; expand domestic exports; and enhance productivity. Their explicit aim is to foster economic growth through market adjustment (Michalopoulos, 1987).

Interestingly, stabilization policies are not a new phenomenon in Latin American policy making. Long-term structural problems such as the availability of foreign exchange, the rigidity of the tax and expenditure structures of the government, the inability to raise enough internal savings, and the supply of various intermediate inputs – collectively known as 'structural bottlenecks' – have been permanent features of Latin American economies for decades. The main thrust of stabilization policies therefore lies in doing away with the bottlenecks responsible for inflationary cycles. In the 1970s, inflation was gaining momentum; the usual policy responses (state intervention, price controls, subsidies) became less effective at reallocating investments. As Foxley (1983) points out, monetarism as an economic philosophy did not achieve dominance in Latin America because it was new, but because it offered a coherent set of short-term measures directly aimed at curbing inflation and stabilizing the economy. These short-term measures were well adapted to the financial crisis of local states and to the limited political conditions then prevalent in these countries. They corresponded to an authoritarian, simplistic perception of the economy, and could be translated into shock-treatment formulas. Finally, they featured a paramount advantage over others: they were easier to implement in non-democratic societies (where political mobilization is kept low) than in newly established democracies.

Undertaking reforms is one thing; achieving success is quite another. Comparativists have convincingly argued that the policy determinants present at the level of individual countries (whether structural, institutional, or behavioural) should explain the success or failure of adjustment (Remmer, 1990; Nelson, 1990, 1994a, 1994b; Przeworski, 1991, 1995; Köves and Marer, 1991; Haggard and Kaufman, 1992; Haggard and Webb, 1994; Bresser Pereira, Maravall, and Przeworski, 1993; Williamson, 1993, 1994; Diamond and Plattner, 1995; Armijo, 1995). In search of answers, most analyses cluster around the institutional building process associated with democracy and market reforms. From a large number of case studies, authors set out two conditions for the success of any given reform policy: (a) the establishment of a comprehensive set of short-term (less than five years) stabilization measures must serve as an introduction to longer-term (ten years or more) structural adjustment policies; (b) in the medium to long term, most policy goals – that is, correction of the main macro-economic disequilibria and a fair degree of market openness to create favour-able conditions for growth – must be attained. As a consequence, profits of entreprises are expected to rise, unemployment dwindle, and wages stabilize. One of the questions raised in this book is: does an appropriate, rationally designed adjustment program represent a guarantee to achieving durable growth? We suggest that episodic, sometimes acute crises cannot be prevented, since economic theory provides no scientific explanation either of sequential events affecting the outcome of adjustment or of causes of the success or failure of reform experiments. The key to success may reside in a conjunction of fac-tors, many of which are political and domestic, while others remain dependent upon international contingencies, beginning with the sometimes unpredictable cycles of expansion and recession in the global market.

The comparative literature is quite proficient in its analysis of the domestic factors affecting reforms, and many case studies have illustrated the role of political actors in distinct environments. Broadly based comparisons led to some generalizations. The success of a reform program, many authors argued (Williamson and Haggard, 1994; Diamond and Plattner, 1995; Armijo, 1995), is dependent upon: (a) the behaviour of political executives determined to pur-sue reforms; (b) the dedication of an apt team of bureaucrats and economists in implementing reforms; (c) either full state autonomy *vis-à-vis* corporate groups and civil society representatives to impose reforms (the authoritarian option) or a democratic bargaining process between political and social actors over the distribution of costs, with a view to future collective gains. These variables are examined in detail in Part One of this book, and a comparison is drawn among the broad policy changes stated in political discourse, the changes in policy made necessary by domestic determinants, and the process of policy implemen-tation according to political opportunities and the availability of financial resources. Our analysis will encompass political rhetoric, policy adaptation, and the outcome of public action with regard to initial goals.

There are many types of public policies in a newly converted liberal environ-ment. How can we distinguish which of these policies can open a path to democracy, which others can only protect what is left of the privileges of an agro-industrial oligarchy or an entrenched military institution? The bulk of mainstream economic literature suggests that, during the 1980s and 1990s, mar-ket reforms were by nature market-oriented. A weak international bargaining position caused by the debt crisis, along with the influence of the IMF in con-cert with most dominant lender countries, gave no choice to borrower countries but to surrender their nationalistic economic models. It was said that newly industrialized countries such as Brazil, Argentina, and Mexico had lost the race towards development. Thus they had to adopt a new liberal paradigm and strictly implement it, in order to resume growth and tackle the main macroeconomic disequilibria which impeded sustainable growth.

Not surprisingly, this normative approach has raised considerable criticism in Latin America and elsewhere. Even from a liberal perspective, authors such as the Chileans Ffrench-Davis and Meller (1990) question the value of IMF measures and, in a broader sense, the whole concept of an abrupt 'adjustment shock.' Policy consistency and good timing, they argue, are essential prerequisites for serious and comprehensive reforms. These should not be improvised. Incremental reforms, they say, are better suited to situations of underdevelopment, characterized by economic fragility and chronic state impotence. The problem with Latin America, they allege, is that most, if not all, regimes, whether democratic or authoritarian, have been extremely timid in the area of institutional and social issues. An incremental approach may be poorly applicable to the prevailing status quo.

It remains the case that political and economic reforms open up a most interesting chapter for comparative theory about structural change in an area of the world known for its backward social practices, deep conservatism, and state impotence. In such a context, we are inclined to think that we can identify true democracies by the way they commit themselves, not only to liberal and market reforms, and not to conventional stabilization measures, but to a more ambitious program of structural change aimed at bridging disparities. Their ultimate goal, we believe, should be to free civil society from the influence of the conservative, bureaucratic, and corrupt state, and from institutional manipulation by traditional elites. These earlier practices had paved the way for previous authoritarian or clientelist regimes. The restoration of regular institutionalized relationships among state, capital, and labour may be an indication of progress, but it cannot suffice; there must be as well an enduring will to enhance the status of civil society and to seek the expression of public opinion through accepted rules for policy-making purposes. A broader access to basic as well as to higher education, along with social programs consistent with the general level of wealth, and bold income-redistribution policies are public issues to be dealt with in a consistent manner. Their medium-term goal certainly ought to be the extinction of absolute poverty. In the long term, they will wish to cross the boundaries of underdevelopment and reach First World levels of economic participation, along with acceptable consumption patterns for the majority. All these objectives, Maravall and Santamaria (1989) insist, represent the threshold of a pluralist society and the prerequisite of democratic consolidation, as was apparently the case for Spain and Portugal twenty years ago. Without wage redistribution, no political participation is conceivable. Without broad public participation, the state inevitably falls under the influence of traditional elites, and the vicious circle goes on indefinitely.

Hence, the main issue examined in this book is: can new democracies move beyond the strict orthodox definition of economic adjustment in the economically constrained environment of a single nation, to engineer a broader set of public actions aimed at achieving a fair level of redistribution? To our mind, it is at this juncture that international factors are called upon to play a key role. The international environment must either prove understanding and helpful in its support of new democracies and their policies, or remain insensitive to the social agenda that necessarily confronts them. We should look back at precedents. In Europe, throughout the late 1970s and until the late 1980s, subsidies from the European Common Market played a considerable role in upgrading social policies in Spain, Portugal, and Greece while these countries gradually engaged in structural adjustment. In the Americas, throughout the 1980s and 1990s, it remains doubtful that international agencies or individual governments did more than pay lip-service to the cause of social inclusion. Is the European precedent useful for helping us understand the present dilemma of Latin American democracies? Our countries are deprived of a comparable regional, wealthy interstate organization motivated by the pressing need to harmonize industrial strategies and labour practices among Northern and Southern countries, if only to prevent what economists usually call 'unfair competition.' There is no such framework in the Americas, where state-to-state competition remains dominant, and free-trade agreements are still in their infancy. In the absence of a congenial international environment, major doubts must remain concerning the capacity of reformist states to handle, at the level of an exclusively national economy, the issues of economic and social restructuring and market competitiveness, and to move 'beyond' market reforms, that is, to pursue socially sensitive policies while simultaneously consolidating their still fragile democratic institutions.

The Influence of the International Environment

External determinants and their impact on the outcome of adjustment have remained marginal topics in the prevalent literature, probably because their study involved too many far-reaching influences working in parallel with domestic factors. The question raised is about the capacity of the international environment to foster conversion of countries from import-substitution to open-market economic strategies. The 1973 oil shock, the ensuing inflationary wave, the debt crisis, and the collapse of the Soviet bloc may have played a major, yet indirect, role in the revival of economic liberalism. Through international linkages, a community of experts devoted to market reforms may also have an effect, even in countries reluctant to yield to foreign influence.

How far do these factors impinge upon traditional policy making? The answer to this far-reaching question could come only from surveys that compared local decision making with simultaneous global events. However, preliminary surveys suggest that, in most cases, the influence of such constraints is unpredictable, since larger countries endowed with natural advantages manage to retain a large degree of autonomy, while others can never meet the necessary conditions for reform in a rather unstable local arena. In the absence of a sound methodological base for a comparison of external and domestic determinants of policy change, recent research tends to focus on the only measurable factor at hand: conditional aid.

Latin American, African, and eastern European cases offer numerous examples of conditional-aid packages linked to debt-negotiation and adjustment programs, while countries such as Spain, Portugal, and Greece met different, more congenial conditions during their transition to democracy. In their case, the European Community asked for an upgrading of their social and labour policies (an expansionist, not a monetarist, program) and provided financial aid for that purpose. The subsidies were maintained all through the negotiation period that led to the conclusive phase of the Common Market (1986–93) and to the 1993 European Union Treaty, and were even increased twice, in 1988 and again in 1993. Simultaneously, constraints became manifest as the reform of economic institutions and corresponding legislation, aimed at liberalizing trade, services, investment, and manpower, was made mandatory for those wishing to join the 1999 Monetary Union. It remains true that conditions imposed upon these countries were never as compelling as those imposed on Latin America.

The European countries experienced eight years of uninterrupted growth, while a long-lasting recession was about to strike Latin America. In Brazil, Argentina, and Mexico, reformers, inheriting the legacy of the lost decade of the 1980s, engaged in rather nebulous policies. With transition costs on the rise, the opposition rapidly gained political ground and insisted on practicable solutions to a whole array of unsolved issues: ignorance, poverty, health, and marginality. This uncongenial environment sharpened conflict between reformers and conservatives. The turning point occurred in 1989 with the fall of the Soviet bloc, giving reformers a decisive paradigmatic advantage over their opponents.

Hence, our main hypothesis at this point is related to the relationship between domestic and international determinants of policy choices. In the presence of democratic, or at least democratizing, political institutions able to mitigate the worst consequences of adjustment, domestic rather than international actors are called to play a decisive role in the adoption of reforms. Foreign aid, especially if motivated by non-economic variables, and therefore unconditional, will contribute to a favourable outcome, while remaining marginal to decision-making processes. This hypothesis should be tested in a situation where aid flows uninterruptedly into a recipient country undergoing credible market reforms within the context of a reasonable level of consensus.

This hypothesis leads to a second one. In the years following the adoption of reforms, if we acknowledge the flaws of the bargaining process between political and social actors in the context of a vulnerable democracy (and therefore the absence of consolidated institutions), international actors who have played a minor role in the adoption will likely influence the future course of the reforms. The indicator of this influence is a substantial amount of conditional aid pouring out from wealthier countries and international agencies, acting as a powerful lever. This hypothesis can be tested when a failing economy is momentarily unable to tackle the immense transition costs, both economic and political, due to a deep recession, and asks for help. We should therefore pay special attention to 1982 Chile and 1995 Mexico, two countries that experienced post-adjustment crises during those years.

Tackling Transition Costs

The already numerous problems of Latin American democracies are further complicated by the fact that the subcontinent experienced a long series of reform experiments in the last ten to fifteen years, usually conducted in an indecisive manner. These experiments borrowed from the Northern developed countries stereotypes of what ought to be done to reshape economies faced with both inflation and recession, and to strengthen their competitiveness in the world market. To the ears of the architects of authoritarian regimes, theoretical formulas such as 'reducing salaries and incomes,' 'strengthening the private sector,' 'deregulating the economy,' 'restoring the market,' and 'curbing the influence of unions' sounded like music. Removed from their original context and imported into the logic of an authoritarian state and an underdeveloped continent, the otherwise inoffensive philosophical speculations of Friedrich Hayek and Milton Friedman were translated by local dictatorships into stringent policies. These policies meant adding more pressure to civil society, crushing what was left of its representative organizations, depressing already low wages for the working majority, and giving more scope to an already wealthy corporate sector through the privatization of public assets sold off at bargain prices.

The influence of orthodox policies on the Latin American economic agenda must not be underestimated. A discussion of orthodoxy and its alternatives, masterfully conducted by Kahler (1990), allows us to arrive at some preliminary conclusions. The orthodox Bretton Woods model of outward orientation for developing economies, defended jointly by the IMF and the World Bank, has been increasingly challenged by structuralist analyses which focus on distinctive patterns of underdevelopment and 'market bottlenecks.' Public policy ought to deal with them in a bold and genuine manner.

Structuralist analyses set up a special category for developing countries, which in turn is translated into distinct economic policies, each finely tuned to specific domestic determinants. Older structuralist models of the 1960s and 1970s had a radical perspective. Turning their backs on the 'biased rules of unequal exchange,' they advocated self-sufficiency for Third World countries. In response, orthodox economists harked back to the 'basic principles' of a true market economy. The academic debate raged on for some twenty years before being translated into action. The radical structuralist alternative lost most of its academic appeal with the collapse of the import-substitution model in Latin America and, more important on the world scale, the end of Communist rule in Russia and eastern Europe. The demise of Marx's heirs opened the way for the inexperienced to do surgery on developing economies used as guinea pigs; the unwelcome results would not prove long in materializing.

Since comparative analysis should not be a slave of world trends or structural determinisms, there must have been a workable alternative to the condition of poverty and social dislocation that faced Latin America throughout the 1980s. Part of the solution may rest in the fact that downstream policies representative of a new, more autonomous relationship among the state, the military, the oligarchy, and civil society are the necessary, if not unavoidable, outputs of previous reforms. The shift from market-oriented to socially sensitive policies asks for favourable conditions to be met. On the one hand, traditional elites have lost ground with the fall of the import-substitution model, and most of their political prestige from their previous association with authoritarian regimes. On the other, organized labour has been weakened to the point that it has no choice but to accept moderate reforms. In the transition era, both 'hardliners' of the Right and 'radicals' of the Left yield ground to the 'moderates' of the Centre. Given these favourable circumstances, the political reformers enjoy a unique opportunity to engage in some form of redistribution not incompatible with adjustment. Thus, social policies can be interpreted as 'the policies of the moderates' and as the manifestation of a regime that tends to establish itself at the centre of the political spectrum while taking its distance from polarized politics. This is the 'systemic' explanation provided by Schmitter in the Woodrow Wilson project (O'Donnell, Whitehead, and Schmitter, 1986). There is no surprise that moderate elites show their preference for gradual, incremental policies in the social domain, while remaining much in tune with the original framework of adjustment. This is all the more predictable because moderate elites, equated here with political reformers, must constantly counteract attempts from 'hard-liners' and 'radicals' to regain the initiative in a highly volatile political arena.

Behind the forces fostering change lay the forces behind continuity. It seems hard to reconcile the rise of social policies as a systemic development with a more traditional approach to Latin American transitions, known in the comparative field as the 'continuity thesis.' Originating in Alfred Stepan's works, this thesis alleges that the militaries

usually maintained control over the democratization process, therefore managing to extract from democrats significant institutional prerogatives, such as extensive representation on national security councils and other decision making bodies with broad political responsibilities, to shield themselves from civilian control, to keep watch over civilian forces, and to intervene in many areas of democratic politics. (Stepan, 1988, cited in Hunter, 1997: 453)

Military presence would make it impossible for modernizers to engage in social policies that would necessarily affect in the middle term the balance of power between traditional and new elites. The thesis has found its more powerful arguments from the Chilean case, where the military's position in the transition is considered extremely strong.* Thus, it is tempting to link the rise of social policies, whether related or not to the immediate containment of transition costs, with a decline in traditional authoritarian institutions, this in turn suggesting the consolidation of democracy.

It remains debatable whether suggestions made by political comparativists found an audience among members of other scientific disciplines, but it is certain that, by the late 1980s, just as market orthodoxy seemed to have won the theoretical battle over adjustment, a new generation of scholars began to challenge its premises on fresh grounds. They gathered considerable empirical data from a number of case studies and identified the flaws of the first wave of adjustment experiments. Pointing at the blatant failure of recent orthodox pro-

---

* General Pinochet's efforts during the 1973–89 period established a strong political Right and a military that commanded ample power. Through the 1980 constitution and the 1989 Organic Law of the Armed Forces, he hoped to bind the hands of his civilian successors. Provisions for designated senators and a binomial electoral system benefited the political Right. Nine seats in the Senate were reserved for non-elected officials selected by the outgoing military administration. See Hunter, 1997: 456.

grams conducted in Africa and Latin America, these economists had the merit of distancing themselves from theory and looking into facts and files. Sponsored by such venerable world institutions and symbols of market orthodoxy as the World Bank and the IMF, they ended up engineering a somewhat hybrid but nonetheless sophisticated model which called for adjustment reforms that ought to include social concerns (Birdsall, 1993; Psacharopoulos, 1993; Hausman, 1994; Fishlow, 1995). The debate is now open on whether the incipient social experiments represent the concluding phase and a reward of successful adjustment conducted by moderates at the centre of the political spectrum (the systemic hypotheses they tend to favour) or a decisive shift to another economic model, conducted by new, possibly more radical elites (or collective actors) closely acquainted with the excluded fringes of the population. Economic evidence points to the first view, while many other indicators support the 'actors' thesis.' Social democracy as an alternative to market adjustment is a model now advocated by a rapidly growing minority among the new political elites and supported by social movements (labour, marginalized groups, Church-led communities, rural workers, ecologists) swiftly mobilizing in response to unbearable transition costs, as suggested by Przeworski (1991; 1995).

The Organization of This Book

This book attempts to bring up to date the study of public policies in three Latin American countries (Brazil, Chile, Mexico) from the early 1980s through to the late 1990s. Part One integrates a selected number of empirical findings into a comparative, political-economy framework in its analysis of domestic determinants of adjustment reforms. The data gathered represent recent findings from a body of international, as well as Latin American, research on economic policy that provided a framework for the field survey that was conducted. Further, the book attempts to illustrate as much as is feasible the tentative hypotheses put forward in the literature and discussed by the present author.

Since the area of economic adjustment has been convincingly covered by academics from both the United States and Latin America, the contribution of this book lies in more detailed illustration of reforms than is found in the current literature, in the updating of the documentation, and in the final verification of the literature's main hypotheses. Furthermore, we deem it necessary to raise ethical questions related to the consequences of reforms, while documenting public responses to systemic dysfunctions and increased poverty. In a comparative perspective, we wish to relate public policies to the dawn of the democratic process in each of the three case countries (Brazil, Chile, and Mexico), keeping in mind that each country features a distinct path to democratization and uneven levels of democratic maturity. For this reason and others, the three countries are not necessarily discussed and analysed in the order suggested by the title; rather, the criterion adopted is whether a country had the leading role with regard to the analytical categories prevailing in the literature.

Chapter 1 identifies the relevant variables to the study of adjustment, from a selection of comparative categories provided in the literature. Chapter 2 considers the determination of the political executive to undertake market adjustment as a key factor in the launching of reforms. Chapter 3 acknowledges, as a variable of relevance, the role of competent and honest technicians in the formulation and engineering of reforms. For honest, sound politicians and bureaucrats to win office, the fight against corruption must be at the forefront of national politics. Chapter 4 discusses the newly found autonomy of the reformist state *vis-à-vis* traditional and powerful clienteles that supported authoritarianism in other times. This level of autonomy, we believe, is an essential condition for the enhancement of the quality of choices and the prestige of decision makers. In more practical terms, autonomy makes it more likely that transition costs induced by reforms will be reasonably shared among all social categories. Chapter 5 provides some illustrations of public decisions influenced by electoral cycles that may, on occasion, run counter to earlier reforms, possibly resulting in a blurred vision of adjustment and providing new opportunities to weakened social groups. Chapter 6 explores selected examples of privileged linkages between state bureaucrats and interested corporate groups during privatization programs. Chapter 7 acknowledges the new, more sophisticated and healthy relationship between state and labour that could allow for social pacts to materialize in times of stringent, hard-felt adjustment programs. Finally, chapter 8 provides a concise overview and assessment of reforms, pointing to the rising social deficit encountered by adjusting countries in the aftermath of reforms. This concluding chapter builds on statistical data drawn primarily from World Bank and other international agencies' recent reports and country studies.

Dynamic models are put forward to account for the significant political changes which characterize the shift from the authoritarian regime to a process of democratization, leading eventually to a state of democratic consolidation. Public policies are to be our test variables for such qualitative changes. This choice raises a long-standing debate, to which this book contributes; namely, what are the decisive determinants of economic policy in the Latin American context? Some authors point to domestic factors associated with socio-economic realities or to political similarities and differences among nations, which obviously display high levels of complexity. Comparativists try to isolate the specific problems that surround the transition to democracy, documenting the vulnerability of new (Brazil, Chile) or upcoming (Mexico) democracies to the behaviour of political actors, to popular pressures, and even to clientelist and populist practices. Many insist on structural constraints and local uncertainties, tend to overestimate domestic determinants, and thus remain pessimistic over the final outcome of reforms. They come to believe that democracies are less capable than authoritarian regimes of creating sound policy responses to critical economic situations; that, in times of election, voters will show their resentment towards political reformers by sending them back to the opposition. Others prefer to stress international factors and constraints such as the debt crisis and the recommendations of the IMF to account for policy choices, as if reformers were nothing more than local governors translating to their population the decrees of the 'Washington consensus.' Unfortunately, few analysts pinpoint how far developing countries can succeed in organizing among themselves the new parameters of regional cooperation, with a view to future collective gains that may eventually bridge income disparities.

Part Two of this book is constructed around three related questions. First, have world agencies (the IMF, the World Bank) issued to individual countries stringent stipulations related to financial support and aimed at hastening future market integration? We echo Kahler's suggestion that international actors do not always behave in the same way towards adjustment experiments (Kahler, 1992). While the IMF keeps insisting on strict compliance to the rules of a free market, integrative organizations may keep in mind non-economic and other strategic dimensions of international co-operation. The European Common Market has usually stressed non-economic variables, such as the consolidation of new democracies and their strategic stability, and kept its distance from neoliberal economics. For example, it relied on unconditional subsidies to upgrade obsolete industries in Spain, Portugal, and Greece, and foster the convergence of these three weaker economies with the more advanced European countries. In game-theory language, it had more to do with a cooperative game than with an antagonistic one. In Latin America, by contrast, international agencies favoured conditional short-term loans, in order to exert some degree of control over policy choices. They were always stringent about countries evading stabilization measures, and supportive of credible economic teams proceeding with reforms.

Second, does financial support, conditional or not, guarantee that recipient countries will undertake stabilization and adjustment reforms? A distinction needs to be made, on the one hand, between broad policy changes at the level of rhetoric and, on the other, the commitment of authorities to implement such policies in line with the initial design. In the early stages, financial support may prove paramount, notably with regard to Latin America, since aid is conditional on the adoption of stabilization measures. Later on, authorities need to convince and mobilize local actors to have reforms implemented; at this point, domestic determinants become predominant. Favourable conditions allow for recurrent flows of aid in periods of recession and new investments during periods of growth. Unfavourable conditions are likely to lead to a slowdown, or even to the relinquishing of reforms.

Third, will the integration of a country into a free-market zone secure the deepening of its reforms? At first glance integration appears to be a reward for measurable successes achieved through previous reforms. Does this mean that integration is indicative of measurable reform successes? This seems to be the case for Mexico and Chile in the context of NAFTA (the 1994 North America Free Trade Agreement) or MERCOSUR (Mercado Común del Sur). Once these countries are formally integrated in a regional 'family' environment, will the dynamics of integration guarantee the success of the downstream, conclusive reforms? Among members of a regional family sharing common goals and values, will conditional aid become more generous to ailing partners? The Mexican case seems to indicate that international actors may be willing to go to great lengths to support a failing economy. Will this support go as far as integrating concerns about redistribution, as World Bank reports and national case studies (Horton, Ranbar, and Mazundar, 1994) suggest?

Part Two discusses the many, interlinked dimensions of international influence over domestic-policy choices. Chapter 9 examines the conditions deemed necessary for gaining international recognition and financial support for reforms, once the general orthodox blueprint is translated into a feasible policy. Chapter 10 suggests that regional integration and co-operation between neighbouring countries can foster their efforts in undertaking reforms that are better adapted to their specific, vulnerable condition. In chapter 11, it is argued that regional integration can effectively support market-oriented policies in more than one way. Chapter 12 points to obstacles met in partially liberalized markets, resulting in a less conclusive outcome of reforms. Chapter 13 establishes defining linkages between regionally specific determinants and endogenous variables responsible for domestic-policy choices. Chapter 14 suggests that, as a regional project, MERCOSUR is considered by Southern Cone reformers to be a privileged tool for achieving a higher level of democracy in their respective countries, and preventing the return of the military.

Part Three of this book is a response to the rising preoccupation with social, not only economic, reforms. The latest blend of neo-structuralist theory, for example, advocates 'adjustment with a human face': gradual redistributive policies, mild state intervention in the areas of education and health, and incentives to growth. These aspects are in line with Kahler's suggestion that, from a purely systemic or moderate perspective, the principal departure from orthodox positions in any new consensus on stabilization and structural adjustment measures comes less in terms of the composition of programs than in the incorporation of additional objectives in their design, beginning with sustainable growth, ensuring the availability of increased resources to meet these goals, and accepting a lengthier adjustment period to integrate the demands of more social categories in their design.

Of course, in the early 1980s, no such nuances were tolerated. Governments introduced the principle of applying shock therapy without warning. The interventionist state gave way, sometimes brutally, sometimes gradually, to a business-oriented liberal state which viewed itself as a provider of resources to traditional corporate elites engaged in a program of modernization aimed at enhancing competitiveness in a globalizing market. In the following years, this orientation was to exert considerable influence over the way Brazilians, Chileans, and Mexicans came to envision the relationship between the state and civil society, particularly the poor and the marginal. Thus social policies of the former period, insufficient and anaemic as they proved to be, were defined even more narrowly, and their funding was reduced, to channel more public money into business restructuring (De Melo, 1993). This was all the more unfortunate since, in contrast to developed countries which were at the time engaging in orthodox policies, Latin American reformers had from the start very little room in which to manoeuvre. Income-distribution patterns were blatantly uneven; as well, both basic and higher education were obviously insufficient by modern standards. Brazil displayed income figures not found anywhere else in the Western developing world, save perhaps Haiti. Such an environment was incompatible with a process of political inclusion, and invalidated minimal democratic representation. Because it favoured political manipulation, demagogic practices, and class radicalism, it made political participation dangerous to representative institutions, and therefore unfavourable to the consolidation of democracy.

Yet the people had good reason to mobilize. Orthodox policies transferred immense social costs to the populations they affected, who now called for justice. If some degree of success was to be attained from this philosophy of economic stabilization, there are reasons to think that it had to be implemented at the expense of the poor and the middle classes, as suggested by Przeworski (1991). Especially for the former, conditions deteriorated so swiftly over the last fifteen years that short-term economic successes in a few countries (Mexico, Chile, Argentina) did not compensate for the increased marginalization of the less-favoured in cities and countryside. In 1995, out of 200 million people suffering from starvation in the world, it is believed that 32 million were Brazilian citizens, while extreme poverty remains a common feature in all Latin American countries, with the possible exception of Costa Rica (Latin American Data Bank, 1997). There is no question that new democracies had to make a clear statement about this unacceptable situation. Our survey shows that they did move on this issue, even though not in a decisive way. Therefore, Part Three deals with the measurable achievements of our three case studies in relation to agrarian reform, education, and income redistribution, in the context of a democratic transition that may, on the one hand, have benefited from the stabilization of their respective economies, or the move towards regional integration; or, on the other, simply have yielded to the pressures of an increasingly aggressive, organized civil society. In countries suffocated by the consequences of adjustment, it is likely that social movements have gained momentum in response to the worsening of poverty and played a role that will need to be assessed.

Part Three comprises fewer chapters, possibly because accomplishments in this last, downstream area of public intervention throughout the 1990s appear less convincing than actions undertaken upstream, during the 1970s (Chile) and 1980s (Brazil and Mexico). Chapter 15 raises the embarrassing question of adjustment against justice. Do policy makers shift part of their interest to socially sensitive policies and redistribution of wages because the economic system asks for a broader, wealthier consumer market? Because reformers come from new, upper-middle-class elites competing with the old oligarchy for a larger share of economic and political resources? Because moderate or vulnerable policy makers yield to increasing pressures from diversified clienteles: the scientific community and university students, organized labour, rural workers, and economically excluded fringes of the population? Chapter 16 provides new insights into the agenda of agrarian reform. Chapter 17 tackles the issue of science and education in the hard times of adjustment. Chapter 18 tries to explain why public intervention against absolute poverty and marginalization seems to be associated with collective action and social mobilization in the aftermath of adjustment. Finally, chapter 19 provides a framework to the understanding of actions taken on the containment of transition costs.

In the conclusions, we discuss the suggestion made by Remmer (1990) and Przeworski (1991) that the relationship between political-regime characteristics and policy choices should not be exaggerated. Other important variables, as these authors accurately state, may also account for policy formation, such as the as yet unformalized rules of the political game in new democracies, the changing composition of the governing elites, the ideological preferences of individual leaders, the unstable membership of political parties, the importance of regional clienteles, and finally the existence of a cohesive group of economic technocrats leading the process of decision making. Nonetheless, we will link these variables to the general political framework of these new democracies, to which, we think, they clearly belong. Such a framework goes well beyond the study of the 'black box' and ought to be broadly defined. We simply do not believe that a democracy, as a more or less institutionalized system composed of conflicting ideologies, competing political teams, and alternative policy blueprints, can be understood without taking into account its interactions with civil society, the representatives of organized labour, and non-governmental organizations.

This is not to deny that the international bargaining position of a particular country, as Remmer suggests, does have a profound effect on policy formation. Individual countries may provide genuine answers to international pressures and behave in an unpredictable way. Even in the context of an acute debt crisis, large, highly industrialized, export-oriented countries such as Brazil or Mexico will not evidence the least propensity to adhere to orthodox policies or recommendations made by the International Monetary Fund. A stronger bargaining position may temporarily convince a given country that profound changes in its traditional economic policy are less necessary to it than to its smaller, less influential neighbours. Large, newly industrialized countries may erroneously believe that structural reforms can be postponed forever (Hirschman, 1992). However, without reforms, the bargaining power from which they benefited initially is likely to decline. A conservative policy is of no help to economic recovery, and therefore to the consolidation of democracy. The same dilemma will reappear in the near future, with less space left in which to manoeuvre. Therefore, we are not convinced that Remmer's deterministic analysis fully translates the continuing process of adaptation of the scope and means of domestic politics to the many constraints imposed by the international environment, which is bound to occur even within large industrialized countries.

One of the main objectives of this book is to link new democracies in the making with the process of policy formation and implementation they pursue, in search of significant achievements in the economic and social domains. It is through this process that new democracies mark their distance from the previous authoritarian regime, seek support from civil society, and eventually consolidate. To a greater or a lesser degree, what determines policy choice is the interaction of ideologies, political leaders, parties, politicians and technocrats, interest groups, and labour organizations. All are useful indicators of the rise and possible consolidation of democracy. Therefore, democracy in the making is more a gradual process in which values and practices are shifting at their own particular pace than a shining new façade in opposition to the concealed rituals of the military regime.

PART ONE: DOMESTIC DETERMINANTS OF ECONOMIC REFORMS

1

Identifying the Variables Relevant to the Study of Adjustment

Until recently, comparative literature tended to underestimate the relationships among regime variation, the process of policy making, and policy implementation. Either international factors were made responsible for the drastic economic changes experienced in most of Latin America, or other 'structural,' non-political variables in the domestic arena were said to play a fundamental role in determining policy choices. In recent years, sophisticated analyses have made a bold effort to relate international to domestic factors in the making of policy. However, recent experiments undertaken by Latin American governments to restructure their economies have offered few conclusive successes (Mexico's failure being the main case in point) indicating a direct linkage between reform-policy choices and outcomes, on the one hand, and the consolidation of new democracies, on the other. More modestly, most analyses now restrict themselves to the study of national arenas, where individual societies seek their own structural adjustment formula and pray for economic recovery. Yet the motivations and behaviour of the actors, either individuals or organized groups, fit poorly into these predetermined analytical categories.

For several decades, comparative analysts have argued inconclusively about the relationship between regime variations and the implementation of public policies. Scholars asked if an authoritarian regime could be distinguished from a democracy in the way it handled economic issues. What type of regime would be able to administer the unpopular economic medicine required by a state of crisis? Everyone agreed that Latin American countries, from Brazil in 1961 to Mexico in 1994, went through periods of growth followed by sudden, unexpected crises. No distinction was made between the various crises as to the appropriate medicine to administer. To pursue this medical analogy: in the past, physicians agreed among themselves that since accuracy of diagnosis was out of the question, given the diversity of symptoms, all patients ought to be treated the same. Crisis in Latin America was a rampant phenomenon, and medicine was understood as a intangible package of stabilization measures, either monetary or budgetary. Such an approach made no distinction between stabilization measures and economic reforms, or between short-term and longer-term policies. It made no specific reference to a particular country. With no such understanding of reform as 'another model of development,' it is no surprise that most authors came to believe that a conservative authoritarian rule, because it was less influenced by interest groups, was more apt than a democracy to administer such medicine. The simple dichotomy between democracy and authoritarianism in the domain of economic policy did not do justice to the subtleties in the process of policy adaptation to the international environment and to a changing domestic arena. Short-sighted, palliative policies could, their authors thought, provide easy short-term successes, giving the misleading impression that they were the only practical answers to the debt crisis.

Respected scholars such as Remmer were the first to suggest that democracies were as good, if not better, at managing as were dictatorships. In the Latin American context of underdevelopment coupled with blatant income inequalities, and given their intrinsically populist nature, should not democracies be true reformers, and not simply apt managers? In the 1980s, economic reforms, and specifically structural adjustment measures, Remmer argued, went far beyond conventional stabilization goals, responding to challenges of unprecedented magnitude. The debt crisis was reaching unbearable levels. This was nothing new in Latin America, but this time it meant a turning point in most, if not all, countries. It put into question the traditional alliance between state technocrats and a dominant oligopoly under a protectionist umbrella, known as the 'national industrial strategy.' Brazil and Mexico were the leaders in articulating such a strategy. They would suffer the most from the uneasy transition, losing both their pride and many of the economic gains they had achieved in the preceding period. Their respective regimes would be deeply affected. They sought solutions which bore no comparison with earlier policy responses. Like most countries at the time, they resorted to short-term conventional stabilization measures because they were being pressured to do so. A new Latin American world was about to emerge, and nobody knew to what extent democracy could usefully contribute to its emergence and consolidation.

The studies collected in Nelson's ambitious edited volume *Economic Crisis and Policy Choice: The Politics of Adjustment in the Third World* (1990) were aimed precisely at providing the first conclusive answers about the nature and orientation of public policies conducted in Third World countries during the 1980s. She described the content of a government's adjustment choices, using several dimensions, such as the commitment of authorities to the idea of reform; the internal consistency (or inconsistency) of the decision-making process; the pace and sequencing of measures; and the degree to which each policy package adheres to or departs from orthodox prescriptions. She set out a series of variables, related either to international factors or to domestic conditions, as main determinants of policy choices. As to policy formation, she made the perception of the crisis a variable dependent on the organization and sophistication of the state's decision-making apparatus, as well as on its relations with external financial agencies, including the IMF, private banks, and lender countries. The international environment, she admitted, would exert maximum influence at this stage. Concerning policy implementation, however, she believed domestic factors would become paramount. The combined influence of regime type and distributional coalitions among political groups and economic interests would shape the local agenda of measures and reforms, while the role of electoral cycles and other situational variables could explain sudden shifts in policy and possible retreats from an initial blueprint. These variables affect the time horizons and security of the principal decision makers. Nelson's framework offers a sound base for discussing the capacity of new democracies to engage in structural adjustment policies and to pursue them in the long term.

Most authors identify the commitment of the political executive as a necessary condition for successful structural reforms. Nevertheless, the nature and the boundaries of such a commitment are not clearly set out. In the late 1980s and the 1990s, newly elected presidents all around the world have pretended to undertake liberal reforms. How real and deep is their commitment to these reforms? By what means do they convey their beliefs to their party or coalition, to the state apparatus, to corporate and social organizations, and finally to a volatile public? Are they committed only to stabilizing the economy and to defusing potential conflicts? Are they committed to bolder liberal reforms and deep structural changes? Liberal economists state that democracies need strong leaders. Authoritarianism is by nature only moderately reformist, if at all. Who still believes that General Pinochet wished to restore a free network of producer-to-consumer relationships in Chile? Who will claim that China's Marshal Deng Xiaoping was devoted to freeing both society and the economy from state controls and ideological preferences?

In the long run, we are not convinced that the principles of a free-market economy are even minimally compatible with authoritarian rule. Some structural reforms may appear liberal because they seem to resemble or to converge with the common view of such policies in a free-market economy. In Latin America, appearances can be deceptive. Mexico, for example, is an ambiguous case; its regime is not authoritarian, but it is not quite a democracy either. How does theory, we ask, account for less orthodox paths to market reforms, such as

Brazil's, which lead neither to success nor to collapse? We believe that reforms call for a strong commitment on the part of the authorities towards reform. There are, however, many schools advocating reform. Among liberals themselves, there are many paths to reform. Once commitment is expressed, nothing can be taken for granted until coherence and competence are applied throughout the whole process of policy implementation. Even then, the reformist crusader is bound to meet, around every corner, the dragon of deep-rooted corruption.

We felt compelled to seek tentative answers to this set of intriguing paradoxes. It is beyond the province of this research to explain the intricate process by which authoritarian societies shift the weights and balances in their ideas and expectations of what individuals and social groups can freely do to express support or dissidence. Nonetheless, some range of possibilities for those who think differently ought to, and does, exist. In the heat of political debate, new leaders inevitably distance themselves from previous ones, and from the traditional and dominant entrepreneurs. Some leaders are corrupt, many less so, and others not at all. This feature alone marks a strong divergence from previous practices and, in general terms, from the authoritarian state.

In principle, only democrats committed to reforms can be true bearers of structural change. At first, new democracies may look weak, even shaky. Is democratic rule, by nature, weak and paralysed? Remmer makes an interesting point in stressing that new democracies are not as fragile as common wisdom believes. Using data from twenty case studies, she has shown that policy performance is not beyond their capacity, at least as far as stabilization measures are concerned (Remmer, 1990: 321ff). On the other hand, democracy as a political process has to be distinguished from the rule of transitional leaders.

Structural-adjustment reforms have an explicit goal; they mean to enhance competition of a local economy in an open world market and restore the confidence of foreign markets. In the early stages, liberal economists advocate the withdrawal of state intervention, to restore a 'free economy.' The problem with this approach is that the state, being the main actor in the reform process, may not be able to withdraw itself from the economy while still acting as policy maker. What is at stake here is the autonomy of the state *vis-à-vis* powerful private interests, to which it addresses particular policies. This feature involves a changing relationship among the state, the entrepreneurs, and the labour movement.

It should prove interesting here to check how newly established democracies (Brazil, Chile after 1989) deal with such issues, compared with their military (Chile before 1989) or civil (Mexico) authoritarian counterparts. Do they tend to act in an isolated way? Are they seeking a more participatory mode? Are they able, under a strong leadership, to restore the networks of political actuation that were so abruptly interrupted (in Chile), or put an end to the ones that were manipulated by the state (in Mexico)? Does the new democratic context favour genuine formulas of agreement that testify to the importance now attributed by reformist decision makers to free social players in a deregulated, eventually non-politicized market? Contrasting the paths of our three case studies should furnish relevant indications about what characterizes a process of structural change conducted by strongly or feebly committed political elites.

2

The Determination of the Political Executive to Undertake Market Adjustment

Determination means the capacity to persuade oneself as well as others. The democratic leaders should be able to formulate and impose a vision of their own to which the bureaucracy and the corporate elites will gradually but decisively commit themselves. Paradoxically, it is said that relations of dependency upon public subsidies and central planning must be replaced step by step by the informal laws of a competitive market. These in turn will allow the free circulation of capital, skill, and investment initiatives in an economy that was previously highly protected. The state must cease to view protectionism as the prerequisite for government intervention and support to entrepreneurs, and to view bureaucracy as the ideal instrument for conveying such practices. To re-establish the autonomy of the state from dominant entrepreneurs, many strongly entrenched traditions have to be rethought.

As a result of the new, less congenial relationship, the competitiveness of the traditionally protected industries will likely fall for some time. More stringent rules will possibly drive many companies out of the market. Opposition from capitalist circles will therefore arise on the fringe of the political system, and mobilize inter-elite networks of influence. Thus, structural adjustment policies will inevitably create tensions among the new political executives, the bureaucracy, and the corporate elites. Such will be the thorny path of new democracies acting as market creators. Will they be able to ensure the autonomy of the new state from the influence of the oligarchy with other means than did General Pinochet's regime in Chile, who so tightly insulated the decision-making black box? Such adverse conditions are likely to shake the determination of weaker political executives towards reforms.

In much the same fashion, the reformist state is bound to redesign its relationship with labour. Two conditions must be met simultaneously. First, the state must reintroduce institutional channels of communication with representatives of unionized workers. In words at least, the state welcomes a durable process of consultation and agreement on matters related to working conditions, salaries, social security, agrarian reform, and eventually the workers' financial participation in state firms.* Second, unions must remain autonomous from the state, while the state keeps a healthy distance from them. This latter condition may prove arduous to dedicated reformers – who often have made names for themselves as adamant critics of the former regime – now that frustrations have accumulated among their supporters, drawn from civil society, and the call for justice and immediate public action is pressing. As a general rule, political actors must be determined to improve working conditions and wages, along with the workers' participation in the economy. This represents a dilemma to reformers since structural adjustment leaves little space for social policies. Reformers, however, may not be driven by compassion, but by the simple yet nevertheless strong imperative of political survival.

Hence, the new situation represents a decisive shift from, say, the previous model of state corporatism used in Mexico. It is understandable that these two sets of conditions present new democracies with a difficult task. The first raises the question of centralization of decision making in the hands of the executive on work-related matters, and the much-debated usefulness of social pacts (*pactos*), which, in theory at least, come into contradiction with the autonomy of the actors. Above all, the temptations of political manoeuvring and clientelism associated with the practice of traditional corporatism are still features haunting transitional democratic frameworks. None of these challenges will be solved by simple good will. Institutional autonomy is the only long-term guarantee that decision making will not be overly influenced by labour aristocracies with a strong hand over their organized clienteles and direct access to the offices of the political executive.

Are democrats committed to questioning the traditional alliance of state and business in the process of structural adjustment? In contrast to the short-term, sometimes radical, stabilization policies pursued in earlier phases of the liberal transition, whose consequences are felt by the workers and the poor, adjustment policies feature many complementary facets, such as the elimination of extended state subsidies and non-market restrictions, the phasing-out of external tariffs, and the deregulation of foreign investment. These issues are of paramount concern to business circles. The process of exposure to the market will be either a gradual or a brutal one. The International Monetary Fund (IMF) and the International Bank for Reconstruction and Development (IBRD, the World

---

* This can be achieved through the sale of shares to their employees, an interesting option put forward in many countries.

Bank) advocate that all measures must occur simultaneously, as a shock treatment. To reduce potential damage, less orthodox theorists suggest that the process of exposure should be gradual and reflect domestic conditions as well as the fragility of the market. Threatened business circles are likely to agree with this prescription, advocating programs to expand exports first and to deregulate imports afterwards (Ffrench-Davis and Meller, 1990: 25ff).

This preference arises from the fact that business circles have good reason to question the ability of the bureaucracy in engineering honest, market-friendly strategies. Bureaucratic intervention has, traditionally, counteracted the market. Experiences from the 1960s to the 1980s show that there is a high risk that the economy of a given country might react erratically to a radical, poorly designed policy. A drop in productivity and job losses are frequent, if not general, consequences of improvised open-market policies. Argentina's industry, for example, was devastated by the poor management provided by the second military regime of Generals Videla, Viola, Galtieri, and Bignone from 1976 to 1983. Dogmatic and inept decision makers exposed already weakened industries to indiscriminate foreign competition. In a matter of a few years, cheap imports inundated Argentina's market and drove many local industrialists out of business. As the domestic consumer market collapsed, General Motors left the country in 1978. Many more investors followed. In the early years of the Pinochet regime, analysts suggest that Chile might have experienced a similar process, although, in comparison with Argentina's, losses were minor. Such examples indicate that, in these two cases, the authoritarian state was acting independently – and on purely ideological grounds – from the interests of the local traditional entrepreneurs.

In historical perspective, this set of undesired consequences helps to explain why the Mexican leaders in the 1970s and early 1980s, and the Brazilian democrats, have long been reluctant to commit themselves to radical, fully orthodox policies. On the one hand, these policies called for the shrinking of the domestic consumer market. On the other hand, uncontrolled market exposure to foreign competition, with a limited understanding on the part of decision makers of the role of transitional programs aimed at upgrading local capacity and enhancing market competition, threatened the business class. In the short term, decision makers and the bureaucracy would favour authoritarian mechanisms over consultative devices. In the longer term, they would invariably shift the weight of accepted influences from one class to other; that is, from the 'producers' to the 'consumers,' from a minority of corporate players, to a majority of voters. Reformist choices would finally sharpen oppositions, not between, but within, the main political parties, thus threatening democratic consolidation. In the Mexican single-party system, they widened the gap between a 'liberal' presidency and the traditionalist or nationalist *camarillas*.* In the multiparty Brazilian system, no ruling party was decisively committed to economic reforms, thus leaving considerable room for presidentialist practices. In post-military Chile, the opposition parties (Christian Democrats, Socialists, and ten lesser formations) created a ruling coalition, or *concertación*, to make sure that an equilibrium could be reached between Right and Left, and that partisan politics would not influence policy choices, and thus result in discord. In all three cases, and in contrast to southern Europe, market-oriented reforms were to be the project of a narrow 'political team' working in relative isolation from party politics. This is why, acting on their own in the political arena, the commitment of these few leaders to liberalism became a major determinant of policy choice.

Mexico is a remarkable example of the changing, sometimes unpredictable, commitment of political leaders to reform. Along with political liberalization came a very gradual questioning of Mexico's traditional economic policy. Everyone in official circles agreed that a complex and distorted incentive system known for its traditional slowness and annoying procedures discouraged domestic as well as foreign initiatives and did not help restore confidence in the future of the country. Growth figures slowed down all through the 1970s, only to plunge drastically in early 1982 as a consequence of the oil crisis. The reform process was put in place in a very prudent fashion, with President López Portillo cautiously trying to bridge the gap between the regime and the local corporate sector, on the one hand, and introducing more flexibility over international business operations, on the other. The stringent contingencies of the early 1980s only added to the rampant structural problems, and created the conditions for a general crisis that engulfed the transitional scheme engineered by the Partido Revolucionario Institucional (PRI). Reversing his initial preference for a soft transition to liberalism, President López Portillo took everyone by surprise by nationalizing the Mexican-owned banking system in the last months of his presidency. A shaky status-quo was re-established, at the expense of state-to-business relationships. From then on, many entrepreneurs, particularly in the northern part of the country, began to join the ranks of the National Action Party (PAN, Partido Acción Nacional) in a common aversion for state intervention, which they deemed anachronic and threatening to their interests.

Teichman (1992) has brought to light the conditions under which the pas-

---

* A particular wing or cluster of interests within a party, in this case the PRI. Mexicanists usually contrast the Left nationalist wing, or followers of Lazaro Cardenas's tradition, to the Right or Liberal wing, which slowly gained momentum under Presidents Avila Camacho (1940–6) and Miguel Alemán (1952–9), before becoming dominant in the 1980s under Presidents Miguel de la Madrid (1982–9) and Carlos Salinas de Gortari (1988–95).

sage from a populist and paternalist to a business-oriented state took place in Mexico. She accurately observes that President Miguel de la Madrid took office in the worst times Mexico had experienced since the end of the Mexican Revolution in the 1920s. From the start, this liberal-minded president decided on radical measures to open a suffocated Mexican financial market. Responding to the 1982 recession, just as Chile had done, Mexico resorted to immediate budget reductions and phased out subsidies to industry in an unsophisticated manner. Carrying out a drastic 80 per cent devaluation of the peso meant impressive cuts in public expenditures, running somewhere in the order of 50 per cent in public works, or an average 13 per cent cut in all categories, during the first year of President de la Madrid's mandate. This is a further indication that, as a general rule, newly elected executives tend to resort to radical policies in dealing with the powerful corporate actors.

In parallel, the state unexpectedly confronted the popular sector. The fight against inflation was conducted under rigorous orthodox precepts, such as reducing subsidies for food and basic household goods, wage control, and higher energy prices. Stagnation in the domestic market was a natural consequence of this cooling of monetary policy. Anti-popular measures were made possible, as we have suggested above, only by the presence of a state-controlled trade-unionism, acquiescent to the will of the executive. Union representatives were either taken by surprise or bribed, and did not officially criticize the whole policy until two years after its implementation, when it became clear that the policy would be costly even to the organized majority. Emotions ran high and the relationship between the corporatist state and organized labour was seriously shaken. The long lag between policy implementation and the organized social mobilization which developed in opposition to it can only be explained by the tight control the PRI still exerted over official union representatives: a perfect illustration of Mexican corporatism at work (Teichman, 1992).

Understandably, the rise of opposition and the resistance of the bureaucracy weakened the executive's commitment to global reform. From 1985 on, discontent could be felt within the state apparatus as well as in unions, who threatened to officially withdraw their support from the government. The PRI apparatus was increasingly afraid to lose political ground to an actively organizing opposition. Political pressure within the party increased and, as a consequence, the president redesigned its policy. Palliative measures were improvised. The initial orthodox blueprint was temporarily abandoned. Government shifted favours from the Right to the Centre–Left. A much smoother gradualist approach was therefore favoured in the aftermath of the 1981–4 recession. Obviously imposed by mounting disagreements within the executive, among prominent

PRI *camarillas*, and by an increasingly dissident labour movement, the official policy reintroduced concerns for state involvement and a publicly monitored reactivating of the economy. The fight against inflation was confined to strategic areas in energy and basic goods, where prices were controlled. Salaries, public services, and exchange rates remained flexible. Budgetary forecasts were made contingent upon the anticipated level of inflation of 150 per cent in 1987. Thus the currency remained weak, depressing domestic consumption but allowing a better positioning of exports. Nevertheless, a much weakened PRI was paying the price for the transitional costs felt by the population. Unlike the Chilean military regime, which was more autonomous from influences, it made new concessions in order to retain a dwindling political base, thus paving the way for the 1989 elections, which it won by very small margins, and then probably through fraud, in several states. In Mexico, the regime understood in time that it could not survive if the level of interaction among the state, the ruling party, and civil society was excessively reduced.

In short, the Mexican case (much like Brazil) indicates that heterodoxy is the consequence of the fragility of an executive's commitment in a changing political environment. The 1988 *pacto* featured elements of heterodoxy, such as deindexation of exchange rates, and of orthodoxy, against inertial inflationary tendencies. Stabilization of the peso *vis-à-vis* the dollar accounts for the success of the policy, as inflation dropped to less than 20 per cent in 1989 (Aspe Amella and Aguayo Mancera, 1989). There is no question that consensus around these measures, drawn from the entrepreneurs and the labour movement, linked to a flexible interpretation of monetarist programs, is largely responsible for the favourable outcome of the anti-inflation policy in Mexico in the critical period preceding free-trade negotiations with the United States and Canada. With dividends in hand, the new executive was in a better position to resume a path of radical reform. President Salinas was able to deregulate financial markets and interest rates in 1990. In any case, in spite of the reservations stated above, Mexico is a clear example of the importance of a state-monitored bargaining process between potentially conflicting *camarillas*, a situation naturally conducive to a flexible, though possibly unpredictable, set of public policies. Such bargaining implies that concessions have to be made from both sides; a radical package may be temporarily put aside in favour of a moderate one, and rescheduled for a better time.

As a geographic neighbour of the United States, Mexico has a long-standing tradition of market openness, gradually replaced by a so-called national-capitalist model after the 1910 fall of dictator Porfirio Díaz. The Mexican Revolution was the mother of state intervention. The relationship between state and capital was quite simple: the state was the main entrepreneur, especially after the nationalization of the oil industry in 1938, while the local capitalist class was its clientele, acquiescent to a flexible strategy which was designed by Mexico City in an incremental fashion. President Luis Echeverria was quite active on this issue. As early as 1971, the Mexican state invested heavily in a strategy of export promotion, through the implementation of special credit lines called Créditos a la Exportación y al Desarrollo Industrial (CEDI).

A traditional feature in Mexico was the structural tendency towards a negative balance of payments, due to the early competition of low-priced consumption goods from the United States. A usual response in the 1970s was to impose high taxes on such products imported onto the domestic market. In retaliation, the United States also imposed restrictions at its southern border. This level of protectionism possibly slowed down what was to become a rather spontaneous and thriving business network between the Mexican and the U.S. market, as was the case in Canada from the 1960s on. It also favoured a basic, primary pattern of trade, where increased exports of oil, to the United States and elsewhere (more than 80 per cent in the early 1980s), obscured the fact that Mexico's share on the international market was stagnating, despite considerable subsidies offered to exporters. The basic, well-accepted principle of state intervention was not working properly, with the deficit of the industrial sector rising 400 per cent between 1977 and 1980, and exports plunging from a 24 per cent growth rate in 1978 to a minus 2 per cent level in 1981. Mexico's position was increasingly vulnerable to external pressures.

Were the Mexican decision makers of the 1970s visionaries when they came up with an alternative to the rigid protectionist model? The system of *maquiladora* firms was Mexico's response to the structural blockage. To what extent did reformers understand that this new strategy would eventually challenge the very principle on which state-to-capital relationships rested? Since 1965, foreign ownership (mostly American) was allowed in the northern states of Nuevo León, Sonora, Sinaloa, and Baja California to foster industrial development in this backward region. Cheap labour and proximity of the importing U.S. market were decisive 'comparative advantages' which strengthened the practices of direct trade from foreign subsidiaries to the United States over the years. European and Japanese enterprises rapidly entered the game. From 1983 onwards, these firms played a central role in the Mexican export strategy, being a source of strong currency and new technologies, as well as creating more jobs than the rest of the Mexican economy. By the mid-1980s, their share of the GDP more than doubled, with an emphasis on two emergent sectors: electronics and the automotive industry.

Determination is dependent upon political considerations. Yielding to mounting pressures from the *Norteño* business class,* supportive of the opposition National Action Party (PAN), President de la Madrid turned his back on the import-substitution model by quoting this precedent in his July 1985 *Plano nacional de desarrollo* and proclaiming the inefficiency of measures restricting imports. Tariffs were suppressed on an increasing number of imported products, from a high of 80 per cent in 1984 to less than 21 per cent four years later. Advantages in the form of credits from the newly installed PROPIEX, or Programa de Promoción Integral a las Exportaciones, were extended to most national firms, as was the case previously with the *maquiladoras*. It is interesting to note that protectionism was not abandoned altogether; several high-priority national firms are only at an early stage of their development, such as some participating in the pharmaceuticals and the automotive industries. Heavy tariffs were still applied to competitors' imports on the domestic market. This cautious approach was rewarded by a sharp increase in the value of exports of automotive products: in 1977, Mexico exported U.S. $120 million in the form of 200,000 cars and trucks, and in 1989, U.S. $2.2 billion in cars, trucks, and parts, mainly to the United States, Chile, and Canada. Hence, there is no question that President de la Madrid's mandate allowed significant export growth and diversification, from an oil-dependent economy ten years before. Some 2,200 *maquiladoras*, most of them American-owned, now employ more than half a million Mexican workers. However, not only has the shifting of the facilities to Mexico cost some Americans their jobs, but lax environmental standards and poorly enforced regulations have turned large stretches of the 3,000-kilometre border into toxic cesspools.

Compared with other Latin American countries, Mexico has the 'privilege' of sharing a 'neighbourhood' with the United States and other countries of the developed world. Mounting protectionism among Europe, the United States, and possibly Japan (mainly on agricultural issues) bears a responsibility for the Mexican crisis, in defiance of the more fundamental principles of liberal or free-trade orthodoxy. Uncertainty giving rise to more uncertainty, Mexico now has the choice between two options: either it tries to diversify its export base in the direction of newly industrialized countries and other regional partners, much in the spirit of President López Portillo's Caribbean initiative, or it strengthens ties with the developed world: the United States, Canada, Japan, and Europe. It is interesting to see that, in Mexico, the 'Third World' and 'First World' options have always competed for dominance. The decisive shift from

---

* *Norteño*, that is, from the Northern part of the country, around Monterrey, Ciudad Juárez, and further west, at Mexicali and Tijuana; all areas closely linked to the economy of the United States through the *maquiladora* system.

the first to the second option is recent, although the preparation for it took place over nearly three decades.

The development of the *maquiladora* network gave priority to the second choice, which led to the signing of a free-trade agreement with the United States and Canada in August 1992 (ratified by the U.S. Congress on 17 December 1993). This came as a logical consequence of continuing efforts to modernize the economy, mainly, but not exclusively, through American investment and technology. Nevertheless, the first option was not discarded, with the signing of similar bilateral agreements with Chile, and more recently Venezuela. It is no surprise that Chile and Mexico should join in a common free-trade zone; first, they are two different types of economies, more complementary than competitive; and, second, the same is true for these two countries in relation to the United States. Both can provide primary products and, using their 'natural advantages,' take a share of the common hemispheric market in selected sectors, such as agriculture and fish products for Chile, and electronic and automotive products (including parts) for Mexico. It remains to be seen, after NAFTA is fully implemented, what will be left of the autonomy of some strategic sectors such as CODELCO (Corporación del Cobre) in Chile and PEMEX (Petróleos Mexicanos) in Mexico.

The late 1994 peso crisis conveys a clear message. Devaluation was considered inevitable by most economists since Mexico faced an oppressive current-account deficit, which reached U.S. $18 billion in 1994, and was fed by a massive trade deficit (table 10). One of the effects of the devaluation has been to increase the cost of imports and boost exports, which in turn should help reduce the trade deficit, reported at U.S. $13.7 billion for January to September 1994, compared with about U.S. $10.4 billion for the same time period the year before. The Mexican state is bound to intervene massively in the economy to reduce the current-account deficit to about U.S. $14 billion by the end of 1995, primarily by reducing the trade deficit to less than U.S. $8 billion. It is hard to believe that wealth and higher patterns of consumption will be able, in the short term, to repay the heavy transition costs of this intervention. Data suggest that, even on the Mexican side, exchange policies and devaluation measures aimed at attracting foreign investment and revitalizing the export sector proved very detrimental to weaker local industries, faced with the threat of bankruptcy. They also reduced consumption levels and wages among the middle classes and the poor. Rampant recession and spreading poverty have been constant features of Mexico since the mid-1980s, long before they were experienced in developed countries. Altogether, the Mexican experience is a clear indication of the need for an enduring commitment on the part of the state, not only to opening the market, but to stimulating exports through a complete set of subsidy programs.

Experience indicates that there is no 'spontaneous adjustment' to the market for a better positioning of exports abroad. However, the Mexican case also shows that the firm determination of a political executive to undertake and pursue structural reforms may not be sufficient to ensure the success of adjustment.

We shall now turn to the Southern Cone region and to longer-term strategies aimed at opening up the economy to foreign competition. In Brazil, for several decades, there has been a tradition of protection against foreign competition. Even under the military regime, the commitment of 'nation-builders' was not towards opening the economy to foreign competitors. During the 1970s, President Ernesto Geisel (1974–9), fully supported by a thriving technocracy in the newly founded capital city of Brasília, established an apparatus of closely knit measures designed to screen technology imports and foreign investments while completing, through a range of incentives, the downstream phases of import substitution. Selected sectors were hydro-electric and nuclear energy, the automotive industry, heavy industrial equipment, and agribusiness. The goal was that Brazil become a 'global trader' in commodities as well as in industrial goods. The democratic regime pursued this expansionist model because most of the players, from the Right or the Left, agreed that national industries should be protected from foreign takeovers. We simply did not see a decisive shift in policy under the democratic transition.

Quite the contrary, in fact: most local advisers to the government and mainstream economists still devoted their attention to the classical means of reviving the competitiveness of Brazilian firms on the world market. They did not rush to advocate structural change through opening the market to new corporate players. For example, the Brazilian model still preserved the traditional (and powerful) linkages between state and rural entrepreneurs or the automobile firms, which prevented radical changes in areas considered to be of paramount importance to the export sector. Brazil also competed aggressively and successfully for the conquest of numerous foreign markets all over the world.

In Brazil, consistently with other features of economic policies pursued in the 1980s, the network of tight measures implemented in the late 1970s to protect national industry from foreign competitors, and, in more general terms, protectionism as a comprehensive policy, have not been questioned, even after President José Sarney Costa's return to power in 1985. We do not concur with Kaufman, who suggests that the authoritarian regime had been widely identified with shifts away from traditional import-substitution approaches, while popular-sector opponents were identified with inward-oriented policies. In this context, the issue of economic liberalization would have had highly divisive political implications (Kaufman, 1990: 76). We believe Brazil's case to be very different from Argentina's in this respect.

This may explain in part why, throughout the decade, international actors voiced such harsh criticism of Brazil, which, on many occasions, turned down requests from the executive board of the General Agreement on Tariffs and Trade (GATT). It is most interesting to observe that it was under pressure from the local export-oriented producers, who were struggling with the new competition from Mexico and other newly industrialized countries, that some degree of flexibility was introduced in 1987. The import-screening state agency CACEX (Commissão de Apoio e Control das Exportações) then experienced the limitations of its regulating capacities. By 1989, it was becoming clear that attitudes were changing and that the country, although reluctantly, was to follow the Mexican precedent. Many experts, such as Partido Social Democrata Brasileiro (PSDB) intellectual Carlos Bresser Pereira, and economic technocrats of the new republic, openly proclaimed that the previous import-substitution model was exhausted and should be put aside (Bresser Pereira, 1989).

The turning point in this area, as well as in economic policy as a whole, was reached with the election of President Fernando Collor de Mello in 1990, who was personally committed to liberalizing the economy. In March 1990, a series of official documents was released, making clear that the whole Brazilian industrial strategy, as well as its trade policies, were being thoroughly redesigned. The emphasis was put on enhancing productivity and preparing local industry in the short term for full exposure to the market. Brasília moved boldly on the path of import liberalization, reducing the list of prohibited products from 2,300 to 1,100 items. Longer terms for the payment of goods, and tax reductions, were offered to producers. Figure 2.1 shows Brazil's foreign trade from 1981 to 1997 (*Gazeta Mercantil*, 21.12.93; Instituto Brasileiro de Geografia e Estadística [IBGE], *Annual Report*, 1996).

Even so, the reforms were incremental in nature. Three goals were identified: first, market deregulation by a gradual phasing-out of tariff protection; second, enhanced competitiveness through the abolition of most state subsidies to firms along with a case-by-case re-evaluation of fiscal incentives; third, state support of industrial competitiveness, by the selection of the best-performing industries and the fostering of joint ventures between these more dynamic sectors, actual or potential. The state would provide steady assistance and fiscal incentives to restructuring by establishing special tariff protection for high-tech industries or risk-capital ventures (Fritsch and Franco, 1992: 137–9). Average tariffs compounded in President Collor de Mello's *plano* represented a decisive shift from earlier protectionist practices. Tariffs dropped from a high of 60 per cent in 1988 to 40 per cent in 1990, and had fallen to less than 15 per cent by 1993. The import-prohibition list was eliminated, along with CACEX itself. Brazilian firms producing machinery, electrical systems, and textiles were

Figure 2.1 Brazil's foreign trade (U.S.$ Billions)

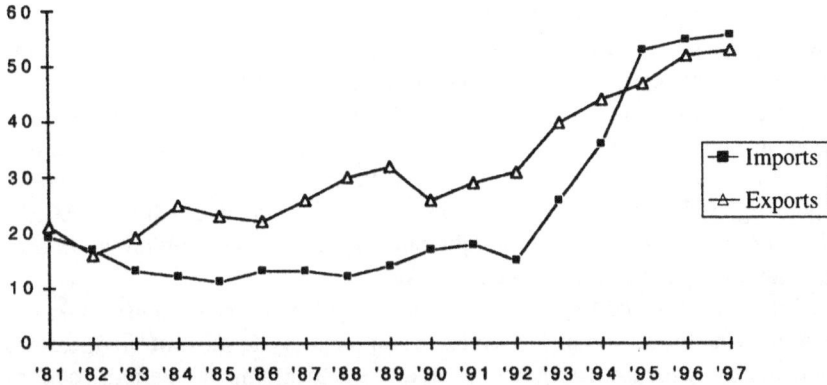

Source: IBGE annual statistical reports, Brasília (various years)

expected to suffer further; while measures to alleviate difficulties were slow to come. Even the national computer industry, a highly protected sector invested with high symbolic value, was, after much painful discussion, opened up to foreign competition. In contrast, agriculture in Brazil – as testimony to the authorities' enduring commitment to this politically sensitive sector – would remain protected for some time to come, on the grounds of unfair competition from heavily subsidized European and American agricultural products (in the general context of the trade war between the two main 'regional blocs' of leading countries).

Being only a minor player in comparison with developed countries, Brazil illustrates in this specific case the best example of a local policy's heterodox adaptation of the liberal blueprint. Its government is apparently committed to pursuing an open-market strategy, in much the same terms as Chile and Mexico, but there are indications that the pace of the whole Brazilian policy depends upon other factors, related to the powerful influence over the state apparatus of technocrats of the Itamaratí and expert lobbyists working for the entrepreneurial class.* The influence of these domestic factors must never be underestimated.

* A long and sophisticated tradition of diplomacy in the External Affairs ministry of Brazil (Itamaratí) has always favoured, in Brazilian politics, multilateralism and independence of action over the temptations of close alliances with First World powers, which carried threats of dependency, particularly in the sensitive area of trade.

State-to-oligopoly linkages are not absolute but relative. They are probably in decline in the new republic, but still important. The government did, for instance, comply with a traditional demand of the entrepreneurs, allowing a floating exchange rate between the cruzeiro and the dollar throughout the 1980s. This policy freed foreign trade from official controls, while fuelling persistently high inflation rates, rising from 89 per cent in 1988 to a 2,150 per cent peak in 1993. These controls are by now practically abolished, while private banks are now allowed to deal directly with trade partners and receive corresponding credit lines under no official supervision from the defunct CACEX. This *laissez-faire* approach brought more than U.S. $12 billion in foreign investments to Brazilian banks over a five-year period.

Fritsch and Franco suggest that import deregulation was not consistently followed by a stimulation of the export sector, contrary to most of the measures undertaken by the military government in the golden 'miracle' period, 1969–74 (1992: 142). Data from figure 2.1 confirm this point, at least for the years up to 1991. As main features, exemptions from the Industrialized Products Tax (Imposto sobre Produtos Industriais, IPI) and the Financial Operation Tax (Imposto sobre Operações Financieiras, IOF) for producers and investors are true liberal measures intended to deregulate the market and facilitate the entry of new cash into the country. In the short-lived Collor de Mello era, much of the debate about possible misconduct on the part of friends of the regime and high-ranking figures was based upon the new conditions created by the wave of deregulation. The ethical problem arose from the simple fact that such unconventional practices contravened the strictly monitored financial system that was still in operation in Brazil up to a few years previous. Corruption is not a new phenomenon in Latin America; it has long been the main threat to incipient institutions. Since President Collor de Mello had to consider the plain fact that the bureaucracy in Brasília was not on his side and was, therefore, moving cautiously, he chose to gather around him a small number of affiliates, among them his brother-in-law Paulo César Farías, the successful organizer of his electoral campaign. Farías proclaimed himself 'regional minister' of the state of Alagoas, channelling considerable money to entrepreneurs and supporters of the president. In Brasília, these activities awakened the interest of the opposition, strongly represented in Congress and the Senate. Therefore, several senatorial parliamentary investigation teams (Commissões Parlementares de Inquérito, CPI), empowered by Congress and independent from the presidency, kept a close watch over the many privatization operations that were swiftly implemented. They also became interested in the subsidies that President Collor de Mello and Paulo César Farías were distributing all over the country, with a clear preference for the state of Alagoas. Members of the CPIs now suspected that the links between the presidency and corporate groups interested in purchasing public assets were nothing more than cases of influence peddling. The Paulo César Farías case infuriated the public not so much because conflict of interest was the issue, but because the villain was obviously working under the new informal rules that he had himself engineered, with total disregard for the new democratic institutions.

As it has consistently done during the previous twenty years, the Brazilian government is building on the basis of a traditional, well-proven strategy, which has the paramount advantage of having the support of a majority of local entrepreneurs. Although faced with recession abroad, it is strongly committed to diversifying its foreign markets even further, as Chile had done in previous years, thereby becoming a 'global trader' (see table 16). Unlike Mexico, which has definitely played the North American card, Brazil shows a new interest in the less-threatening framework represented by regional Southern Cone integration.

Further research is needed to verify a possible correlation between the sharp decline of the developed countries' share in Brazilian exports, on the one hand, and the technological content of such exports, on the other. More likely factors include the mounting trade war between regional blocs and the influence of international recession itself, which favours emerging markets. The fact is that, for 1990 alone, China and the newly industrialized Asian countries as well as Brazil's immediate neighbours, Argentina and Chile, have substantially increased their imports of Brazilian goods, by 56 per cent and 45 per cent respectively (BIC, 1991). The Pacific market has jumped from a mere U.S. $400 million in the 1970s to more than U.S. $8 billion in 1992 (Gazeta Mercantil, 27.10.93). Since industrialized products already account for more than 55 per cent of total exports, it would be interesting to investigate the new trends associated with this relocalizing of markets, and theorize further over the responses of newly industrialized countries to the challenges posed by a mounting competition among partners of the developed world, the formalizing of regional free-trade agreements, and worldwide recession as a general phenomenon.

The reformers' commitment to stable growth leads them to create favourable, easily achieved trade conditions for the local entrepreneurs. In this endeavour, political executives can be at once conservative and surprisingly creative. This is our understanding of bilateral free-trade agreements such as MERCOSUR, signed a few years ago by Southern Cone countries, and NAFTA, involving Canada, the United States, and Mexico. MERCOSUR certainly accounts for the encouraging results in trade among Argentina, Brazil, Uruguay, and Paraguay, while it opens a new chapter on new democracies consolidating through regional-integration agreements. These regional agreements are a response to harsh economic conditions, as the rules of the game become tougher. Rescheduling of debt is kept between strict parameters. Aid, which is made conditional upon significant and measurable achievements in the domestic arena (in environmental protection, for example) is more closely monitored by international agencies. The Brady Plan made Latin America's creditors new sponsors of local state firms, and gave them a voice in decisions about how local economies ought to be managed and how new democratic governments should behave in the new world environment. Such an environment raises doubts about the capacity of the local bureaucracy to pursue its traditional mission. This is why the question of the technicians' competence and proper behaviour becomes paramount.

3

The Role of Competent and Honest Technicians

In the context of reform policies, two categories of Latin American political regimes were identified from the data gathered in our survey. The first was characterized by the presence of strong political executives such as those in Chile and Mexico. Both these countries meet Remmer's precondition for economic stabilization, to wit 'the existence of a cohesive group of economic technocrats' closely associated with decision-making circles. These regimes were obviously not democratic at the time liberalism was adopted, although the relationship between the character of a regime and the cohesiveness of its economic team is not clear. Under the military regime, Brazil's successive finance ministers and technocrats engineered a different policy (more nationalist and protectionist in character) than did other authoritarian regimes, such as Chile's. In Pinochet's Chile, policy implementation was brutal, exhibiting strong ideological preferences. Orthodox liberalism was the mandatory reference of a narrow, strictly monitored team of decision makers (Ramos, 1986; Ominami and Madrid, 1989):

These experiments in economic policy making have been undertaken by strong military governments. By repressing dissidence and not allowing the normal expression of public opinion as is common in a democracy, the authoritarian regimes have sought to impose a new discipline on the social body, one that is supposed to rectify previous trends and disorders. Economic policies play a key role in the process. (Foxley, 1983: 1)

Out of three monetary *planos* conducted in Chile under the military regime, two can be considered truly orthodox in nature. They feature a drastic path to reform designed by a team of motivated technicians. The 1975 Plano de recuperación económica, under Minister of the Hacienda Jorge Cáuas, who was invested with extraordinary powers, was intended to restore financial equilibrium to state expenditures. It concerned itself chiefly with the balance of payments and the curbing of inflation, while Sergio de Castro, leader of the Chilean liberal-minded economists,* was responsible for long-term reforms. General Pinochet expressly asked that policy be designed without any social or corporate influence. The military cautiously kept clear of the decision-making process. We can therefore consider the Plano de recuperación económica to be an almost pure expression of liberal thought, designed in absolute macroeconomic abstraction. A strict monetary policy was then implemented, leading almost immediately to a reduction in the volume of circulating currency. There is no doubt that such drastic measures were aimed at reducing domestic consumption; they directly affected the middle class as well as the workers, whose income was reduced by half in subsequent years (Tironi, 1982: 26ff; see figure 18.1, years 1974–83).

The 1982 world recession hit Chile hard, and the economic team retreated from the initial orthodox blueprint in response to unfavourable international factors and to mounting criticism from an almost bankrupt private sector. A new stabilization plan was put forward, still under IMF prescriptions, though surprisingly short of structural adjustment procedures. Policy makers were in fact reacting to unforeseen constraints, and began to integrate the concerns of the corporate groups, the export-oriented industries, and a much weakened banking sector. The model was swiftly moving away from pure liberal abstraction. Fiscal austerity was strengthened, and imports, which had expanded in recent years, were reduced, with tariffs climbing from 10 to 35 per cent between 1982 and 1984. Additional limitations to credit confirmed the enduring commitment of the authorities to the fight against inflation, in a classical monetarist fashion (Tironi, 1982).

Bolder and more orthodox in nature was the structural adjustment plan of 1985 under Finance minister Hernan Büchi. With recession behind them and corporate opposition satisfied with the corrective measures previously adopted, the path to a radical policy resumed. Büchi, a colourful and authoritarian personality, made it clear that he needed absolute freedom of action to conduct a full-fledged policy of his own. Public expenditure was drastically reduced, and a reform of the taxation system was implemented to encourage private spending. The steady decline of inflation was therefore interpreted as a dividend of strict monetary policy, and explains the support of IMF and foreign creditors to the orthodox liberal approach consistently pursued by Chile (Cox Edwards and Edwards, 1992).

---

*Who graduated in economics from the University of Chicago, and therefore were called the Chilean 'Chicago Boys.'

The presence of an active state, even in the context of ultra-liberalism, as well as a package of state subsidies and incentives to industry, cannot be excluded on ideological grounds. Peter Evans's recent research on Taiwan and South Korea points out that the central role of an autonomous, probably competent bureaucracy acting under an authoritarian state is to define new rules and practices, and to enforce minimal, although stringent, regulations favouring export-oriented activities (Evans, 1992). In authoritarian Chile, the state has constantly played a significant role in the definition and implementation of a diversified export strategy. In the overall process, it appears that initial failures made necessary an adaptable policy, whose outcome was far too dependent upon international factors to be fully predictable.

The Chilean economic team was keen from the first to take action on the issue of trade liberalization. By late 1973, it reduced tariffs to less than 60 per cent, a significant figure for the time, over a three-year period. It was also formally committed to regional integration, with the signing of specific agreements with the Asociación Latino-Americana de Libre Comercio (ALALC) as well as with countries of the Andean Pact. All measures were aimed at keeping tariffs between trading countries at a minimal level. Results in this field were nonetheless meagre; neighbouring Peru, under General Juan Velasco Alvarado, did not follow the Chilean liberal revolution and turned to a model of 'nationalist-military revolution' that endured for five years.

As a means of accelerating market adaptation, imports were encouraged, as the average tariff barriers were reduced from 94 per cent to 52 per cent. Sergio de Castro consistently advocated the deepening of market reforms, and tariffs went down to historical lows of about 10 per cent (much ahead of any other Latin American country at the time). Exchange rates followed a downward path, and stabilized at the end of the 1970s. This open-door strategy, along with the indebtedness of the private sector consecutive to the first wave of privatization, greatly contributed to the economic mess of 1982. The country's traditional industries, inherited from the earlier import-substitution model, were in no condition to stand up to foreign competition. Textile and mechanical industries were devastated as well, losing the main bulk of their players, to recover only slightly in the second half of the 1980s.

Technocrats can also change their mind, under adverse circumstances. The deficit in the Chilean balance of payments became so large that Finance minister Escobar Cerda suggested that General Pinochet retreat from liberalism and raise tariffs again, by 10 to 35 per cent, in a more protectionist fashion (Cox Edwards and Edwards, 1992). This illustrates the powerful, though unstable, influence of the international environment over policy choices. Because they belong to an epistemic community conscious of global trends, economists are the only group able to translate into domestic policies the prescriptions of international actors. They give a workable, non-dogmatic interpretation of a given moment of 'crisis.' They convey to decision makers their perception of the threat it poses to domestic growth, and engineer practicable answers. Under changing conditions, their policies may therefore shift from orthodox to heterodox, or the other way around. Under Hernan Büchi, the road to liberalism opened up again. Tariffs were lowered to 15 per cent, but foreign investment in the export sector, as we have seen, helped to protect the Chilean survivors from further competition.

While import figures showed a growth in luxury goods, an export strategy was not consistently designed before the early 1980s. Copper, which accounted in 1973 for 80 per cent of sales, dwindled to 50 per cent ten years later, and to less than 40 per cent in recent years. As dissatisfaction with the regime grew among entrepreneurs, it became imperative that rewards from the international market be provided to Chilean businesses. In response to the mounting opposition to the military, the authorities launched in 1985 a far bolder export-oriented strategy, which initiated state subsidies and other incentives. The timing was apparently good; the copper industry, dominated by the public entity CODELCO, had undergone an extensive modernization process. A new sector of industries closely linked to the bold expansion of international demand for Chile's natural resources (metals, pulp and paper, sea products, and fruit) began to thrive. In less than ten years, more than 500 new firms entered the market and rapidly expanded, in parallel with the reduction of the traditional textile and metal-mechanic sector. In 1990, the new democratically elected government of President Patricio Aylwin showed clear indications of *continuismo* in selecting the moderately liberal academic Alejandro Foxley as head of the new economic team. Foxley had often criticized ultra-liberalism in the Pinochet years, but had no intention of shifting away from market-friendly policies. He immediately reduced tariffs to less than 10 per cent. The Chilean strategy of *continuismo* was more defensible in times of economic recovery than under a severe recession (Luders, 1991; Salman, 1992; Vial, 1992).

For local producers, the export strategy included incentives such as the exclusion of export goods from the Impuesto al Valor Agregado (IVA), the 18 per cent sales tax. Of paramount importance to this success was a new exchange-rate policy fostering investment. State entities such as Pro-Chile, whose role was to provide easy access to credit for producers, were activated and given new means of intervention. In late 1985, U.S. $600 million was offered to investors at below-market interest rates, another indication of the increasingly active economic role of the state in favour of investment (Echenique, 1989). In response, the whole sector heated up, with average annual growth rates of about 15 per cent, from 1987 on. Exports tripled in value between 1983 and 1990, although, as figures indicate, product diversification was far from satisfactory. Fewer than ten primary products (with copper, wood, fish, and pulp and paper being the main contributors) still accounted for 75 per cent of the performance. The export sector remained heavily dependent (although less so than in the recent past) upon copper and other commodity markets (Ominami and Madrid, 1989).

It is understandable that this kind of export structure was by nature highly sensitive to fluctuating prices and shrinking demand from developed countries plagued by the 1990–2 recession. The price of copper, for instance, as a result of an oversupply on the world market, has fallen a full 25 per cent in a three-year period, reducing the value of a product which accounts for 40 per cent of all Chilean exports; fishmeal, accounting for 10 per cent of all exports, now suffers from increasing Peruvian competition (Agosin, 1993). Most Chilean economists are now concerned about the fragility of Chile's 'miracle.' They are becoming strong advocates of extending the export strategy, based upon products of a higher technological content, which could allow for more profitable returns to the local economy as a whole (Spencer, 1991: 15ff).

There is no easy solution to this problem. On the one hand, it is well known that the traditional Chilean industry (or what has survived of it) is not suited to competing on the international market, and is further hindered by the limited size of the domestic consumer market. On the other hand, everyone in Chile agrees that the new non-traditional industries associated with the processing of natural resources offer a rather narrow base for industrial diversification. Trade statistics have revealed a startling figure: for 1993, the fifteen largest state and private firms operating in Chile were responsible for 65 per cent of all exports. Between this highly concentrated oligopolist structure, on the one hand, and a multitude of scattered small and medium-sized enterprises, on the other, there is a chasm that cannot be bridged without a thorough industrial strategy. Until now, no such strategy has appeared in Chile. Its economic team is competent, but not particularly imaginative.

A first solution may lie in an enduring interest in foreign investment, which amounted to U.S. $2.68 billion in 1993, the highest annual figure on record, an increase of 87.5 per cent over 1992. Given our comments above, it comes as no surprise that the mining industry took the lion's share, with 51.7 per cent of the total. As a single example, Lac Minerals of Canada and Cyprus Minerals Company of the United States are investing $1.5 billion apiece in the development of the El Abra copper mine, as partners of the state-owned corporation CODELCO (Caputo, in *Latin American Weekly Report*, 03.02.94).

Another way out of the rather weak export base lies in regional integration agreements. If Chile encounters structural problems in diversifying its exports, it will understandably wish to diversify its customer base. This certainly explains, for the most part, the bilateral treaties it recently signed with Mexico, Argentina, Venezuela, and Colombia. The Chilean government has also expressed a desire to adhere to the NAFTA. We should not be lulled into believing that such agreements exclude Chile's commitment to diversifying its export markets. In recent years, for instance, Japan became (without any formal agreement between Tokyo and Santiago) the first among Chile's trading partners, with figures increasing threefold between 1989 and 1991, and reaching U.S. $1.6 billion by 1992 (*Gazeta Mercantil*, 27.10.93). Chilean investment abroad in the first eight months of 1994 totalled U.S. $553 million, the highest level since 1975, when the outward drive began. In almost twenty years, Chileans have invested U.S. $1.6 billion in foreign countries, U.S. $659 million of it in neighbouring Argentina. About half of the accumulated investment has gone to finance and services (*Latin American Weekly Report*, 13.10.94). Such initial successes confirm that, notwithstanding all the reservations stated above, Chile shows signs of a significant economic recovery, with new resources now available for other – possibly social – purposes.

In any case, the Chilean economic team has featured in its trade strategy a degree of energy and adaptation to circumstances not easily found elsewhere in Latin America. The somewhat improvised first phase of total exposure to market forces showed that Chile did not wish to remain the hostage of a traditional industrial oligarchy. Technicians have therefore established strong links with the rural producers, to design a comprehensive export-diversification strategy based on agricultural goods. To succeed, the strategy needed massive involvement of the state apparatus and long-term investments. With the tacit agreement of the international financial community (Chile's bargaining position was obviously good), the technicians engineered regulation mechanisms hardly compatible with the Chicago Boys' early teachings.

Although ruled by civilians, Mexico is not a democracy. The PRI, which has remained in power since 1929, has exercised constant vigilance over communities and organized groups within the framework of white-collar-worker and peasant unions under tight state control. Loyalty to the party line meant jobs and wealth; opposition meant exclusion. In Mexico's case, a genuine solution was found to the difficulties of combining strong political commitment and technical capability when a team of able economic managers was established through the initial selection, by Miguel de la Madrid, of Salinas de Gortari, a candidate from the ranks of the PRI 'liberal' *camarilla*, and an economist who had graduated from the University of Chicago. Conditions for policy consistency were therefore in place during his six-year mandate (1989–94). On the other hand, a rift between the Salinas team and the traditional PRI organization widened.

In the 1980s and early 1990s, the maturing of economic policies depended largely upon the capacity of local reformers, along with their technical staffs, to translate and pursue a long-term strategy under the new paradigm imposed by prominent international actors, often called the 'Washington consensus.' A reasonable degree of success, at each stage of this strategy, would allow for a further deepening of reforms. Some conclusive outcomes, such as lower rates of inflation or an increase in foreign investment reflected in the creation of more jobs, would help to legitimize further steps in the same direction, consolidate the power of the new elites committed to liberalism, and tighten ranks among bureaucrats.

Meanwhile, transitional costs will remain high, although an economic recovery may alleviate some of these and gain the support of the entrepreneurs and of the middle class, whose level of income depends mainly on economic cycles. On the contrary, if an unsound strategy bears inconclusive results, the initial scheme may be all the more difficult to follow. Palliative and short-term measures may blur the initial design. An economic crisis sets in; inflation soars; social transitional costs prove higher than expected; and sacrifices are imposed upon the entrepreneurs, the middle class, and the poor. Under the new democratic conditions, the discontented find political expression at the polls, and structural transformation may be abandoned (Przeworski, 1991). If most authors agree that orthodox policies are more likely to be associated with authoritarian regimes (where there is no risk because there is no vote) and are less compatible with a 'democratic transition,' there are still many reasons to believe that democratic governments may be prone to undertake them, taking into account the vital necessity of getting rid of a discredited, possibly corrupt, bureaucracy.

In this regard, Brazil offers a puzzling case. Orthodox liberalism characterized the first phase of the military regime (1964–70), while an original blend of heterodox liberalism marked the new civil regime from 1985 onwards. Political executives came from broad political coalitions, while a new technical staff was drawn from universities and research institutes, such as the Rio-based Fundação Getulio Vargas, and put to work in the ranks of a well-established bureaucracy, in some cases one with a long and prestigious tradition, such as the Foreign Affairs ministry Itamaratí. The reformist team was thus made up of new politicians, traditional technocrats, politicized scholars, and technicians. This was an unlikely assemblage, prone to engineer unconventional economic policies.

A major condition for carrying out a reformist agenda successfully is that the reformer bureaucrats must gain legitimacy. Public opinion, informed or not, easily gains unanimity when breaches of law and poor public behaviour are at stake. Furthermore, opinion is now easily informed and mobilized through the media, which can act quite independently from state control, particularly in Brazil; hence, the campaign launched against institutionalized corruption in Brazil, which in recent years gathered unanimous support among the population and fostered a process of deep systemic change unique in Latin America. The Brazilian campaign points out the increasing influence of both modern media and activist elements of the new democratic institutions over public opinion. This social movement, we believe, creates the minimal and necessary conditions for a future democratic consolidation. As the prime mover, the Left-to-Centre coalition of the Workers' Party or Partido dos Trabalhadores (PT) and the Brazilian Social Democratic party or Partido Social-Democrata Brasileiro (PSDB) in Congress managed to create investigation teams, the CPIs, aimed at discrediting the right-wing coalition responsible for the amendment of the 1988 constitution, a precondition for an agreement with the IMF. Shortly after, the CPIs diverted their attention to the Budget Commission. In October 1993, they publicized horrific tales concerning the behaviour of its acting president, Alves Dos Santos, accused of openly accepting large sums in bribes. This affair was at least as important for Brazil in crossing the line from transition to consolidation as the 'mani pulite' campaign had been for Italy (see the national magazines *Véja* and *Isto É*, October and November 1993 issues).

Political corruption in Brazil has a long history, involving close and undemocratic relationships between state and business. It was a tradition reinforced by the military regime under President Ernesto Geisel (Duquette, 1989: ch. 3, on the 1978 Jorge Wolney Attala scandal), making the transition to democracy all the more difficult to achieve. The corruption issue being at the forefront of Brazilian headlines from 1992 to late 1993 is a sign of the significant progress of civil society's own organizations in their ongoing struggle against the traditional order, which had survived the formal transition from authoritarian rule to democracy. As a primary condition, we suggest that reforms can progress only when clientelist and corrupt practices are kept under control and become marginal. To achieve such a goal, there is no doubt that reformers must distance themselves from the older generation. Traditional elites do not allow for radical changes in social and macroeconomic areas, and in periods of transition impose narrow limits on the will of reformers. Such a situation indicates an immature process of democratization.

Although there is no easy recovery from decades of political corruption in Latin America, technical ability at least is progressing rapidly. We suggest that, among new players and true reformers, cohesiveness on the part of credible decision makers and capable economic advisers at the onset of public decision making is likely to widen the scope of choices. For one thing, credible political executives will seek public support in the domestic arena to weaken particular groups opposed to reforms. Second, a capable economic team working in close relationship with them and free from clientelist influences will more effectively and decisively convey the demands of international institutions to local opinion. They are likely to express an accurate and workable interpretation of the economic crisis in which the country is involved. The team and its technical staff may be able to issue a comprehensive blueprint of 'what ought to be done,' given specific domestic conditions. A practical proposal achieves a better bargaining position with the international actors, especially in the case of larger, more industrialized developing countries endowed with numerous economic advantages. In such conditions, public policy is likely to be less dependent upon a whole range of particular interests constantly flowing from the domestic political system. It may also distance itself from the prescriptions of the international actors. Nevertheless, in all cases surveyed so far, the ideal situation is never fully met. Public policies are, in varying degrees, the outcome of pressures from both the international environment and domestic contingencies.

Nelson poses as an inescapable condition for the success of policies a close and enduring collaboration between a fully committed political executive, on the one hand, and an able team of economists, on the other. If containment of inflation is the goal of a true monetarist policy, one is bound to admit that Brazil, in spite of its Plano Cruzado, its Plano Bresser, and other less dramatic attempts, has achieved little success. We suggest that the essential level of collaboration was simply never reached before the mandate of President Fernando Henrique Cardoso, which began in 1994. As a result, Brazil has been extremely fickle in its adjustment models, and this has led to constant policy changes. The transition era (1984–94) can be seen as a series of erratic and short-lived attempts to either stabilize, cool off, or stimulate the economy according to the contingencies that affected the political system. The first Finance minister of the transition, the conservative Francisco Dornelles, tried to steer the new regime into a negotiated agreement with the IMF. His attempt was short-lived. By August 1985, President José Sarney Costa, yielding to the pressing demands of his party of adoption, the Partido do Movimento Democrático Brasileiro (PMDB), replaced him with Dilson Funaro, who immediately engaged in an heterodox experiment, thus cutting bridges with the IMF. Funaro's Plano Cruzado can be labelled a radical heterodox reform. It exhibited bold measures, such as freezing prices, wages, and even financial assets; rapid growth of public expenditures; and easier access to credit. It also featured more orthodox measures such as budgetary cuts or the interruption of publicly financed energy projects (Schwartz, 1990). This is all the more understandable since the 1986

Plano Cruzado was designed by a large, heterogeneous group of economists and scholars who came from the left wing of the PMDB. Many, such as Finance minister Dilson Funaro and renowned academic Maria de Conceição Tavares, were firmly committed to handling *pari passu* the issues of inflation and social backwardness. On the one hand, Funaro temporarily reduced the state deficit through significant budget cuts. On the other, he expanded the purchasing power of the middle classes. The most unprecedented measure, however, was to call directly on consumers to denounce to the authorities cases of abusive pricing on the part of traders. At first, public opinion was enthusiastic, participation ran high, and inflation abruptly stopped. Popular support for the new policy was achieved, but unfortunately Dilson Funaro was unable to rally the president to his views. With the prospect of the coming 1987 elections in mind, President Sarney Costa began meddling with the Plano Cruzado, yielded to businessmen's complaints, and unfroze prices, which immediately soared. Inflation went up again, and the new currency gradually lost value. As the executive's commitment wavered, conditions for policy consistency were not met; the Plano Cruzado was a total failure. Establishing comparisons between President Sarney Costa's and Filipino leader Ferdinand Marcos's behaviour, Haggard accurately suggests that the intrusion of a president's 'plebiscitary style' in the realm of economic policy can be explained by political concerns related to his own electoral agenda, not to a preoccupation for economic performance (Haggard, 1990). The consequence is a tendency to disrupt internal coherence within the decision-making apparatus, which in turn leads to policy inconsistency.

Contradictory measures are the result of a blurred vision of the role of budgetary policy in the economy. Should it contribute to growth and a global warming of the economy to create jobs, or should it, in compliance with IMF advice, play a restricting role? As a result of the constant intrusion of presidential power in the realm of budgetary policy, favours to corporate elite friends, and the mixed signals sent to entrepreneurs and consumers alike, neither Funaro's very unorthodox approach nor the more liberal Plano Bresser succeeded in curbing inflation. A highly credible and internationally known intellectual and a successful businessman, Carlos Bresser Pereira made, in 1988, a bold attempt at stabilizing public spending and curbing inflation. Public opinion showed signs of scepticism, and once again the president failed to support his minister when decisions had to be implemented. Plano Bresser had no more luck than its predecessor, the Plano Cruzado.

Under such adverse conditions, conflict among members of the executive on the issue of monetary policy provoked a high turnover of personnel; Bresser stayed only a few months, then left his duties in apparent disgust. The population's total lack of confidence in any newly proposed policy and a declining presidential credibility paved the way for electoral manoeuvres and further uncertainty (Bresser Pereira, 1989). After several failed attempts at monetary reforms, weak executives swiftly retreated to a situation nearer to the status quo. Inflation reached intolerable levels by mid-1989, and the political executive was in no position to offer the kind of economic rewards necessary to resume a minimal program of structural transformation. The road was therefore open to a return of the Right.

Brazil's rugged path to financial stabilization featured, as its most drastic measure, the introduction in 1986 of a new currency, the cruzado, which, after various attempts to consolidate its ever-fluctuating value, did not survive the 1989 hyper-inflation threat. President Fernando Collor de Mello, who was elected in late 1989 on a truly liberal platform, replaced it with a new currency, the cruzeiro. The Plano Collor, similar in some ways to President de la Madrid's 1983 shock policy, featured drastic orthodox measures such as budget austerity and a freeze of 75 per cent of private-sector assets (Zantman, 1990). The impeachment of the president in October 1992 created further uncertainty until, in June 1993, President Itamar Franco appointed Fernando Henrique Cardoso as Finance minister. Anything but liberalism was expected from this prestigious São Paulo academic, who had been, in the late 1960s, a main contributor to the Marxist dependency theory. This nomination was a further sign of the unconventional and rather gradualist political choices Brazil made in its attempts at democratic consolidation.

The first example in Brazil of a policy designed by a close collaboration of the political executive and able technicians is the 1994 Plano Real. With Cardoso stepping in as the PSDB candidate for the presidency, by March 1994 Minister Rubens Ricúpero, a moderately conservative figure and Cardoso's collaborator, was appointed under a program of continuity. Forging ahead with the Cardoso's stabilization program, he implemented a new currency: the 'real,' whose value was theoretically to be that of the U.S. dollar. At the time the last monetary reform was introduced, inflation was running at highs of 45 per cent a month, up from a mere 25 per cent when Cardoso came into office as Finance minister nine months before. The Plano Real, launched in July 1994, was the latest attempt to tackle the unresolved issue of inflation. It succeeded in driving inflation down from a monthly figure of 40 per cent in May–June to an average figure of 5 to 4 per cent in the last months of 1994.

The complexities of Brazilian political life bear no comparison with those of Mexico and Argentina, and even less so with those of the smaller countries of the continent. Such conditions, if they are reflected in the political process, must inevitably lead to heterodox economic measures in a mixture of liberal market-oriented policies, monetarism, economic nationalism, and concessions to the unions. All these are designed to gain immediate political support for the executive from a variety of pressure groups – thus the Spanish term *inmedia-tismo*, to account for improvisation and sudden changes in policy, as was clearly the case in 1986 with Plano Cruzado. It may also happen that leaders faced with dissension in the ranks do not hesitate to act in a manner, termed *decretismo*, that bypasses the fragile institutions of new democracies: Congress, the judiciary, and the technocracy. This occurred occasionally during the Sar-ney Costa (1985–9) and Collor de Mello (1990–2) presidential mandates. Such practices undoubtedly undermine presidential credibility. Democratizing the political process and building up a sound institutional framework from scratch is no easy task, in Brazil or anywhere else. It is quite clear, however, that the more cohesive and technically sound the implementation process is, the greater the degree to which the ensuing policy package is likely to depart either from the simplistic orthodox prescriptions or from the status quo advocated by the traditional local elites. There is more room for political elites to manoeuvre, and the road is open to heterodox experiments.

4

The Autonomy of the Reformist State

It is expected that the orderly orthodox blueprint of a reform package echoes the usual, well-publicized IMF monetary tenets. Foxley is convinced that there is a rationale behind the measures taken. What is at stake here is not a collection of independent policies but a process of closely interlocked measures whose ultimate goal lies in a comprehensive reorganization of the relationship between state and society, labour and capital, the local and the foreign:

I was firmly convinced that the piecemeal approach of evaluating an economic program, so frequently advocated by monetarist-conservatives – that is, examining each economic instrument separately and evaluating whether or not each policy action was 'efficient' – is insufficient and may be seriously misleading. It will certainly be misleading and incomplete when Latin American experiments with radical conservative economics are examined, given the all-encompassing nature of the phenomena. (Foxley, 1983: 6)

Given the 'all-encompassing nature' of these experiments, less importance is likely to be accorded to the study of individual regimes in their relationship to 'the single unavoidable policy agenda of the 1980s.' So puzzling to observers has been the interest in liberalism demonstrated by the new democracies, especially Chile from 1989 on, Carlos Carlos Menem's Argentina, and Brazil in the New Republic, that many authors began to question the very meaning of a democratic transition associated with liberal experiments. At first, authors paid little attention to democratization and regime change, while focusing essentially on the reforms themselves. New democrats, they alleged, keep up appearances but are essentially acting as political affiliates of big-business lobbies. Institutions are restored and apparently respected; the same is true of freedom of speech; free elections are held, wherein all citizens may – and, in Brazil and Chile, must – vote. Noticing a lack of enthusiasm and some degree of fatalism on the part of voters, they attributed it to the absence of a genuine political alternative. Since new democracies are merely 'neopopulist' regimes concealing the traditional autocratic alliance between state and business, they came to conclude, there was no point in opening a special category for democracy or a niche to policy makers who present themselves as 'democrats.'

To account for the systematic process of theatrical manipulation of public opinion by a cluster of corrupt individuals acting behind a screen of formally democratic institutions, neopopulist analysis invariably turns to sociology. It focuses on aspects of cultural values, low levels of education, and depoliticization inherent in most Latin American societies. Self-proclaimed leaders are either performing virtuosi or clumsy actors. The Mexican PRI is unsurpassed in the forging of fake ballots, while the inexperienced and corrupt Brazilian president Collor de Mello could not even complete his first term. There is no democracy because decisions are taken behind closed doors by an elite of corporate executives and bureaucrats sharing common interests. Bresser Pereira insists on the cyclical character of populism in Latin American politics. Once economic crisis sets in, populist leaders invariably return to old practices of clientelism, grant special privileges to powerful interest groups, and allocate financial resources according to their own political agenda. 'Populism uses economic levers to satisfy political ends,' Bresser Pereira adds. As a consequence, corporate groups are prone to escaping social responsibilities and manage to avoid income-tax payments, causing a chronic fiscal crisis, which is considered to be one of the main problems of the Latin American state. The Brazilian word *sonegação* (hiding revenue from the Treasury) captures the whole idea of the special treatment extended to the wealthy by the populist state (Bresser Pereira, 1993). In all cases, populism in underdeveloped Latin American societies is a perverted manifestation of democracy. Has populism, we may well ask, anything to do with democracy?

Neopopulist analysis may explain deeply rooted cultural practices alien to Northern democratic rituals, while concealing clientelist traditions inherited from colonial times. It may account for breaches of constitutional law which have taken place in both one-party regimes (Mexico) and multiparty democracies (Brazil). It is, however, unsatisfactory on theoretical grounds because it does not account for the complex and irreversible phenomenon of change, to which a variety of long-term determinants contribute. As a more adequate reading of populism, the O'Donnell approach of a 'delegative democracy' is stimulating, since it makes room for the concept of transition and does not exclude a democratic consolidation. Among other variables, it integrates dynamic elements such as the changing nature of political elites, the growing influence of civil society, and external factors related to the crisis in the world economy, which affect the capacity of elites to attract wide political clienteles and specific interest groups (O'Donnell, 1994). We should not be lulled into taking democracy for granted, once an authoritarian regime collapses. Democracy had no choice but to extricate itself, in Przeworski's words, from the rules of the previous order. Even though there are few examples of democrats being able to act freely on their own, this is not to say that they always remain conservative.

In Latin America, many reforms have been conducted by regimes which were neither democratic, authoritarian, nor presidentialist; who managed to bring about reforms without any popular support; who paid no attention to the potential role of parliamentary institutions; who acted freely as self-proclaimed reformers in a desert of public opinion. To most liberal economists, the Chilean decision makers did very well indeed. The literature makes it plain that reforms effected by authoritarian means are nonetheless reforms, although different in nature from the ones designed by broad coalitions. It does acknowledge, however, that 'democratic' adjustment policies differ from 'authoritarian' ones since, in theory, the state lacks a minimal degree of 'autonomy' from civil society.

Theorists argue over whether policy choices are rationally determined, or rather, simply represent practicable alternatives offered decision makers at a given moment by domestic opportunities. Our approach stems from Nelson's suggestion that 'there is a continued process of implementation that defines the coherence of reform measures. The degree to which policy decisions are carried out [is more important] than the economic outcomes of the measures taken' (Nelson, 1990: 13).

As encompassing as they may seem, policy choices are obviously not driven by intangible economic laws, but by political preoccupations. Nelson writes that the first phase of reform policies stems from political concerns and is devoted to restricting state interaction with the domestic environment. Its intention is to reshape domestic conditions in such a way that local actors will be called to react, positively it is hoped, to market stimuli offered by the international environment rather than to state intervention. This means shifting more or less abruptly from an almost Keynesian state-controlled economy to one that is deregulated. There is, however, a definite prerequisite to reducing the interaction between the state apparatus and these actors. To do so, the executive has to establish new rules affecting the relationship between state and society, capital and labour. In some cases, political mobilization and participation can be silenced (Chile); in others, political participation is manipulated and reduced (Mexico). In both cases, decision-making circles and their economic teams try to achieve internal coherence and the autonomy of the state by non-democratic mechanisms.

Chile, in the aftermath of the 1973 military coup, offers the blatant example of brutal, outright destruction of social forces and political parties. Because of

extreme polarization of public opinion on issues related to politics and economic policy, it is no surprise that Pinochet re-created the harsher forms of an
ultra-right *caudillismo*, which followed in the steps of Franco's 1939–43
Normalización. Invested with all the powers of the state and the army, the self-
proclaimed Chilean *caudillo* was in an excellent position to preach the lessons
of liberalism while conceding nothing to the popular movement. In this case,
we are justified in referring to authoritarianism as the easier, classical mode of
pursuing orthodox pro-market policies.

The situation in Mexico is complex because, since the constitution of 1917,
state and society have traditionally enjoyed a close relationship. One ought to
remember that the common interests of the elite and the enduring practices of
state trade-unionism, under a single one-party regime, gave rise to forty years of
unanimous or enforced nationalistic policy making, oriented towards industrial
development. In Mexico, as in such countries as Argentina, Turkey, India,
Egypt, Italy, and France, the ideal of national capitalism has been followed for a
long period of time, giving rise to such powerful state institutions as PEMEX
(Petróleos Mexicanos, established by President Lázaro Cárdenas in 1938).
Other state firms, together with their counterparts in the official trade unions,
helped to restructure civil society under strict hiring regulations. Personal compliance with official PRI orthodoxy was a requisite condition for any career.
These bodies are responsible for the rise of a 'working-class aristocracy' which
prevented, for many decades, the development of any autonomously organized
opposition to the dominant corporatist regime (Middlebrook, 1989).

Signs of political liberalization were discernible by the mid-1970s, as Interior minister Jesus Reyes Héroles was asked by newly elected president López
Portillo to design a 'political reform' to restore multipartism and party competition in national elections. The Tlatelolco student uprisings of 1968, along with
the mounting difficulties of the Mexican model (the import-substitution crisis,
which provoked a massive crowding-out of private investment in the late
Echeverria years) certainly opened many eyes to the increasing discrepancy
between the regime's official revolutionary rhetoric and the suffocating political and economic environment into which the country was slowly sinking
(Middlebrook, 1986).

The shift from national capitalism to a liberal economic policy was most certainly accelerated by serious debt problems associated with the end of the oil
bonanza in the early 1980s (Grayson, 1988). It was also fostered by the mounting
competition from the conservative PAN (Partido de Acción Nacional), particularly successful among industrialists in the northern part of the country. Established in 1938, in response to the nationalization of the oil industry, this party was
given new impetus by the dissatisfaction of the *Norteño* entrepreneurs with the

PRI regime. Through their policies, all PRI governments of the period tried to bridge differences with this thriving and influential class. Other political parties (officially recognized in the political reform of 1977) also began to compete with the PRI on its left, mainly in towns and big cities. It is also acknowledged that, under an accelerating process of urbanization, the traditional PRI political base, lodged mainly in the southern countryside, was rapidly dwindling. In the Mexican case, and in total contrast to Chile, a redefinition of state corporatism was conducted *pari passu* with economic reforms. It was not seen as a prerequisite to reforms, but rather as parallel to them. The regime understood that, to survive as the dominant force in Mexican politics, it had to diversify its clienteles. President López Portillo avoided controversy and would not move much further than trying to resume economic growth through an ambitious oil-exporting policy, which appeared promising in its early years. He did, nevertheless, choose the liberal-minded Miguel de la Madrid to succeed him in office.

The Mexican case suggests that the autonomy of reformer statesmen from domestic influences is felt most strongly at the outset of a new presidential mandate, and less so as the mandate continues. This pattern, we suggest, is likely to replicate itself from mandate to mandate. A new executive ostensibly draws the line between itself and the previous regime; this level of autonomy is then gradually eroded. In his first year in office, as we know, President Miguel de la Madrid decisively engaged in a stringent monetary stabilization program, which created turmoil inside the PRI and elsewhere for the regime. Measures such as the Ley de Obra were gradually taken, from 1984 on, to contain union influence on the work force.* Further confrontation within the PRI led to the splitting of Cuauhtemoc Cárdenas, leader of the Left nationalist wing of the PRI. The son of Lázaro Cárdenas, president from 1934 to 1940, who had launched an agrarian reform and nationalized the oil industry in 1938, he became the leader of the older, still minor Partido de la Revolución Democrática (PRD), which attracted the New Left and gained considerable momentum. On occasion, PEMEX and other union leaders went as far as to voice their support for the PRD. In response, President de la Madrid shifted policies in an attempt to preserve what he could of the historical alliance between state and unions: in one instance, the process of inter-elite bargaining, in Middlebrook's terms, was fully re-established while reforms slowed down markedly.

In much the same fashion, mounting dissent between his own economic team

---

* The 1984 Ley de Obra, inspired by the 1977 political reform, gave authorities a new framework of intervention against abuses of influence peddling in the labour market, by self-proclaimed union leaders loosely connected with the ruling party. It is on the basis of the Ley de Obra that President Salinas de Gortari later intervened against high-ranking leaders such as La Quina.

and union representatives justified President Salinas de Gortari's decision, in the first year of his mandate, to take decisive action against La Quina, the president of oil workers, and other influential union leaders (Prévot Shapira, 1989). The presidency chose to take direct control over PEMEX. Restructuring of its operations went on under a new, docile leadership, with massive lay-offs, until at least late 1992. In the oil industry, protest and discontent with government policy marked the first years of the Salinas presidency. Ex-workers promptly organized, with the support of opposition parties. By early 1994, 187 wells and more than 134 PEMEX plants were still blocked by ex-workers, while huge demonstrations challenged the regime in the streets of Mexico City. By 1993, President Salinas de Gortari finally yielded to these pressures, hastily restored channels of communication with the traditional PRI networks, and abandoned his commitment to the pursuit of strict monetarism. In early 1995, newly elected president Ernesto Zedillo marked his distance from the Salinas administration and the traditional Prista wing in a still bolder way. He had Raúl Salinas, brother of the former president, charged with the murder of Francisco Luis Massieu, president of the PRI.* This measure was aimed at enhancing the image of his own, much-criticized leadership, and possibly at putting an end to the intolerable settling of accounts between increasingly conflict-ridden PRI *camarillas*.

Working under democratic rules poses a challenge to reformers. A democracy's depth, power, and degree of 'refinement,' to use the vocabulary of David Hume, is dependent upon conditions encountered in its specific environment. A particular environment shapes the process and the rules of interaction among the actors, the realities and constraints of decision making, the difficulties of policy implementation, and the usefulness of short-term political rewards. In an inescapable situation imposed by the conservative paradigm of the 1980s, reform policies proved to be the battlefield where democracy and authoritarianism struggled for dominance in Latin America.

In a ground-breaking article on the prospects of democracy in Spain, Maravall and Santamaria stated that the main challenge facing the new regime would be to mobilize sufficient popular support and build a significant parliamentary base around reform policies. This support was necessary to undertake the profound economic, social, and political reforms needed to modernize Spanish society. Only such reforms could overcome structural obstacles to democracy, and neutralize the threat that both terrorism and ultra-right activism represented for democratic consolidation (Maravall and Santamaria, 1989). Central to their analysis is the idea that committed, strong executives are a pre-

*Francisco Luis Massieu was assassinated in September 1994, six months after candidate Luis Donaldo Colosio.

requisite for coherent governmental action, but that popular consent is needed to create the conditions for policy implementation. The authors' conclusions did not specifically address, however, the issue of state autonomy. They left the impression that momentum could be gathered through some sort of 'popular consensus' around the idea of reform. While remaining sceptical over the 'popular consensus' hypothesis, we suggest that the heterodox components of reforms are sound indicators for measuring the degree of state autonomy *vis-à-vis* domestic influences. Orthodoxy means that the state is acting in full autonomy from civil society, while more heterodoxy in reform policies indicates that state actors are prone to yield to particular demands.

Whitehead defines heterodoxy as an odd mixture of Keynesian and monetarist policies in a single economic package, such as a *plano*. Heterodoxy offers a pragmatic, not a rational, answer to a double set of constraints (Thorp and Whitehead, 1987). In Hirschman's terms, public action must reconcile the domestic consolidation of democracy with financial stabilization and market competitiveness abroad. However, Hirschman refuses to define 'one best way':

I shall plead that the intellectual path I have followed is not altogether bizarre. Repelled by a policy prescription (balanced growth) that seemed to me excessively demanding, dangerous in its policy implications, as well as simply wrong, I elaborated an alternative approach. Later I looked at some situations where events had taken more or less the course I have advocated and noticed that this course in turn harboured some dangers and risks of its own. This is only natural, for there is no riskless action. Recognizing and attempting to avoid those risks does not mean either that we should not act at all or that the proposition against which I argued originally is rehabilitated ... Looking for uniform solutions to development problems invariably leads us astray; this is for the imperatives of either simultaneity or sequentiality, that is, for the insistence on 'integrated planning' as well as for the injunctions to postpone certain tasks in the name of 'one thing at a time.' (Hirschman, 1992: 18)

For Hirschman, explicit in the heterodox approach is the emphasis upon easing the harsher consequences of orthodox policies. It translates as a sustained commitment to domestic growth, over monetarist distrust for growth-oriented public expenditures. Since these expenditures are a main contributor to inflation, Thorp and Whitehead tend to relate 'heterodox' choices with the persistence of 'inertial inflation,' which renders the usual adjustment responses inefficient:

With continuing inflation, a large part of the rise in prices in any one year can usually be explained simply by 'inertia,' as the effect of past price rises. In our case studies this is not often or necessarily the result of formal indexation, but of policy responses and private sector expectations revolving around four crucial 'prices': the exchange rate, the interest rate, certain public utility prices and the wage rate. Certain other controlled prices (typically food prices) may also play a strategic role ...

As inertial inflation becomes entrenched, so inflation becomes less responsive to demand, and therefore to the typical adjustment package used. This, together with the significance of the increased interest burden, goes far to explaining the diminishing returns to conventional adjustment measures and the growing appeal of so-called 'heterodox shocks' such as the plan Austral adopted in Argentina in mid-1985 and the plano Cruzado in Brazil in early 1986. (Thorp and Whitehead, 1987: 6)

Such policies are almost orthodox, but allow a little more time to ease the process of adjustment and reduce associated political tensions. The same final outcome is intended as under orthodox policies, in contrast to policies that only pretend to be attempts to stabilize while essentially rejecting the underlying objectives of orthodox policies.

Heterodox adaptations of adjustment packages may also indicate that decision makers are increasingly influenced by a volatile domestic environment. In contrast to authoritarian regimes, which reduce the opposition in such a way as to minimize the interaction of decision making and social demands, while exerting no influence over international factors which might alter the outcome of their policies, democracies are facing both sets of challenges. They are exposed to the intangible international environment, on the one hand, and are sensitive to the flow of social demands, on the other. Political pressure, and even opposition, comes from such social forces as corporate organizations and trade unions, but also political parties. Coalitions are bound to accommodate, at least minimally, every party that participates in government.

Heterodoxy faces political problems of its own. It may happen that discord develops in the ranks; ministers and high-ranking technical personnel may diverge on the orientation of a given policy. Democratic leaders can neither crush social forces nor eliminate political parties. Instead, heterodox policies are designed to incorporate distinct political opinions and paradigms, and to restore coherence to the coalition. They ask their economic technicians to design practicable policy blueprints. The commitment on the part of executives to achieving medium-term reform objectives becomes paramount. The need to translate these goals into sound heterodox policies which will offer manageable solutions to a situation of intense crisis is crucial for the success of the endeavour.

The point of departure of heterodoxy is that political players agree among themselves that public policy should keep 'transitional costs' within limits acceptable to civil society. They are prone to accepting that measures ought to be taken to minimize the harsh consequences of adjustment. Only highly credible executives can handle this thorny issue properly, and gain further credibility from the very sacrifices they ask every social group to make. It is also obvious that rewards must be provided to some of these groups, and to the economy in general, if structural reforms are to be pursued any further. The main problem with heterodox policies is that, because their rationale is primarily political, they may not work properly as economic reforms.

More interestingly, heterodox experiments indicate that policy choices can depart, to a certain extent, from the general prescriptions of international actors. Policy implementation eventually features more elements of heterodoxy than did the initial blueprint. In a democratic transition, the personal and ideological background of the new leaders is paramount. Their own preferences in terms of the political line they belong to will influence public opinion. As they face recurrent electoral deadlines, decision makers may be tempted to loosen a given policy, thus relying on heterodox growth-oriented measures to attract popular support. With or without an institutional framework, their jurisdiction eventually collides with that of the economic technocrats, whose main concern is to keep in line with the original blueprint. Internal coherence gives way to concealed or open conflict. State capacity is eroded. The initial policy is abruptly modified, or even abandoned, according to the electoral agenda, as suggested by figure 4.1.

Poorly designed heterodox policies eventually result in palliative measures, 'populist' in Bresser Pereira's terms, which send mixed signals to both corporate elites and civil society. They blur general policy goals by adopting short-term political manoeuvres. Their design is time-consuming; they are prone to opportunism and vulnerable to clientelism; they give rise to sudden shifts in policy. Moreover, they point at the difficulties in building a majority on either a nationalist or an open-market liberal strategy. Lack of experience on the part of the new political personnel also accounts for myopia and clumsy decision making. The whole democratic transition should not be reduced, in our view, to mere 'neopopulism,' on the grounds that occasional discord occurs at the highest level of government, or between government and the bureaucracy inherited from the previous military regime. Populist politics seem to be closely associated with transition to democracy. We believe they will not endure in a consolidated democracy. First, political confusion is hardly compatible with sound policy making. Second, an unpredictable economic policy is likely to be poorly rewarded in terms of economic performance; transitional costs are likely to rise beyond acceptable levels.

Populist presidents in the context of a 'delegative democracy,' to use O'Donnell's term, may temporarily resort to 'plebiscitary politics.' Delegative democracy has the apparent advantage of allowing swift policy making, but not

Figure 4.1 In a democratic transition, domestic contingencies weaken policy implementation during elections or periods of social unrest.

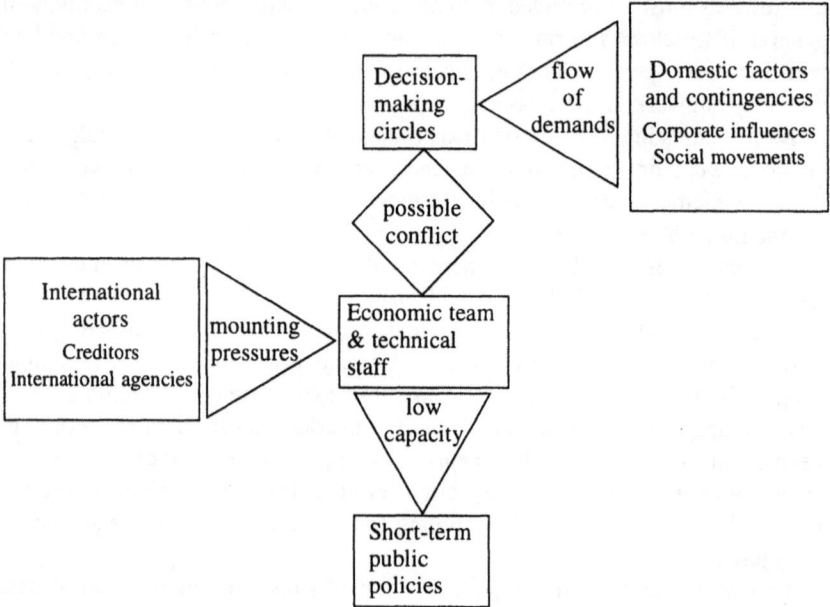

```
                        Decision-      flow      Domestic factors
                        making          of       and contingencies
                        circles       demands    Corporate influences
                                                 Social movements

                          possible
                          conflict

 International                        Economic team
 actors        mounting               & technical
 Creditors     pressures              staff
 International agencies
                                        low
                                       capacity

                                      Short-term
                                      public
                                      policies
```

without costs, including the high likelihood of gross mistakes, and erratic implementation (O'Donnell, 1994: 62). In our view, only a sound institutional framework, providing accepted rules of the game to all players – decision makers, economic technocrats, interest groups, popular and labour organizations – is able to create the conditions of stability in which public policies can be pursued to their ultimate goals. We refer here to the definition and characteristics of a functioning democratic institutional setting, as depicted by O'Donnell (1994: 57–8). This framework channels the flow of demands issuing from civil society. It protects the decision-making process from electoralism, personalist politics, and internal conflict. It reduces the impact of interest groups and electoral deadlines on decision making. It eventually translates social demands into a comprehensive economic strategy, thus affecting the sequencing of measures, programs, and growth incentives. It encourages the formation of linkages between state officials and strategic producer groups who support reforms (Evans, 1992). Institutionalized systems mitigate the fundamental problems of collective action. In older, consolidated democracies, associational life is dense; reforms can be explained in terms of shifting alignments among interest groups

(Haggard and Kaufman, 1992). These alignments create flexibility and open the way to long-term perspectives, in which the patterns of state intervention can be modified and updated, under changing conditions, in ways which are not overly detrimental to particular groups. Because the time-horizons of actors are lengthened, state capacity gains strength in the process of policy implementation and economic adaptation. Most authors will agree that such a framework is the threshold of democratic consolidation.

If the institutional framework is the necessary condition for engaging in a comprehensive strategy, is it sufficient? We are inclined to think it is not. In Latin America, structural-adjustment experiments are launched in times of unfavourable international conditions. Individual countries are unable to assert their autonomy from market factors. There is nothing these countries can do to set the price of commodities they export through the New York or London exchange markets, and even less to prevent a world recession detrimental to their own program of economic recovery. Mexico, and Chile before 1989, put forward comprehensive strategies under a coherent, although non-democratic, framework. Working under a regime of continuity, they were able to reproduce the orthodox blueprint, with minimal adaptation to achieve their initial goals. The Chilean dictatorship was able to keep up the pace of reforms. The Mexican decision makers favoured a 'stop and go' strategy that betrayed the influence over presidential policy making exerted by state-dominated organizations channelling intense flows of social demands.

On the one hand, Chile provides an example of non-democratic means used to interrupt normal linkages between the state and civil society and to ensure state autonomy during the implementation of liberal reforms. On the other, Mexico shows that the usual corporatist approach to achieving state dominance may not work properly in the long term. Bold steps must be taken by political players to reassert the very foundations over which the executive power lays. It is unclear, however, if this strategy can be pursued for a full mandate. Official Mexican reformers believe that, once a new president comes into office, reforms may progress insofar as civil society is manipulated, and its elites tightly controlled by the regime. However, the democratization of institutions, particularly the introduction of an 'honest' electoral process, will increase the vulnerability of a manipulative state system. Faced with upcoming elections, politicians become all the more vulnerable to popular pressures because they are organized and integrated into an already established bargaining system, which has institutionalized a continuous process of interaction.

5

The Influence of Electoral Cycles

This chapter examines a limited selection of public policies that can be related to electoral cycles. A selection was made because a thorough review of all electoral events and the study of their relationship with each and every decision affecting reforms would need a book in itself. As we suggested earlier, electoral politics may play a significant part in influencing government policy. A few examples drawn from our three case studies should substantiate this point.

The year 1994 being an electoral one in Mexico, the Salinas de Gortari administration resorted to much the same practices it had adopted on previous occasions, apparently losing all interest in market reforms. The state hastily rebuilt its bridges with PEMEX and other unions. The company's support to social programs was resumed: five thousand oil workers' families were offered new housing facilities, while financial restructuring was suddenly abandoned. A decision to end social benefits and cancel workers' pensions, part of the initial plan, was set aside. Furthermore, following a mid-March agreement, most of the laid-off workers were swiftly rehired. As was to be expected, social unrest came to a halt. By 1 May, President Salinas, Rojas Gutierrez (chief executive of PEMEX), and Romero Deschamps (the union's leader) were marching side by side at the head of the traditional Labour Day parade, while a mass contingent of oil workers from around the country marched past with banners stating: 'Solidarity with your policies, Mister President.' This act of 'renewed friendship' happened simultaneously with a strong statement by PRI candidate Ernesto Zedillo that PEMEX would never be privatized, and neither would it be exposed to foreign competition. With this declaration, essentially intended for domestic consumption, the presidential candidate showed no intention of provoking the United States, which issued no official statement on the affair.

Electoral years can be expensive for the national treasury and can even weaken the whole economy. Moreover, even with signs of crisis looming on the horizon, a ruling party seeking re-election may not give the government any leeway to undertake stabilization measures before the elections are held. This situation is evidenced by the peso crisis of late 1994. Analysts blame former president Carlos Salinas de Gortari for pursuing economic policies that left the peso overvalued, while freely spending in the public sector in order to defuse opposition and attract voters. They suggest that Salinas deliberately delayed a much-needed devaluation until after he left office. The newly elected president Ernesto Zedillo had no choice but to implement a very unpopular stabilization package in the first weeks of his mandate (*Latin American Weekly Report*, 05.01.95). In doing so, he replicated a pattern well known in Mexican politics, that of implementing drastic reforms at the outset of a presidential mandate.

In Mexico more than in any country under study, state firms and unions have traditionally served the government's purpose of conveying to their members the general orientations of the regime (Couffignal, 1990). One must conclude that, if the traditional corporatism has been on occasion seriously shaken by the shift towards reform policies, it has nevertheless adapted to complex and changing circumstances. On the one hand, the new model offers less autonomy to the political clienteles and official unions and fosters the influence of the political executive over public opinion and the labour movement. On the other hand, the Mexican executive is increasingly vulnerable to the voters' decision, and takes steps to restore a shaken ligitimacy. State corporatism, however, has remained an enduring characteristic of the relationship of the state to civil society well into the 1990s. It goes along with other, more subtle forms of control, which render the Mexican process of democratization unique and quite confusing.

In an electoral year, mass media are of paramount importance to the orienting of public opinion. Remaining under government control, radio and television networks are kept under close scrutiny, with their badly paid journalists privately receiving money as gifts from PRI officials to ensure that programming reflects the political line of the executive. Censorship is less obvious as far as the print journalists are concerned, probably because only 15 per cent of Mexicans read newspapers on a daily basis. Those who do read them are mostly intellectuals and businessmen whose political mind is already made up, and whose position is usually known to authorities. A common practice is the inclusion in newspapers of full pages of governmental advertising and articles, for which editors receive as much as U.S. $30,000 for a front page. Traditionally, more than 50 per cent of advertising comes from the state and its various agencies. In September 1993, a radio program was suppressed by decree, after Opposition leader Cárdenas was invited to speak on the air. Cárdenas *was* seen on television in October, the first time since 1988 for the PRD contender. The Mexico City–based newspaper *Reforma*, whose editor is Alejandro Junco de la

Vega, a politically independent intellectual who is no friend to the PRI, has attracted readers with his harsh front-page denunciations of alleged electoral frauds in the 28 November 1993 elections in the state of Yucatán. It is impossible to foresee the reaction of PRI authorities to the media's growing autonomy; the simple fact that such things have occurred in recent years is an indication that the official party does not have the stranglehold on information that it enjoyed for many decades (*Gazeta Mercantil*, 24.12.93). This situation may explain why, at the Guadalajara meeting of the Inter-American Press Association (Sociedad Interamericana de Prensa, or SIP) in October 1997, the SIP's freedom-of-the-press committee singled out Mexico as a country where press freedom is in particular jeopardy.*

The Brazilian situation offers a completely different picture. From the early 1980s on, it has been characterized by mounting social demands and union or party reorganization, occurring simultaneously with the New Republic civil government's gradual integration of liberal measures. There is no state-controlled unionized sector, as there is in Mexico, nor is there a strong military hand, as there is in Chile, to enforce the power of the executive. The press has been independent since the mid-1980s, with *Folha de São Paulo* on the forefront of all opposition campaigns against corruption, mismanagement, and human-rights abuses. It contributed to the demise of President Collor de Mello in 1992, when a series of well-documented articles publicized cases of misconduct and made it plain that the president was unable to exert control over his own team. In fact, the press went so far in its accusations against politicians that President Fernando Henrique Cardoso submitted a bill to the legislature that would make journalists liable for fines up to U.S. $90,000 for libel resulting from their stories (Latin American Data Bank, October 1997).

In association with the press, the popular movement has acted with full autonomy through a series of political campaigns, such as Diretas Já in favour of general elections (1984), and through numerous strikes. The Worker's Party (PT) of Luis Inacio da Silva (Lula) emerged as a social democratic alternative to the Right, and is proving very active on all levels of civil society, and even of government, sending more than one member to the executive. Adamant defence of the poor, support of the public sector against privatization, and a bold program of social policies and agrarian reform attract voters from the whole country. Often compared to the Polish Solidarnosç movement in its early years, the PT in the late 1980s shed its image as a São Paulo–based party representative of unionized workers, and successfully won a national audience.

---

* It was alleged that three journalists had been slain and four others abducted, and that twenty documented attacks against journalists have occurred.

The reformers of the New Republic devoted much effort to restoring democratic linkages between independent unions and government (Buchanan, 1989a). The goal of the Social Democratic party (PSDB), founded in 1988, was to bring together the demands of the marginal and of the hard-pressed middle classes into a single moderate, practicable political program. As a main competitor, the PT remained active, if not dominant, among the working class of the southeast. The resurgence of a militant and more pragmatic Left was so spectacular in the aftermath of the military regime that it succeeded in imposing upon the elitist democracy the rules of 'social agreements' (pactos sociais), and the integration of its dominant political figures in the state machinery. This presence, which remains to be assessed, has undoubtedly neutralized the influence of liberal corporate elites. Thus, there is little in Brazil that compares with the Chilean and Mexican situations. In Chile, the popular movement was crushed by General Pinochet's repressive regime. In Mexico, during the 1980s, it was manipulated and partially neutralized by the PRI corporatist network. In Brazil, even in the last years of the authoritarian regime, it thrived, in absolute freedom from a weakened state and the discredited traditional parties. It engaged in activism as quickly as the political conditions for a democratic transition could be met (Tavares de Almeida, 1987).

The best and most recent example of a stabilization program aimed at curbing inflation in the context of an electoral campaign is the Brazilian Plano Real. This attempt was launched in July 1994 by Finance minister Ruben Ricúpero, from a blueprint previously designed by the former Finance minister and PSDB presidential candidate Fernando Henrique Cardoso. The new currency, the 'real,' which began circulating three months before the election, was an electoral exercise designed to bring down inflation for a short time and thereby enhance the chances of the PSDB candidate, who, after many difficulties with traditional interest groups and members of Congress, had engineered the plan before leaving office in February 1994. The contender acknowledged the fact that the new currency was not a solution to the economy's many problems; he promised, if elected, to undertake massive reforms by returning to the constitutional reform thwarted earlier that year by Congress and thereby to 'reorganize the state, create a new federation and promote a broad fiscal, tax and social security reform.' He also proposed to press ahead with the privatization of state-owned monopolies such as telecommunications and oil, both of which require a constitutional amendment before they can be auctioned off (Latin American Weekly Report, 07.07.94).

In addition to confronting other presidential contenders – PT candidate da Silva and Partido Democrático Trabalhista (PDT) leader Lionel Brizola, former governor of Rio de Janeiro – candidate Cardoso faced a wall of opposition against his new stabilization plan. Maria da Conceição Tavares, one of the brains behind the Plano Cruzado, surprised the public by criticizing the Plano Real, describing it as 'yet another shock,' an allusion to the four previous new currencies introduced since 1986, and the false hopes generated by the initial but short-lived successes of the Cruzado and Collor plans against inflation. In any case, Cardoso won the election, with 47 per cent of valid votes, albeit with a considerable abstention rate. The Plano Real was therefore to become the most successful case of short-term electoral politics designed by weak executives in the stormy waters of a democratic transition. It remains to be seen if such leaders are capable of rallying a majority around the blueprint of deeper structural reforms conducive to a greater level of autonomy of the state *vis-à-vis* powerful interest groups.

Stabilization programs conducted in parallel with an electoral campaign make an easy target for organized labour, as was also evidenced by the Plano Real. Seeking the voters' support, decision makers had no choice but to yield to social demands. In September 1994, the stabilization program was shaken by a combination of higher-than-expected inflation rates and consequent legitimate labour demands for compensatory pay increases. Workers at the car-assembly plants in the industrial belt of São Paulo went on strike, demanding pay increases to offset the 12 per cent rise in the official price index since the 'real' was introduced. An agreement was reached within three days, with ministers directly involved in the settling of a deal; the pay increase was agreed to, in the form of a one-off bonus for extraordinary participation, as a productivity reward to vary in accordance with the cash available in each of the firms or groups of firms. Since auto sales in recent months had remained high, auto-maker managers had no problem in paying such a bonus (*Latin American Weekly Report*, 29.09.94). This agreement points at a growing difficulty on the part of decision makers in pursuing the initial goal of the Plano Real, which was to end the automatic indexing of prices and wages, a main contributor to inflation.

6

Privileged Linkages with Corporate Interest Groups

Notwithstanding the necessity for the democratic state to achieve a level of relative autonomy from interest groups, Nelson has convincingly argued that an alliance with mobilized interest groups is a precondition for pursuing deeper economic reforms. This is especially true of the privatization agenda. Once monetary policy is set, stabilization achieved, and political executives equipped to handle their social consequences, the stage is set for subsequent more complex policies. Less dramatic than monetary policy and budget cuts, but still invested with a strong nationalist component (most important in Latin American political culture) is the paramount issue of privatization. As is well recognized in the literature, privatization has as its goal the elimination of an often underproductive, deficit-ridden public sector in order to restore public-finance equilibrium. It also reduces the influence of bureaucracy over the decision-making process, theoretically freeing both policy and the market from the alleged inertia of the state apparatus. Opponents of privatization argue that it puts an end to the capacity of the state to act as a main entrepreneur and co-ordinator of the economy. It remains to be seen, however, if a 'lean state' is condemned to impotence. The advocates of privatization answer that it all depends on the regulation mechanisms which are set up, and on the administrative capacity of the state to enforce on a daily basis the minimal, nevertheless inescapable, regulations imposed upon the corporate players. This condition is not always met.

The issue of privatization has long roots in Brazil. As early as 1953, the ultra-liberal São Paulo entrepreneurs mounted a campaign of such intensity against the creation of Petróleos Brasileiros (PETROBRAS), intended to be another public monopoly, that nationalist President Getulio Vargas, in power from 1930 to 1945, and elected again in 1950, was given no choice by the military but to resign. He resorted instead to suicide in August 1954, generating considerable public outcry. More recently, in 1974, under the Geisel pro-business presidency, privatization of public assets was again at issue (the wealthy corporate São Paulo–based Grupo Visão being adamantly in favour of it), but the former military regime had by then a strong commitment to the public sector, which it envisioned as an engine of growth. Military presidents were the main contributors to its development. For instance, state-owned PETRO-BRAS was becoming, by the mid-1970s, the major corporate group in Latin America, with twenty-nine branches and an annual, continuously growing, budget of U.S. $7 billion.

In retrospect, one may view with irony the 1979 initiative of President João Batista Figueiredo to create his Programa nacional de desburocratização, which achieved nothing but the creation of more bureaucracy. In the transition period, only thirteen firms were effectively sold to the private sector; that is, a meagre 0.6 per cent of the public sector's equity, for U.S. $200 million (Werneck, 1989). President José Sarney Costa, who inherited a classical state-oriented political program designed by President Tancredo Neves's advisers, was in no position to shift decisively from the initial scheme. Recalled to office after much manoeuvring and yielding to corporate political pressures, he reactivated the whole issue in 1987 and created the Comissão nacional de privatização, which later identified a list of seventy companies which were candidates for privatization (Schneider, 1988).

The privatization program met such strong opposition from the unions and from a majority in Congress that the whole process came to a sudden halt. A few months after their improvised privatization, such entities as the Instituto Nacional de Colonização e Reforma Agraria (INCRA) and Empresa Brasileira da Terra (EMBRATER), the state company responsible for supporting farmers, were returned to the public sector. At the time, the power of the executive to implement policies was in a shambles. Privatization would not again reach the forefront of national policy until the beginning of President Collor de Mello's mandate in 1990.

As the first democratically elected president since Jânio da Silva Quadros in 1960, President Collor de Mello came to office with a level of legitimacy not seen for a long time in Brazil. He intended to follow a liberal policy that was both radical and orthodox. Given his narrow political base, he understood that swift action was to be taken if some degree of success was to be achieved (Schneider, 1992). The Programa nacional de desestatização was a major element in the Collor de Mello liberal 'package.' Unfortunately, ambiguous signals sent on various occasions, such as the June 1991 Guadalajara summit of Latin American leaders, showed that his political commitment towards liberalism was not without nationalist overtones. Collor de Mello also had to consider the plain fact that the bureaucracy was not on his side and, therefore, was moving rather cautiously. Investigation teams, or CPIs, empowered by Congress, also kept a vigilant eye on how privatization was implemented. Many believed that the links between the state apparatus and the interested corporate groups were nothing more than cases of influence peddling.

One year after the formal phasing-out by the Plano Collor of twenty-four public companies, all the firms were still operating. Amidst mounting controversy and frantic opposition from the PSDB and the PT, the process was accelerated slightly in late 1991, when several subsidiaries of PETROBRAS and USIMINAS, the Minas Gerais iron mine company, were offered to private buyers, this last for U.S. $1.2 billion. State-owned air transporter Viação Aérea de São Paulo (VASP) was offered to local investors, but, as a result of overbidding (a practice typical of the Collor de Mello era), the whole transaction came under investigation. Generally, privatization operations were restricted to the industrial sector: mining (USIMINAS), steel (AÇOMINAS, CST [Companhia Siderúrgica de Tubarão], CSN [Companhia Siderurgica Nacional], COSIPA [Companhia Siderurgica de São Paulo]), petrochemicals (PETROFLEX) and fertilizers (PETROFERTIL, GOIASFERTIL), as well as air transportation (VASP). But the blueprint made clear that operations would eventually embrace telecommunications (TELEBRAS [Telecomunicações Brasileiras] as well as aeronautics (EMBRAER [Empresa Brasileira de Aeronaútica]).

The first six months of President Itamar Franco's mandate were marked by even more than usual confusion, as three ministers of the economy (*fazenda*) stayed in office for periods varying from a few weeks to a few months. The third one, Eliseu Resende, tried to follow up the original Collor program and managed to privatize both CSN and CST in April 1993. Nonetheless, he could not pursue his program any further (*Gazeta Mercantil*, 21.12.93). It became evident that President Itamar Franco was an undecided and transitional figure who wished to avoid political turmoil as much as possible during his short mandate, so that for the time being, the high-risk radical path was to be put aside. In June 1993, the PSDB senator and renowned intellectual Fernando Henrique Cardoso was appointed to pursue a gradualist program of his own, to be cautiously implemented according to the unpredictable and highly volatile domestic conditions. With new elections set for late 1994, politicians and their respective parties prepared for political manoeuvres on a broad scale, which left little room for heroic struggles around the thorny issue of privatization.

In Maravall and Santamaria's terms (1986), when there is no popular support or parliamentary majority in favour of reforms, the executive inevitably becomes powerless. Only general elections can provide a decisive breakthrough and restore a level of political legitimacy from which genuine public policies can be designed in accordance with the new conditions. Although it is more than dubious that Finance minister Cardoso was anywhere close to becoming the inquisitor of the public sector, whose role in the realm of a 'self-sufficient economy' he had so highly praised in his earlier 'dependency school' writings,* privatization was tentatively resumed in the metal industry, when COSIPA (São Paulo's steel company) and AÇOMINAS of Minas Gerais were auctioned off in August 1993 to dominant corporate groups such as Votorantim, a gigantic Brazilian conglomerate.

The main reason for governmental action in this area was that the financial contribution of the state to these poorly performing industries was considered to be far beyond its financial capacity, while local private players seemed ready to take charge. Public investment in steel transformation was estimated at U.S. $7,390 million; at U.S. $3.6 billion for petrochemicals; at U.S. $670 million for fertilizers; and finally at U.S. $425 million for machinery and aeronautics (Werneck, 1992: 272). More recently, the same logic was to prevail in further privatization operations. By the end of 1994, thirty-three undercapitalized industries were put on sale. These included firms involved in river transportation (Lloyd Brasileiro), mining (Mineração Caraíba), computers (COBRA), and aircraft assembly (EMBRAER). Other manufacturing firms and the electric-power distributor Rio Light and Excelsa were also auctioned off. Total sales amounted to more than U.S. $8.3 billion (Banco Nacional de Desenvolvimento Econômico Social [BNDES], Annual Report, 1994). The sale by auction of 50 per cent of the shares in Petroquímica União in early 1994 raised U.S. $271 million. Other, more valuable, petrochemical firms are expected to be sold in 1995, for an estimated value of about U.S. $4.5 billion.

It is revealing that no significant foreign investments have been included in these deals, a fact which is quite consistent with the dependency tenet stating that national industry ought to remain in local hands. Brazilian corporate actors made it a condition of their support for reforms, particularly when consensus was building around the Cardoso candidature against PT leader Luis Inacio da Silva (Lula). Another interesting policy, definitely inspired by the British model of privatization, was being designed; it would allow for employees of public firms, including the second-largest state firm, Companhia do Vale do Rio Doce (CVRD), to purchase shares in their respective firms. Nevertheless, compared with Chile and Mexico, and as far as 'strategic' areas of the economy are concerned, privatization in Brazil has maintained a relatively slow pace that gained momentum only after Fernando Henrique Cardoso's election in October 1994;

---

* With Enzo Faletto, *Desarrollo y dependencia en America latina* (1968); *O modelo Brasileiro* (1971).

57 per cent in value of the entire program was achieved during 1996–7 (table 12). And more important, it is different in nature. Foreign capital is allowed into the process, up to a maximum of 40 per cent of total voting shares. As an example, a consortium of three multinational companies has been formed to bid for the Bolivia–Brazil gas pipeline. Broken Hill Proprietary of Australia, British Gas, and Britain–based Tenneco Gas are expected to take part in all stages of the project, which involves construction of a 2,300-kilometre pipeline from Bolivia to Campinas in São Paulo State, for an estimated total investment of U.S. $4.2 billion. The World Bank has expressed its reluctance to back the project, which is under the control of the two state monopolies: PETROBRAS and the Bolivian oil and gas state firm Yacimientos Petrolíferos Fiscales Bolivianos (YPFB). Brazil has signalled its intention to go ahead with the project, even without World Bank support, thus indicating that there was still room for public initiatives in the strategic energy field. PETROBRAS keeps a 51 per cent control for itself, while YPFB retains 20 per cent (*Latin American Weekly Report*, 10.02.94).

Brazil has remained committed to its nationalist paradigm for two reasons: first, both the organized working Left and the corporate Right, although divergent in their assessment of the role of the public sector, are in full political agreement when it comes to the protection of 'national property'; second, in direct opposition to Mexico and Chile, the weight and magnitude of the industrial sector in the tenth-ranking country in terms of gross domestic product makes the issue of attracting new multinational corporations a secondary one in Brazil. There is no question that throughout the structural adjustment process, and despite its poor showing in reform policy, Brazil has enjoyed in the aftermath of structural change a much better international bargaining position than any of the other Latin American countries under study.

In Chile, the 'Chicago Boys' created environments highly favourable to corporate ambitions, which on occasion proved rather weak on financial grounds. Two phases characterize the privatization of the public sector in Chile. The first, from 1973 to 1982, began with a swift return to the private sector of most of the 450 companies and banks nationalized under President Allende's National Unity government. A core of major industrial enterprises engaged in copper and energy production, with CODELCO the main player, remain in public hands on grounds of their high contribution to the state Treasury (Yotópoulos, 1989). Throughout the discussions, which involved military as well as civil technocrats, it appeared that financial stability was the main criterion for rejecting total privatization of the public sector, an indication that Chile's policies were capable of flexibility in terms of ideological preferences (Marcel, 1989).

The late 1970s saw an extension of the process to non-strategic areas, with

the privatization of companies which had not been touched by previous legislation. As the main recipient of fiscal incentives and state credits (up to 20 per
cent), local holdings such as Cruzat-Larrain and Javier Vial came to control
more than half of the two hundred largest Chilean companies. Concentrated
ownership of the privatized companies was thus an explicit objective of the
regime. In 1980, the social-security funds, to be administered by Administradoras de Fondos de Pensiones (AFP), were included in this process, and health
and education insurance companies were also privatized (International Bank for
Reconstruction and Development, *Trends in Developing Economies* [1992]).

Crippled by debts and low profits, the bulk of Chile's private sector almost
crumbled as a consequence of the 1982–3 crisis associated with the world
recession. As a response to this unforeseen challenge, the state deemed it necessary to intervene in favour of the corporate elites: a decisive shift from a pro-
market to a status-quo policy. An odd, non-public/non-private sector was temporarily reinstated, to be gradually sold again to the surviving entrepreneurs. As
a consequence of the restored profitability of the so-called strategic sector, the
second phase of privatization was undertaken in the mid-1980s. These essential
companies were once again returned to the private sector, in which the domestic
pension-plan holdings (AFP) and foreign investors appeared as new players.
Local spending, now circulating from the banking system to industry, under a
new and genuine legislation of *capitalismo social*, contributed to investment in
modernization projects (Luders, 1991; Business International Corporation,
1991). By the early 1990s, the process of privatization in Chile was significantly advanced.

In figure 6.1, it is interesting to observe the lag which characterizes many
privatization operations in Chile. It is worth observing that the chronogram of
devolution to private owners differs, sometimes significantly, from the original
calendar. Almost a year elapsed before Chilmetro was fully privatized. The air-
line LanChile was expected to be fully privatized by 1987, but was still 23 per
cent publicly owned by 1991. The privatization of the Edelnor operation is even
less conclusive, with only 18 per cent of total shares sold into private hands by
1991. This lag attests to the difficulties encountered by authorities in their
desire to transfer to the private sector a series of state firms. Either these companies do not meet the necessary standards of financial soundness (Endasa), or
cannot deliver the minimal profit levels which would make them attractive to
buyers (Colbun) at the deadline set by the privatization blueprint, or there are
no reasonable or acceptable offers on the part of particular buyers (LanChile).
Sometimes, all three constraints are observable, and privatization is simply
postponed *sine die* (Santiago Metro).

Other data (Sáez, 1993) reveal an interesting feature which we suggest is

Figure 6.1 The lag between the privatization agenda and its effectiveness for selected firms in Chile (in years)

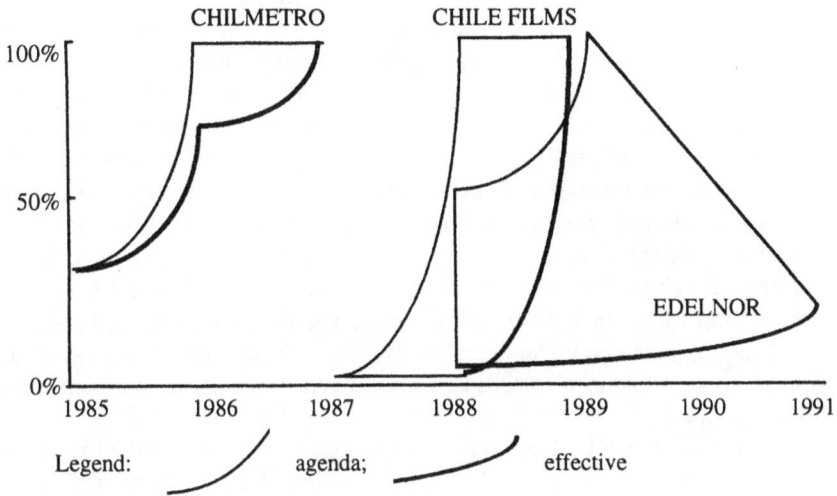

Source: Based on data gathered in Muñoz, 1993: 95

related to the emergence of a democratic executive in this country. All privatization processes which had not met their goal of 100 per cent private ownership by the end of 1989 were still not concluded by 1994, four years later. Furthermore, the Concertación did not launch any new privatization operations after 1990, and demonstrated no hurry in concluding those already begun, even those at an advanced stage of the process (LanChile). The paradigm on which the previous policy was based had changed. Simply put, the new economic team did not display the same level of generosity towards corporate groups as had the previous regime.

Long-term orthodoxy therefore characterizes the Chilean privatization process, although the state has closely monitored individual operations, particularly in difficult circumstances. It has therefore frequently played a very active role, which is not sufficiently accounted for in the theoretical literature. These elements should motivate us to look beyond simplistic views about classical *laissez-faire* and think about a new chapter to be written on the role of the active state in the privatization agenda. When the Concertación came to power, the privatization process was slowed down, if not interrupted. Though Chile was a pioneer in the area of privatization, the state still retains a considerable entrepreneurial role. The copper corporation CODELCO, Empresa Nacional de

Mineración (ENAMI), Empresa Nacional de Petróleos (ENAP), and forty-odd companies administered by the Corporación de Fomento (CORFO) are still in public hands. They range in size from giant firms such as the Colbun–Machicura hydro-electric power complex and the national lottery, through the Iquique free zone (already owned by private investors for 49 per cent of its assets) and several regional power distributors, to firms devoted to mining, rail transport, shipping, wheat marketing, and supplying Easter Island (Rapanui). As a group, they are profitable. In 1993 their combined profits reached U.S. $42.3 million, more than double the sum of a year earlier. The only loss-maker was the coal-mining Empresa Nacional de Carvón (ENACAR). This good performance most certainly accounts for the continuing public interest in such industrial activities. The new democratic state did not move away from this practice until 1994, when the second Concertación government, under President Frei-Ruiz Tagle, issued a plan which offered the private sector participation of at least 10 per cent in all CORFO–administered firms (Latin America Data Bank, 03.02.94).

Compared with Chile, Mexico had a steep road to climb if it wished to privatize extensively an already gigantic public sector of 1,155 firms, which, in 1982, included the banks nationalized under López Portillo. The success of the endeavour, with almost 1,000 enterprises returned to the private sector, has been of such magnitude that Mexico is the champion of privatization in Latin America. It must be remembered, though, that domestic factors such as the opposition at the very core of the PRI accounted for the politicization of the issue under President de la Madrid. An incremental and less conflictive strategy was therefore introduced by the executive to forestall controversy. As in Chile, a 'strategic sector' was excluded from buy-outs, and only smaller companies in a wide array of activities, ranging from a soccer team to public hotels and a bike-assembly line, were privatized. In 1988, these 758 firms amounted to less than 3 per cent of the state sector's contribution to GDP (Aspe Amella and Aguayo Mancera, 1989). The privatization program had been conducted in a shrewd manner; more symbolic than not in terms of value of assets, it nevertheless prepared public opinion for what was to come.

More dramatic was the end of the state banking monopoly, in which individuals were allowed to acquire shares up to a 1 per cent limit of the total value of equity. Such limitations to capital concentration helped to defuse fears of a massive takeover by important private holdings in this critical area of economic activity. The Mexican model differs drastically from the Chilean as far as monopolies are concerned. The last phase of President de la Madrid's mandate was almost entirely devoted to restoring profit to potentially saleable public firms, while waiting for favourable market conditions to implement the process.

This was done by President Salinas, with an emphasis upon the banking sector, and in the radical manner most representative of the first two years of his mandate. The operation proved quite profitable to the Treasury: assets worth U.S. $5.8 billion were sold to domestic and foreign investors for an estimated U.S. $11 billion. Thus, the Mexican government eased its budgetary crisis and was able to channel new money into projects such as the Programa Nacional de Solidaridad (PRONASOL). Another set of 226 public companies, including strategic ones, were also privatized. If PEMEX remains a public entity, because of the high symbolic value attached to it, financial crisis has put an end to its monopoly. Practices such as contracting-out, and investment opportunities for foreign capital have been allowed by PEMEX since 1991. Finally, in order to cope with the rather narrow capital base which has been an obstacle to further private shares in the banking sector, Salinas put forward the initiative of a national pension plan, similar to the Chilean Administradoras de Fondos de Pensiones (AFP) model.

7

A New Relationship between State and Labour

The political problems associated with structural change and labour unrest have received a somewhat impressionistic and unsophisticated treatment in the conventional economic literature. Such scholarship was obviously more concerned with quantitative results than with the political and social consequences of government intervention.

Governments must first run the political juggernaut of public opinion and interest groups, and implement these broad changes before beginning to sell off firms. This is why the most successful privatization efforts in major Latin American nations have been accomplished in those countries with the strongest political executives. (Business International Corporation, 1991)

Simplistic as it may seem, the final statement quoted above addresses the real question. Let us try to formulate in terms of political analysis what policy implementation means for organized labour groups. How do 'strong executives' run the political juggernaut of public opinion and organized groups? Through repression and the use of force, which is the easiest way, or rather through democratic means? Are they strong because they are authoritarian, or because they manage to make dextrous use of the rules of democracy to gather political support around heartfelt, nevertheless defensible, economic policies, as in Felipe Gonzalez's Spain or Patricio Aylwin's Chile?

   Going back to Remmer's (1990) question: is economic policy essentially related to regime variation? Are policy choices constrained by socio-economic characteristics or by the political similarities and differences among national situations, which can be very complex? We agree that the complexities of a given society are likely to produce unconventional, distinct policies. In Brazil, for example, one of the largest countries in the world, with 160 million citizens, many more players, organizations, and institutions are likely to mobilize around the issue of structural reforms than, say, in Chile. In a larger country with many distinct regions, the issue of reform is likely to provoke more debates and raise harsher conflicts than it would among the tight network of politicians and technocrats in smaller countries. All actors are capable of providing their specific interpretation of a foreign reform blueprint, given their respective set of interests. Others will voice their concern for a national non-partisan interest. These expressions of opinion, when they are formally recognized in the political system, are a valuable contribution to the democratic debate. Thus, the interaction of the ideological orientations of the leaders and their followers (whether motivated by particular or by national interests) with autonomous and politicized public opinion, fragmented as they may be, over the blueprint of a policy imposed by international conditions, is in our view the locus of democratic processes. A common language has to be developed from many vocabularies. As institutions democratize, this interaction with civil society is bound to grow in size and scope.

Unfortunately, civil society is as weak as the democratic state itself (Przeworski, 1995: 53). Among the many conditions that seem to make it weak is the absence of prestigious organizations. Political parties were prohibited after the 1964 Brazilian and the 1973 Chilean *golpes*, or, in Mexico, kept at the margins of the political system throughout the PRI's sixty-year rule. In all cases, party members were either kept under close supervision or the parties were disbanded and the members dispersed. They had to reorganize, bearing new names, with new leaders. In contrast to the Middle East, political and class radicalism, lacking influential leaders, declined rapidly in Latin America. Such radicalism lost most of its appeal among the masses, probably because it was deemed incapable of playing a useful role in incorporating them into the political system. Therefore, at the outset of democratization, the absence of strong popular parties led by radical intellectuals left the labour movement, more closely associated with the struggles of ordinary workers, with an important role to play. If no party was in a position to force the economically disadvantaged masses to pursue their interests within the 'accepted rules of the game,' then the unions would have to do it. The prerequisite for keeping the masses in line was to discipline the organizations themselves, a task to which a younger generation of popular leaders committed itself.

Recent research about and from Latin America demonstrates that, in two cases out of three, labour mobilization is closely associated either with the opening of the political debate in a democratic transition, or with the implementation of liberal economics. Strikes represent a relevant variable in this context. In Brazil as well as in Chile, the number of strikes grows in parallel with the transition itself, from 1985 onwards in Brazil and from 1989 on in Chile. Strikes may be linked to the enormous costs entailed for labour in terms of both wages and employment. Strikes in Brazil went up from 312 in 1983, in the context of democratization, to 4,189 in 1989, at the end of President Sarney Costa's mandate. In Chile, they were up to 101 in 1989 in the phase of democratization, from 41 in 1983, under General Pinochet. In both cases, there is a link between the country's political process and the open expression of labour-organized opposition to adjustment reforms (Heredia, 1993).

One would expect Mexico to replicate this pattern, since structural adjustment went forward more decisively than in Brazil, and possibly as much as in Chile. Surprisingly, data show that it is not the case, with strikes declining in number from 216 in 1983, before the launching of reforms, to 118 in 1989 at the beginning of President Salinas's *sexenio*. To account for the low level of labour unrest in Mexico, the literature stresses two main factors. First, the salaries of unionized workers were to some extent protected from the costs of economic adjustment, and public employment grew by 18 per cent during President de la Madrid's mandate. Second, union management was always kept under tight control by the state apparatus; in other words, union elites remained loyal to the PRI regime, and seemed eager to avoid the heavy political costs to themselves and to the state associated with labour unrest. Mexico's case clearly points to the capacity of non-democratic (or partially democratized) regimes to integrate into the framework of adjustment policies mechanisms for reducing transitional costs. These are 'spontaneous' mechanisms, in Heredia's terms, through which manipulation by the elite, and even its corruption practices, can be used in an *ad hoc* fashion, to ensure that public employees remain under control. Of course, sound data on this rather sensitive issue cannot be found, but Mexico is an example that there are other, less democratic means than institutional bargaining by which structural adjustment reforms can proceed without damaging the relationship between organized workers and the political executive in the volatile context of a regime transition. Such are the lessons to be drawn, we suggest, from the *peso* crisis of late 1994. The *pacto* agreed upon by political players in January 1995 is a clear indication that the state has not lost its grip over organized interest groups, and that institutionalized interaction with labour elites is still used as a dominant mode of governance.

Stabilizing a failing economy is an endless task, to which Mexican presidents have devoted all the energies of genuine firemen. Structural adjustment policies may seem ripe in all fields of public intervention, but analysts should be very cautious in proclaiming the enduring success of reforms. In January 1995, President Ernesto Zedillo's administration drafted an emergency economic plan to help counter the effects of a sudden, sharp devaluation of the peso that took place in December 1994. The peso devaluation happened in two stages. The first was a decision to raise by 15 per cent the level at which the government would intervene to support the currency; this stage was implemented on 19 December, announced on 20 December, and discontinued the following morning, ushering in a second phase, in which the peso was allowed to float freely against the U.S. dollar. The policy of propping the peso at the 3.46 level had cost the Central Bank, in these two days alone, an estimated U.S. $4 billion (*Latin American Weekly Report*, 05.01.95; see also table 9).

This emergency plan was heterodox in nature, as are all stabilization plans that are state-monitored social pacts (*pactos sociales*). The *plano* was drafted after hours of consultations among representatives of the government, labour unions, and the business sector. It was primarily aimed at preventing inflation from spiralling out of control as a result of a 60 per cent devaluation of the currency. The central components of the plan called on business and labour to hold down wages and prices, while committing the government to reducing its expenditures. Under the plan, labour unions agreed to limit their requests for wage hikes to a maximum of 7 per cent, which would include a 4 per cent wage increase, plus up to 3 per cent in productivity bonuses, a meagre compensation for a 60 per cent wage loss. For its part, the corporate sector accepted a moratorium on price increases, except for 'justifiable' price adjustments on imported products. The government, in turn, agreed to lower some taxes for businesses as an incentive to abide by the price moratorium. In addition, the government would work to lower the fiscal deficit through two measures. On the one hand, it would attempt to increase revenue by expediting the privatization of petrochemical plants, harbour administration, and power plants. On the other, it would reduce public expenditures by an equivalent of 1.3 per cent of GDP (*Latin American Weekly Report*, 05.01.95).

The twilight of a PRI-dominated labour movement was marked, in July 1997, by the death of Fidel Velasquez, leader of the mighty Confederación de Trabajadores de México (CTM) and the most influential representative of blue-collars within official decision-making circles. Velasquez had been responsible for the anti-inflation social pacts. In late August 1997, members of the Congreso del Trabajo (CT) elected as his successor Hector Valdes Romo, who was also acting as director of the union representing government workers, Federación de Sindicatos de Trabajadores al Servicio del Estado (FSTSE). The two official state-controlled unions faced a difficult period, as dissent within government-led unions became increasingly apparent in consequence of the measures implemented in the aftermath of the peso crisis. Opposition grew from the powerful Asociación Sindical de Pilotos Aviadores (ASPA) and Sindicato de Telefonistas de la República Mexicana (STRM), which were both fighting for autonomy. Experiencing a loss of their traditional influence with an inflexible Zedillo administration, unable to check the influence of business organizations who rejected their proposal of a 23 per cent minimum wage hike, both the CT and the FSTSE faced growing competition from a new, independent labour organization, the Foro Sindical Unitario (FSU). Understandably, the opposition parties PRD and PAN were also pushing for an end to the long-standing system by which the CT, the CTM, and subordinate unions gave preference to workers affiliated to the governing PRI (*Los Angeles Times*, 08.20.97; *La Jornada*, 08.21.97). In November, the new interim leader of the CTM, Leonardo Rodriguez Alcaine, called for an end to the annual anti-inflation agreements, emphasizing the deterioration of wages during President Zedillo's administration. Both CTM and CT demanded changes in Mexico's labour laws to increase the Christmas bonus for workers, and questioned the government's ability to create jobs. This unusual, belligerent position was probably influenced by the recent creation of two independent labour organizations: the FSU and the Unión Nacional de Trabajadores (UNT), which broke away from the CT and the CTM. Both organizations claimed that they had no affiliations with other institutions, either the PRI-dominated government or opposition political parties. They made progress in the *maquiladora* area, not without considerable resistance from official unions (*El Nacional*, 04.11.97).

State corporatism is traditional in Latin America, and still plays (as it has done remarkably in Mexico) a significant role in the political quiescence of organized labour. But other phenomena are also at work, such as the modernization of the opposition forces themselves. For one, the upsurge of strikes in Brazil is a clear indication that organized labour can achieve a considerable degree of autonomy from state control, while authoritarian institutions swiftly crumble in the process of transition under weak political executives. The anticipation of political participation and material gains are attracting a new generation of sophisticated leaders and intellectuals. By gaining autonomy, labour organizations are likely to regain some of the prestige they had lost in the previous era.

While it distances itself from the previous Marxist activism of the older generation, the Latin American Left is becoming much more active in the domestic political arena, as democracy gains ground. It is possible now to establish a more peaceful, institutionalized relationship between a state apparatus dominated by moderate reformers and organized labour. In much the same way as was Lech Walesa's Polish movement Solidarnosç in the early 1980s, the Brazilian Partido dos Trabalhadores (PT) is an example of a regional labour movement converted to address broad national issues. This displays a firm trend towards political inclusion of labour in the decision-making process, and not simply on the basis of elite manipulation. Even in the Brazilian case, where confrontation mounts in parallel with market reforms, strikes and hard anti-government rhetoric do not exclude institutionalized arrangements among unions, business, and state bureaucrats. Such agreements point to a degree of acceptance, on the part of labour elites, for liberal economic policies that include some social components.

The social democratic blueprint is not foreign to Latin America. There is, however, a standing controversy around the principle of 'social pacts.' These pacts involve mutual agreements among business, labour, and representatives of the government. In Brazil, the automotive industry and the unions signed the 1992 automobile pact (*pacto automobilístico*). All three parties agreed on a single plan aimed at restructuring the automotive sector and restoring its profitability. The federal state was to provide strong incentives. Business would engage in modernization of its assembly lines, while unions accepted cuts in salaries to save jobs (Castañeda, 1993: 312ff). The plan was rewarded by surprisingly good results in 1993, the best year in the history of the Brazilian automotive industry, with growth rates exceeding 15 per cent (Scheuer, 1993: 39).

Social pacts have also been used in Chile, where the anticipated privatization of CODELCO always remained a divisive issue. The first clue to how the incoming Frei administration sees the future of state-owned enterprises will come from its decision on Radomiro Tomic, a major copper ore deposit. In 1993, the Finance ministry refused to fund its development costs, estimated at U.S. $450 million. CODELCO's management proposed developing it as a separate enterprise from Chuquicamata, with a new labour regime, and a total workforce of about six hundred. Harsh competition was expected to come from the El Abra project, involving Canadian and U.S. investments. It is worth noting that, while state bureaucrats were calling for full privatization of CODELCO, there were many who mobilized in the opposite direction. Former Mining minister Juan Hamilton, a Socialist party member, along with the CODELCO unions, fought to stop partial asset-stripping, such as had occurred at the El Abra operation. The battle was lost in 1992 when a law was passed to allow CODELCO to exploit its holdings in joint ventures with foreign investors. Nevertheless, CODELCO management has been gradually winning round the unions to accept such proposals as productivity-linked wage increases.

Unfortunately, this important labour pact was abruptly jeopardized when it became known that CODELCO's erratic management was responsible for financial losses amounting to U.S. $206 million on speculative futures trading on the metals market. This scandal resulted in the dismissal of the company president, Alejandro Noemi, and also damaged former Finance minister Alejandro Foxley's image in the country. Foxley, a Christian Democrat, was committed to keeping CODELCO in public hands. The case fuelled a harsh controversy between the Right's political opponents of the Concertación, who called again for CODELCO to be privatized, and the unions, mobilized against privatization. Labour proclaimed that, given the situation, it would accept no further wage cuts and would even reclaim salary money from the previous bargain. This incident clearly points to the importance of correct public behaviour on the part of policy makers, to ensure that, in a new democracy undertaking structural reforms, an early equilibrium can be reached between conflicting interest groups and conflicting visions of public policy. It also raises other important questions about the practice of equity in times of structural change.

The problem with changing already fragile economic systems is that short-term and long-term agendas often come into open conflict, and may result in worsening economic conditions for the poor. During the 1960s and 1970s, the long-term national industrial strategies of Argentina, Chile, Brazil, and Mexico all followed a logic of relative self-sufficiency, which had the merit of supporting the slow rise of a middle class in urban areas. The challenge of the debt crisis subsequently began to undermine both the planning capacity of the state and the vitality of the middle class. The crisis imposed a shift from long-term objectives to short-term stabilization measures. All through the 1980s, top decision makers in these countries paid less attention to structural reform issues than to stabilization and external bargaining with creditor countries or agencies.

Chile, more than Brazil and Mexico, provides an interesting example of the civilized environment new democracies can provide to both capital and labour, in total contrast to the earlier authoritarian style of macroeconomic planning and insensitive state management. The democratic debate is also mother of change. We have seen that Chilean democrats were interested, from the outset of the transition process, in seeking social development strategies to generate growth that would translate into some sort of redistribution in an enhanced labour market. This is an absolute necessity for competitive economies based upon acquired know-how and sophisticated technologies. Their intention was to widen a rather narrow domestic market and to act against marginality. However, it is unlikely that their general policy would shift away from its initial preoccupation with achieving a market-regulated economy, given low levels of private savings and restrictive public expenditures. The question is now opened to discussion: how will they handle a challenge of such magnitude?

Governments that want to eradicate poverty while minimizing losses of efficiency are not helpless in capitalist economies. The social democratic model is theoretically viable. Governments can encourage technological innovation; they can counteract economic fluctuations; they can facilitate labor mobility; they can deliver welfare services and maintain incomes. The degree of irrationality in capitalism is not a given. Governments elected with a mandate to assure everyone of material security do have instruments with which to pursue their mission. (Przeworski, 1991: 133)

We believe that this mission will take as its foremost goal the reduction of the effects of transition costs. The new measures will try to tackle the problems induced by the previous, upstream adjustment policies. They will be envisioned as the maturation process of adjustment itself, though they will nevertheless display many differences with upstream reforms and should include new concerns. In response to a more sophisticated economic environment and to a stabilized, growing economy, some authors suggest they are likely to restore an active role for the state:

Government has a special role in promoting the development of human resources. By extension of agricultural services, it can improve the skills of farmers. By providing unemployment assistance and retraining facilities, it can help workers to accept more readily new labour-saving technologies. By providing information and conducting research, it can help to reduce monopolistic practices. By investing in physical infrastructure (such as irrigation to raise agricultural price elasticities, rural feeder roads to bring products to markets, harbours and communications), it can provide the conditions for price incentives [such as devaluation] to work, and stimulate private investment. (Streeten, 1993: 1283–4)

In political terms, these interventions are truly reformist, in the sense that their avowed intention is to shift the balance of power from the traditional elites to the middle classes, from an oligarchy to a thriving class of new entrepreneurs. Threatening as they are to the traditional order, these policies may be pursued only if moderate reformists prove strong enough to overcome the resistance that they are likely to provoke; to deter, for example, any attempt on the part of the military, supported by conservative elites, to regain power.

The experience of our three case studies shows that abrupt changes in monetary and macroeconomic policy, which involve drastic consequences for almost every group in society, are possibly the thorniest issue new democracies have to deal with, one which requires both a strong reformist commitment on the part of the authorities, and a competent decision-making process. Chile and Mexico were more favoured than Brazil in this respect. Despite the obvious distinctiveness of their examples, many of their features can be generalized to a whole array of reform experiments which took place in the 1980s in Latin America. Adjustment reforms fuel harsh opposition, undermine state legitimacy, and stir discontent in intellectual and political circles. All executives lose popularity.

These experiments, particularly in the case of Brazil, made innumerable victims among finance ministers and their technical staffs. This is one reason, as we came to see, why these transitional governments have been so reluctant to engage in them.

8

Assessing the Economic Performance
of Reforms

Brazil, the Clumsy Reformer

Brazil had a thriving economy in the 1960s and 1970s, with annual growth often exceeding 10 per cent; these rates have never been matched since (table 1). Although the 1973 oil crisis affected growth, Brazil remained a respectable newly industrialized economy until 1981. The following decade presented a very different picture, as the country failed to pursue a consistent set of adjustment reforms in response to a changing world economy marked by growing competition. Per capita growth peaked, the net flow of foreign capital dried up, and savings fell sharply, which strongly affected government reserves. Sporadic attempts at structural reforms and stabilization programs proved insufficient to curb inflation, which moved from an average yearly rate of 42 per cent in the late 1970s to rates above 2,668 per cent in 1994. Then came the Plano Real, with rates falling under 12 per cent (table 2). The public contribution to gross domestic investment remained fairly consistent during the period (table 3), and state intervention remained high, as evidenced by trade restrictions, import licensing and exchange controls, subsidies to nationally owned firms, and an extensive public sector, most pervasive in infrastructures (oil, power generation, nuclear facilities) and in industry (armament assembly-lines, steel, and mineral extraction).

Many policy changes were initiated in 1990. Trade regulations for more than 1,500 products were liberalized, restrictions on imports of technical and computer equipment were abolished, though generally without the necessary transition phase, while privatization and financial sector reforms were slowly and sometimes clumsily initiated. In March 1990, the Collor de Mello government introduced a stabilization program involving a temporary freeze of financial assets and a broad set of policies and programs aimed at restructuring the economy by reducing the interventionist role of the state. These efforts, however, had only temporary and partial effects.

In 1990, the government achieved a consolidated operational budget surplus equivalent to 1.4 per cent of GDP (gross domestic product), thanks to cuts in public expenditures, a tax on financial gains, and below-market interest rates on frozen government bonds. This surplus shrank in 1991, and a deficit, amounting to 1.7 per cent of total GDP, reappeared in 1992. Under President Itamar Franco, the government has not interfered with contractual financial arrangements nor imposed price controls. If it was successful in avoiding hyper-inflation, it could not end the massive flight of domestic assets caused by volatile interest rates in the country (table 15). Net flows of capital were noticeable in the direction of Portugal, the United States, and several tax havens such as the Bahamas. By mid-1994, a new stabilization program was put forward, including a new currency and a tight monetary policy, which sharply reduced inflation (table 2).

Until then, it is no surprise that successive governments found it hard to restore foreign confidence in the Brazilian economy through negotiated agreements with government creditors and international agencies. Brazil had until 1995 the heaviest debt burden of all developing countries (table 4). Following a tight phase in 1985 during which the ratio of total debt burden to total GDP and to exports (table 5) reached high levels, the Brazilian government in 1991 arrived at a first agreement with foreign commercial banks concerning 1989–90 arrears. Short-term interest payments culminated in 1992, while amortization of capital slowly accelerated (table 5). A second agreement was reached in 1992 with the creditors of the Club de Paris (a regrouping of the main Western creditors to Latin America), which was followed by bilateral ratification. International Monetary Fund (IMF) credits were never significant, in comparison with Chile or Mexico (tables 6–7). The same can be said about the Brazilian debt to foreign official creditors (table 8). By late 1992, foreign banks, along with the local government, announced a reduction of the debt and the debt service for U.S. $44 billion commercial debt. Negotiations were also conducted over the composition of debt instruments, given that more than U.S. $3.2 billion would be necessary to enhance old-to-new instruments. Brazil therefore agreed to raise debt service payments to 50 per cent of interest due after the new term sheet was signed in November 1993. Brazil was among the last Latin American countries to come to an agreement with its creditors on the issue of debt restructuring. Hard currency reserves followed an upward slope (table 9), as a result of cuts in public expenditures and good export performance, until the mid-1990s (table 10).

Even though Brazil has been a latecomer in adjustment reforms, bolder steps were taken in March 1990 to privatize many publicly owned industrial firms. In parallel, trade liberalization and deregulation went ahead, albeit in the face of considerable opposition, as we have seen above. The adoption of a new constitution in 1988 also had a major impact on economic management, reversing the trend towards a highly centralized state in favour of more decentralized activities, particularly at the level of municipalities.

Import prohibitions and most quota restrictions were abolished, while import control through foreign exchange allocation was eliminated. A market reservation law protecting high technology products was abolished in 1992, and foreign companies were allowed to set up new facilities. In parallel, direct export subsidies and export regulations were abolished. The average tariff was lowered in 1990 from 35 to 14 per cent, while the highest tariff was down from 45 to 35 per cent. Tariffs will be entirely phased out among members of the Mercado Común del Sur (MERCOSUR) agreement, which took effect in 1995.

Brazil's trade balance remained highly favourable until the Plano Real (figure 2.1 and table 10), while trade patterns are highly diversified with respect to geographic partners and export categories (table 11). Approximately 28 per cent of exports are to the European Union, 20 per cent to the United States, 20 per cent to the Asian market, and 22 per cent to other Latin American countries (table 11). The Asian market is on the rise, thus exposing Brazil to setbacks in that region. More than two-thirds of total exports consist of manufactured products, a pattern designed to protect Brazil from external shocks and restrictions (tables 10 and 13). The balance of payments remains generally favourable, despite a heavy debt burden and current-account annual deficits (table 13). The bulk of dominant local firms remain in Brazilian hands: around 350 among the 500 larger ones (table 14).

All transition governments favoured multilateralism and participated in the General Agreement on Tariffs and Trade (GATT) negotiations, helping the European Union to exclude the cultural sector from direct foreign exposure to the international market, at the outset of the Uruguay Round of negotiations in December 1993. Brazil shows a growing interest in the MERCOSUR initiative, while it fears the negative impact of the North America Free Trade Agreement (NAFTA) on its exports of shoes, orange juice, textiles, ethanol, and steel products to the American and Canadian markets. Furthermore, the deregulation program has suppressed domestic production and distribution quotas, licensing, price approval of investment plans, and other macroeconomic restrictions. Transportation is also largely deregulated, while new laws permit a certain level of privatization of harbour services and a freer contracting of labour.

In the field of privatization, eighteen firms (for the most part, in the energy – mainly power-generation and distribution – and manufacturing sectors) had been auctioned off to local entrepreneurs by mid-1992. After an interruption arising from a change of administration in Brasília, the program slowly resumed and has extended to areas such as utilities, oil, and banking. The program regained momentum during the 1996–7 period, counting for 60 per cent of total operations (table 12). Privatizations, however, required significant amendments to the 1988 constitution; by early 1998, these changes had not yet been completed. In the field of administration, decentralization of responsibilities went forward. Local states were themselves responsible for auctioning off utility firms falling under their jurisdiction. The much-debated 1988 constitution reduced the federal government's share of tax revenues from 50 to 35 per cent and raised state and municipal shares to 41 and 24 per cent respectively. Less clearly defined is the devolution of responsibility for expenditures. The fact that the federal government's share of expenditures has declined less than has its share of tax receipts probably added to the difficulties in stabilizing its budget.

In short, Brazil has advanced quite decisively, though not without considerable difficulties, on the path of adjustment. Its efforts, however, have been repaid by the formal, although cautious, recognition of main official creditors and international agencies such as the U.S. government and the Club de Paris. In parallel, private foreign investment has literally poured into Brazil: an indication that, for many corporate players, Brazil represents promising opportunities for short-term profits, which will then be taxed at lower rates than in other, probably more disciplined, Latin American countries. Plano Real helped the São Paulo Exchange (Bovespa) to experience steep levels of appreciation, from 1995 on.

The Politics of Austerity in Chile

Compared to Brazil, Chile until recently featured rather backward patterns of development, mostly as far as industrial diversification and export structure are concerned. Chile's private savings and investment have traditionally been low compared to other countries of similar income levels, but they rose steadily over the late 1980s. Overall private domestic savings rose from 2.2 per cent in 1984, following a major economic crisis, to 14.5 in 1992. Savings increased as a result of a number of factors, including the 1981 pension and tax reform, a genuine housing subsidy program which up-fronts private savings, and a stable policy environment. Public savings, enhanced by improved levels of tax administration (by Latin American standards), wage containment, and encouraging performances in the public sector, rose from 0.8 per cent of GDP in 1984 to 7.8 per cent in 1992. This figure includes the Copper Stabilization Fund.

Gross investment has traditionally been low in Chile, with average figures below 15 per cent of GDP over the last thirty years, and never exceeding an average of 17 per cent in any five-year period. In contrast, the last years have seen a remarkable shift from the previous situation, with investment rising to more than 25 per cent annually. Since 1988, foreign investment resumed, while project financing provided an important stimulus to overall investment. In the late 1980s, GDP figures rose decisively (table 1), while inflation rates were gradually controlled (table 2) and gross domestic investment featured a new pattern, in which private savings and foreign investment gradually replaced public domestic expenditures as main contributors to growth (table 3).

This favourable situation was apparently made possible by a series of adjustment policies involving both stabilization measures and market-friendly strategies. Understandably, the first paid off in the shorter term, with inflation rates gradually declining to less than 9 per cent in 1994 (table 2), while liberalization achieved significant results only in the late 1980s; exports rose over these years and usually managed to match imports (table 10). Structural adjustment measures involved privatization of nearly 50 per cent of the public sector, including pension plans, banks, and a whole array of industrial activities, but excluding copper mining, a public monopoly invested with high symbolic value by a majority of Chileans. Privatization operations, accomplished in two phases, were never spectacular nor did they involve considerable fresh money. Many simply involved returning property to former owners, either in the banking sector or in agriculture. Land reform measures dating back to the Frei and Allende periods were never entirely rescinded. Many nationalized domains remained in the hands of new entrepreneurs or co-operatives; only a minority were given back to landowners or *latifundistas*.

The first wave of privatization was launched during the years 1976–9; twenty-five public firms and banks were sold at below-market prices. Nevertheless, as financing was scarce at the time, most sales resulted in the near-bankruptcy of their new private owners as early as 1981, and the state then took on a new role, backing and restructuring this private debt. A première for Latin America, the IMF came through in support of the local government and financially guaranteed the operation, which resulted in the creation by official authorities of an odd, tightly monitored semi-private/semi-public sector in the so-called liberal Chilean economy. The second phase of privatization was conducted, in a more cautious manner, during the mid-1980s. It involved fewer firms, and conditions offered to potential buyers were apparently stringent. The whole program, however, slowed down under the democratic government elected in 1989. It is widely accepted abroad that this privatization program, although incomplete, helped to stabilize public expenditures. Improved public finances made an important contribution to Chile's economic recovery in the 1990s. The overall non-financial public sector progressed from a deficit equal to 2.4 per cent of GDP in 1985 to a surplus equivalent to 4 per cent of GDP in 1990 and to 3.2 per cent in 1992, with savings at 7.8 per cent of GDP. The figures for the two following years, however, seem less promising, since expenditures have consistently increased in parallel with the imposition of new taxes on corporate profits.

There is no question that rising copper prices on the world market contributed to this outcome. In 1990, the recently elected government reversed the tax reduction trend in order to finance social and employment-sector programs, raising the value-added tax from 16 to 18 per cent, changing the basis for collection of corporate income tax to actual rather than distributed profits, and increasing income taxes. This reform paved the way for a new wave of social expenditures. Nonetheless, the non-financial public sector surplus reached 2.3 per cent of GDP in 1991, of which 0.7 per cent was channelled into the Copper Stabilization Fund. State revenues increased, and expenditures dropped as a result of lower interest rates on the international market, which resulted in lower interest payments on external debt.

In the field of industrial policy, a major modernization process was launched in the mining sector as well as in wine and fruit production. In 1991 national current accounts registered a dramatic improvement, with a trade surplus of U.S. $143 million – compared to U.S. $824 million the year before. A decline in copper exports was more than compensated for by an 18.6 per cent increase in the value of non-copper exports, resulting in an 8 per cent increase in the value of commodity exports. Imports increased at the moderate nominal rate of 4.5 per cent, reflecting a 12 per cent decline in capital goods imports. As a result of positive current-and capital-account movements, the overall balance-of-payments account showed an encouraging surplus of U.S. $1.2 billion, a remarkable figure for a country still characterized by a rather narrow export base (consisting of about a dozen main commodity goods products). International reserves reached U.S. $14.8 billion in 1995, representing approximately a year of merchandise imports (table 9). Foreign capital inflows contributed to this result. Net foreign direct investment also increased to U.S. $540 million. These statistics, however, understate the significant increase in gross foreign direct investment by U.S. $480 million, since they include an increase of U.S. $426 million in Chilean investment abroad, mainly in Argentina. Since 1992 domestic as well as foreign capital investment inflows and outflows have remained, for the most part, stable. The currrent-account balance progressed markedly from the 1980s to the 1990s, with the continuation of a tight monetary policy coupled with enduring efforts to stimulate productivity and exports (table 13).

Faced with a very strained situation in the early 1980s, Chile has made significant strides in reducing its external debt. Debt-equity conversions reduced Chile's external debt by U.S. $900 million from 1985 to 1990 (table 4). As the main Latin American recipient of IMF Structural Adjustment Loans (SALs) (tables 6–7), it is obvious that Chile was rewarded not so much because it was a 'success story' of liberal policies (quite the contrary, in fact) but because it exhibited the good behaviour expected from a developing country in a rapidly changing international environment. Furthermore, in September 1990, Chile reached an agreement with creditor commercial banks that included rescheduling the total U.S. $1.8 billion in amortization from previous multi-year rescheduling agreements falling due before 1995. The country's annual interest payments reverted to the previous semi-annual schedule, and major banks purchased U.S. $320 million of Chilean five-year bonds in 1991.

The debt situation remained tight, with total debt outstanding at U.S. $20.6 billion at the end of 1993, equivalent to 50 per cent of GDP, or 1.9 times the level of merchandise exports. Nevertheless, debt reduction operations have contributed to a reduction in the ratio of total external debt to GNP from 141.7 per cent in 1985 to 45.5 per cent in 1994, and in the ratio to exports from 48.4 per cent in 1985 to 19.2 per cent in 1994 (table 5). This significant improvement in debt indicators, added to the reduction of international interest rates, has led to an increase in the secondary market price of Chile's external debt, from 53 cents to the dollar in 1987 to over 90 cents by early 1993. Shortly after, Chile became the first Latin American country (far ahead of Brazil and even Mexico) to regain an investment grade rating, a definite milestone in the Latin American debt crisis. Hard currency reserves were increasingly sound (table 9).

Unambiguously devoted to regional integration, and actively involved in multilateral negotiations with both MERCOSUR and NAFTA partners, Chile is the often-quoted example of an indebted developing country boldly engaged in an overall scheme of world-market restructuring. Given the openness of its economy, Chile still remains highly dependent upon recurrent world cycles of expansion and recession, a situation worsened by the narrow base of its manufacturing export base (table 10). Therefore, constant foreign capital inflows favoured by increased trade, low international interest rates, and overall economic growth will likely play a crucial role in the country's medium-term performance. The state, however, must prove its ability to support and finance social programs aimed at enhancing the quality of the workforce and furthering the inclusion of the poor in a slowly – too slowly – expanding domestic market. This market, in turn, will play a significant role in compensating for the ups and downs of foreign demand for Chilean commodity goods. To do so, a comprehensive industrial strategy will have to be designed by a government that must look beyond day-to-day politics to the horizon of longer-term structural and development policies. The diversification of a technologically advanced production base ought to be the target of such a strategy, to ensure that the Chilean economic performance will endure and prove to be more than a short-lived speculative 'bubble' in a changing world environment.

Towards an Adjustment Crisis in Mexico

Before the debt crisis, Mexico enjoyed a prolonged period of high economic growth and price stability. Between 1973 and 1980, GDP grew at an average 6.5 per cent annually (table 1). Conservative fiscal policies kept inflation low until the mid-1970s, but large increases in public expenditures pushed inflation to double digits and led to the collapse of the exchange rate in 1976 (table 2). In the following years, fiscal accounts continued to show marked deterioration; the country was, however, still able to finance its increasing imports from rising oil exports. This strategic sector benefited from considerable public investment in drilling and refining facilities, which made Mexico one of the main exporters of petroleum products in the Western hemisphere. Imports expanded fourfold, however, causing capital flight. Foreign debt reached U.S. $78 billion in 1981, from a U.S. $7 billion level in 1972. In 1982 rising world interest rates and falling oil prices gave a fatal blow to the postwar Mexican growth cycle. Foreign creditors refused to roll over Mexico's short-term debt, provoking the exhaustion of foreign reserves and a temporary suspension of foreign debt service. Shortly after, the government nationalized the banks, eager to establish control of domestic reserves already shrunk by a massive capital flight. Inflation reached 60 per cent by late 1982, and the peso was depreciated almost 30 per cent.

In 1983 an IMF-supported stabilization program was launched. In less than twelve months, the primary fiscal balance went from a 3.5 per cent deficit to a 4.8 per cent surplus; but the peso depreciated further, while inflation skyrocketed to 100 per cent. A severe recession followed, but an upturn in the non-interest current account occurred, showing a U.S. $15 billion surplus during 1983–4, and hard currency reserves could be partially restored. This stringent stabilization plan continued until mid-1985, yielding some encouraging macroeconomic results, such as the recovery of GDP growth to 3 per cent and the decline of inflation to 60 per cent. Then two major external shocks threatened the Mexican economy: first, the Mexico City earthquake, which caused destruction evaluated at 2 per cent of total GDP; and second, the collapse of oil prices in early 1986, which further reduced government revenues.

A second stabilization plan was therefore launched in July 1986, adding rigorous fiscal austerity measures to a gradual exposure of the Mexican economy to foreign competition, in order to support its greater integration with the rest of the world and attract new investment from foreign creditors. Results were slow to materialize and could not be achieved until an 'economic solidarity pact' (referred to as *el pacto*) was signed by government, union, and business representatives. The *pacto* was in fact a compromise, halfway between a stringent stabilization plan and a more expansionist vision of economic management. A major tax reform was initiated in 1987, which simplified the system, modernized its administration, expanded the tax base, and reduced rates. Individual and corporate tax rates were brought in line with international levels. The message of the tax reform was one of relative equity, with corporations now contributing to the national Treasury more than they ever had in the past. The highest personal tax rate and the flat corporate tax rate were both reduced to 35 per cent, from 60 and 42 per cent respectively. This transition phase was, however, relatively short.

From the moment President Salinas de Gortari came to power in 1989, structural adjustment reforms progressed swiftly. Drastic cuts in public spending were made, amounting to almost half of total government expenditures. Most of the large projects of the late 1970s were abandoned, but expenditures for maintenance and the social sector were maintained throughout the period (table 7). Political support for the reforms was carefully engineered through the *pacto*, later renamed the 'pact for economic and social growth' (pacto para la estabilización y crecimiento económico, PECE). The PECE specifies two key figures: the minimum wage and the depreciation rate of the peso. Adjustments in the minimum wage have consistently lagged behind inflation, resulting in the halving of the real minimum wage. As for the peso, its value fluctuated from one to the dollar in 1989 to 20 cents in 1991, and up again to 33 cents in 1994.

A bold trade reform has been at the centre of the structural adjustment program. Until 1983 all merchandise imports were subject to quantitative restrictions. Ten years later, less than 20 per cent, of tradable production was subject to such restrictions. The maximum tariff is now down to 20 per cent and the weighted average is at 12.5 per cent, representing one-fifth and one-half of 1985 levels. Mexico adhered to the GATT in 1986 and, in 1993, shared common views with the United States and Canada on the details of NAFTA. Unfortunately, Mexico has never in recent years been able to reach a point of equilibrium with its trading partners. Trade with the United States, Japan, and most of the developed and industrialized countries is still showing a severe deficit, which has worsened over the last years, contributing to the 1994 peso crisis (table 10).

By 1989 Mexico had been successful in achieving an agreement with the commercial banks for the rescheduling of about U.S. $48 billion worth of debt. The debt deal reduced annual transfers abroad by about U.S. $4 billion, thereby reducing pressure on the exchange rate. This, in turn, was reflected in a drop of 20 percentage points in domestic interest rates, reducing the annual cost of servicing the domestic debt by 4 per cent of GDP. The new situation made it easier for investment to locate in Mexico, and thus stimulated production. Along with the deregulation of financial activity, lower interest rates stimulated a rapidly growing stock exchange, whose transactions increased by 266 per cent, in real terms, between 1988 and 1992. Foreigners were allowed to purchase securities, including Treasury bills. These rates, however, also encouraged further borrowing from corporate players; U.S. $10 billion were added to the publicly-guaranteed debt burden between 1992 and 1994 – mainly from and to the private sector (table 4). This increased pressure on interest rates, which began to climb again in 1993 (table 15) and skyrocketed over 50 per cent in the aftermath of the peso crisis.

The privatization program was cautiously introduced in 1984 and almost completed by 1994. A majority of public firms (1,155 firms in 1982 alone) were sold to local or foreign investors, mainly in the telecommunication and banking sectors. The operations, conducted under President Salinas between 1990 and 1992, yielded almost U.S. $16 billion in fresh money, which was allocated to the debt service, mainly to domestic lenders now faced with an almost certain bankruptcy. An exception was made for the 'strategic' petroleum sector, and Petróleos Mexicanos (PEMEX) remains in public hands (a frequently made promise, reiterated by President Zedillo after his election in August 1994).

In the early 1990s, Mexico seemed to be harvesting the fruit of its earlier adjustment policies. In 1994 economic growth was at 3.5 per cent, down slightly from 4.4 per cent in 1990 (table 1). Fostered by lower interest rates, private capital inflows were unprecedently large, reaching U.S. $17 billion (table 3). The current-account deficit increased to about U.S. $13 billion in 1991 and displayed a strong tendency to plunge to unprecedented levels in the 1990s (table 13). Strong currency accumulated in foreign exchange reserves (table 9). This was a result of higher-than-expected imports (mainly capital and intermediate goods) and lower oil exports (table 10). A massive and costly modernization process in the industrial sector was undertaken, aimed at strengthening the manufacturing export capacity of the Mexican economy. This effort may have gone beyond the capacity of the local banking system. Foreigners were invited to invest in it, by acquiring shares on the Mexico City *bolsa* or stock exchange.

Nonetheless committed to the recovery of the national private sector, the government applied U.S. $4.5 billion from the privatization fund to reduce public debt held by Bancomex. A further U.S. $4.5 billion was added to this sum in

March 1992. This led to fast rates of growth in monetary aggregates and credits to the private sector. The overheated economy slowed down somewhat in 1992, to turn upward again in 1993 with the support of lower world interest rates.

The Mexican program of structural adjustment is thus characterized by tight fiscal and monetary policies coupled with a still inconclusive process of trade liberalization (unable so far to achieve a positive trade balance). While dependency on oil exports has dwindled to less than 60 per cent of total exports, and integration with the North American developed countries is in progress, the debt burden has increased sharply in the last two years because of low world interest rates. Gross external debt rose from U.S. $96.8 billion in 1990 to U.S. $118 billion in 1993 (table 4), but fell from 43.8 to 33.2 per cent of GNP (table 5). Reflecting the effects of the external debt restructuring, the debt service to export ratio fell from 51.5 per cent in 1985 to 33.9 per cent in 1994. As an encouragement to its efforts in implementing bold reforms, Mexico was also granted substantial structural adjustment IMF loans, the first among Latin American countries (table 7).

Triggered by uncontrolled public spending and the heavy cost of swiftly modernizing industry, Mexico's economy collapsed in December 1994. Coming twelve years after the 1982 Chilean precedent, the Mexican melt-down was an 'adjustment crisis' in the sense that it was triggered by the forces unleashed by market reforms: speculative investment on an overheated *bolsa*, the financial burden of industrial modernization, a low level of protection against the unregulated import of techological inputs, an eroded state capacity, a fragile, heavily indebted banking sector, and, last but not the least, political turmoil induced by infighting among elites and regional economic disparities. More noticeable was a widening chasm between a thriving northern *maquiladora* belt and the stagnant, backward southern states. This crisis was considerably more serious than it had been in Chile a decade earlier, and resulted in lasting consequences on wages and levels of consumption for the majority. International aid poured in, as we know, but currency reserves melted from U.S. $25.3 to U.S. $6.4 billion within a three-month period (table 9). In a matter of weeks, Mexico sank to an even worse financial situation than it had experienced twelve years before. The debt jumped to U.S. $165 billion (table 4). Under such adverse conditions, it seems difficult to talk about Mexico as an example of an enduring success. Thus, neither 1982 Chile nor 1994 Mexico substantiates the view that adjustment reforms represent in themselves a shield against brutal setbacks and social or economic disruptions.

PART TWO: INTERNATIONAL DETERMINANTS OF
ECONOMIC REFORMS

9

Gaining International Support for Domestic Reform

The international environment has become less than congenial to democratic experiments, and by the early 1990s, new democracies were feeling the weight of international factors more heavily than ever. A rampant, long-lasting recession has hit Third World countries particularly hard. Political leaders, opening their eyes to the legacy of the 'lost decade' of the 1980s, now question their previous policies. The performance of their respective countries in a global economy, and therefore of the liberal reforms themselves, has been more limited than expected. Political and clientelist schemes involving systematic corruption diverted large amounts of money from public, social, and economic programs towards particular interests, while dishonest corporate elites withheld their corporate income tax from the national treasury. Thus it is not surprising that true reformers should raise a sustained outcry over the decaying state of the bureaucracy, and put forward bold alternatives to economic stagnation and persistent underdevelopment. As it rapidly gains political support, such opposition also continues to raise a whole array of unresolved issues, including ignorance, poverty, health, and marginality. These influences add up, and serve to underscore the contradictions between the policies' present means and their ultimate goals.

Moreover, reform policies need the support of international players. Whitehead wrote that international conditions were markedly less favourable to Latin American democracies than they have been to their southern European counterparts in the unstable transitional period of the 1980s (Whitehead, 1986). A developing nation's resources and capabilities are limited in size and scope. Many authors and even international agencies now openly question the strict 'open market' approach to structural adjustment. They share the view that tangible and significant support must be provided to new democracies. There is no growth without fresh money. Institution-building is a long and delicate process which cannot be improvised. The consolidation of democracy therefore depends upon international support, particularly in moments of crisis. Interesting examples can be drawn from the recent past. In postwar Europe, the Marshall Plan greatly assisted the resumption of growth and thereby consolidated democracy in Continental non-communist countries: Belgium and the Netherlands, France, West Germany, and Italy. Again, during the 1970s, when Spain, Portugal, and Greece engaged in a decisive process of democratization, the support of the European Economic Community (EEC) gave the initial impetus to their reform policies. Subsidies from wealthy northern countries helped update social programs and foster regional development, thus creating better conditions for a sufficient level of popular support to the subsequent structural reforms.

International diplomacy is always active (at least verbally) in promoting democracy and human rights. Foreign nations may also resort to other, more tangible means, in the form of bilateral or multilateral aid, economic complementarity, or trade agreements. A genuine form of aid conditionality is not without precedent. Aid in the name of democracy puts powerful mechanisms into motion, which were experienced in Spain and Portugal and may have proved decisive in consolidating these new democracies. Figure 9.1 suggests that financial support from the international community can play a significant role in the creation of an economic strategy at the crossroads. Is there any indication that the European precedent applies to Latin America?

Authoritarian regimes have left deep scars on the reputation of Latin American countries on the world market, with the possible exception of Chile. Foreign investors and international agencies tend to see the state, especially in the larger countries, as the representative of entrenched local corporate mafias indulging in unfair practices on the export market. Everyone remembers the accusations of dumping which were a regular feature of GATT members' complaints to Latin American countries in the 1970s and early 1980s. A small but significant number of areas of international trade were at stake. The armament industry is often quoted as one of the success stories of the Brazilian authoritarian model. Fattened with public subsidies, the Brazilian weapons industry successfully provided heavy armament to both Iraq and Iran as well as to Third World countries. They were not alone on this market, as we came to know. Brazil ranked last on a list of eight weapons traders to the Middle East and other unstable strategic areas. With the twilight of the Cold War and the rise of democratic regimes all over the world, exports had come almost to a standstill by the end of the decade (Proença, 1993).

The automotive sector was not entirely successful. Brazil's tightly protected multinational car industry – Volkswagen alone being in control of 49 per cent of the local market – was no match, on the consumer markets of developed

Figure 9.1 A consolidated institutional framework counteracts domestic and international influences, and strengthens policy implementation.

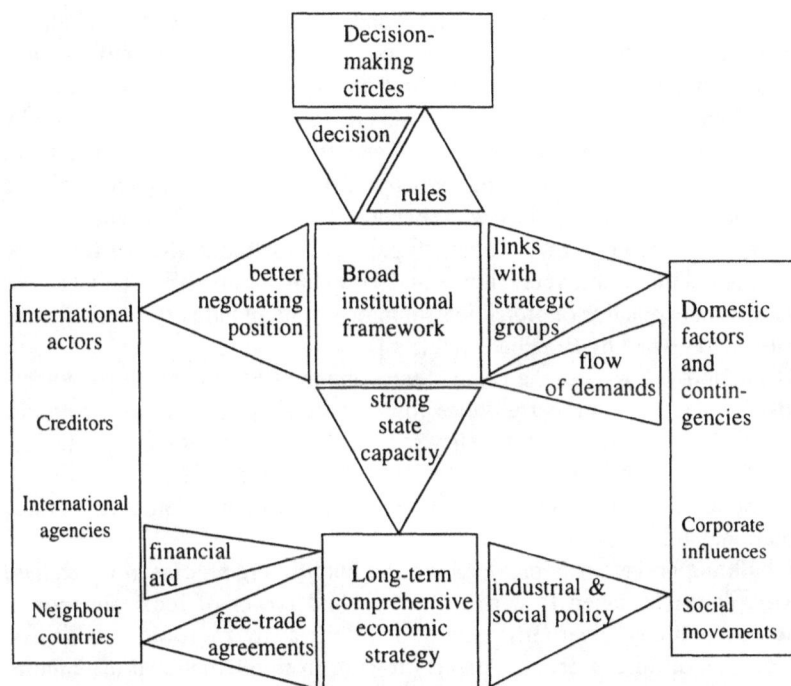

countries, for its astute and more technologically advanced Japanese and Korean competitors. Attempts to carve out a niche in North America for local, less expensive products such as the Volkswagen Fox were inconclusive (Scheuer, 1993). The thorniest issue, however, was Brazil's highly protected fledgling computer industry. Engineered in the Figueiredo years and given full political support from the Sarney government in 1986 in the highly controversial Lei da Informática, this policy was the last in a series of initiatives taken in Brasília under the logic of 'national security.' A locally based hardware and software industry of high technological level was expected to provide computerized systems to the thriving armament sector as well as to mini- and personal computer assembly lines; the plan was to be implemented in 'technological poles' at Campinas and São José dos Campos in the state of São Paulo.

Emotion ran high in Washington when Microsoft's MS DOS technology was prohibited from entering the Brazilian market in 1988. Otherwise, Brazilian dreams of competing with Japan and the United States in this strategic, highly sensitive area were short-lived. Government funding to the new research centres never materialized, and researchers were left without much in the way of support and means. Brazilian industry and consumers showed little interest in local products. In some cases, when computerizing their operations, they ordered smuggled hardware and software from Japan and South Korea. In such uncontrolled conditions, the road was wide open to abuse. Clones were built by local researchers, which attracted GATT attention and fuelled accusations of unfair practices. Under mounting pressure from leading competitors in the United States, the whole policy was abandoned a few years later under President Collor de Mello, not without much pain and frustration (Moniz Bandeira, 1989). Behind this controversy, it was understood by all involved that what was at stake was the practice of protectionism in favour of an industry which was for the most part owned by Brazilians (table 14).

By the mid-1980s, both the United States and the EEC had begun to retaliate against Brazil, imposing extra duties (up to 100 per cent) on car, electronic, paper, alcohol, and steel exports. They repeatedly voiced their concerns to Brazilian officials in Washington, in the IMF offices; and at the Club de Paris, when time came to negotiate on matters related to the conversion of debt and to international aid.

Rebuilding bridges may prove a long and humiliating process in which hard decisions must be taken to curb the entrenched power of local oligopolies, frame constitutions, create institutions, and shift away from old nationalistic practices; all of this, under continuous pressure from international institutions, from lenders, and governments of industrialized countries. There is no question that foreign debt is a strong lever in the hands of dissatisfied creditors and investors. Mounting international competition, with ensuing 'buy local' policies adopted by Japan, the EEC, and, increasingly, the United States, leaves the political executives of the underdeveloped countries little room for political manoeuvring. Thus the whole process of structural change faces tremendous challenges, to be met always under the scepticism about the future of Latin America that is shared by both local and foreign investors.

Many authors, Remmer (1990) and Stallings (1992) among them, attribute a decisive role to international factors in the adoption of reform policies in developing countries. On this subject, we refer the reader to the lengthy discussion provided by Stallings, who sees three distinct ways in which international factors impinge upon domestic policy choices: first, new developments in goods and capital markets, which determine the availability of external resources (less resources mean a limited range of policy options); second, international linkages or networks of transnational actors who share common views and philosophies about 'what ought to be done' in the realm of public policy; third, leverage constraints (financial and political power exercised by creditors over those who are indebted). This last variable is often pointed to as the decisive factor.

Structural reforms, if pursued with some degree of consistency, will obviously offer a better footing to local governments for a renewed dialogue with foreign creditors and potential investors, which in turn may reverse their previous unfavourable judgment towards Latin American democrats and democracies (Whitehead, 1992). International actors – foreign creditors, funding agencies, and the governments of developed countries – are quite indifferent about which political leader, party, or coalition is undertaking reforms, as long as these are consistently undertaken. And if they are not? Even then, international players may not react in the same way. According to Kahler, leverage is diminished by diverging interests among international actors. While funding agencies such as the IMF are the crusaders of the orthodox philosophy, governments are pursuing highly political and strategic interests that go beyond the strict compliance to orthodox prescriptions by a given country, be it Mexico, the Philippines, or Turkey. In this sense, the Cold War bore a logic of its own; the desire to support a strategically important client-state frequently overrode the interest in enforcing a comprehensive reform package (Kahler, 1992). For the same reason, we suggest that, throughout the 1980s, international players did not particularly favour democracies over dictatorships, a situation that has, however, begun to change in the 1990s. What is fully acknowledged, though, is that some countries were economically, as well as diplomatically, rewarded for what was considered to be the 'proper sequencing' of their reform strategies, with regard to a changing international environment.

The concept of appropriate timing is developed in the comparative literature as an attempt to account for the influence that international factors come to have, over a specific period, on the outcome of a given policy undertaken in a particular domestic arena (O'Donnell, 1986). It refers here to the presence of significant achievements in the domestic arena, such as financial stability and the reduction of inflation, occurring simultaneously with debt negotiation. In such a case, the presence of these policies should be a true indication of fairly integrated steps in the implementation process of a given reform package. Foxley cleverly summarizes the holistic character of these measures as a complete set of orthodox remedies to a situation which is being diagnosed, by dominant conservatives, as an ill or failing economy. The procuring of badly needed capital to finance the trade deficit and raise investment goes hand in hand with tight conditions set by creditors and investors abroad:

In order to restore the confidence of these groups and make the economic program credible as a long-term solution to the country's problems, the new policies must conform to certain rules. These rules of 'sound economic management' are codified by the international financial community, including the IMF, large private international banks, and business groups ... Given such an explicit codification of what constitutes sound policies, the restoration of confidence requires strictly abiding by them. (Foxley, 1983: 31)

International lending to Latin America was characterized all through the 1980s by the enforcement of the principle of conditionality: sometimes simple conditionality, when an IMF stabilization program was already under way and accepted by a local government; but more frequently, double conditionality. The latter applies to a comprehensive framework of coherent and complementary policies, some being oriented towards financial stabilization with IMF funding, others being rather growth-oriented adjustment programs with funding from either the International Bank for Reconstruction and Development (IBRD), or the World Bank, or from the Inter-American Development Bank (IDB). Each lender sets its own conditions, theoretically independent from one another. In fact, international agencies came to understand that double conditionality would be hard to enforce. They tended to impose the practice of cross-conditionality, to ensure that stabilization and adjustment programs were carried out *pari passu*. This implied that if a given country was complying with one of its lenders, the failure to comply with the other would result in the curtailment of all sources of international funding (Ffrench-Davis and Meller, 1990).

   More generally, and as the mechanisms enforcing conditionality were gradually implemented, most countries understood that they had to be fair players under the new rules. Mexico, Alwyn's Chile, the New Brazilian Republic, and Carlos Menem's Argentina all stated their commitment to a freer market at every opportunity. Rules were undoubtedly stringent for each of these countries, but felt more severe to the weaker ones. On the one hand, it was understood that the international community was justified in imposing conditions on its renewed interest in investment. On the other hand, Latin American decision makers expected the international community to be of some help in supporting the process of structural adjustment in their debt-crippled countries by allowing for more flexibility in its interpretation of what IMF or IBRD structural adjustment packages should entail. This flexibility would foster the implementation of such policies. Conditional aid could possibly worsen transitional costs, the most feared consequences of structural change, and, under certain contingencies, disorganize a momentarily depressed domestic market. The process could affect social as well as political stability, and weaken democratic experiments in periods of economic transition. Conditional aid and the packages it intended to impose were in absolute contradiction to the previous model of state intervention, given the size of the public sector in most Latin American countries. Let us examine a single example.

Sector studies shed an interesting light on the mechanisms whereby foreign players influence decision making in a specific domestic arena. Among the issues on which the principle of conditionality has been based, protection of the environment began to play an increasing role in the second half of the 1980s. It is well known that in the case of Brazil, World Bank funding is paramount to the completion of an ambitious infrastructure program, which slowed down significantly after the 1982 debt crisis. The Brazilian electrical sector, and consequently the public utility firms responsible for its development, became vulnerable to the IBRD's pressures. Beginning in 1985, more than fifteen projects – many of them in Native lands of the Amazon Basin – were questioned on the basis of their unsatisfactory environmental procedures. First, a U.S. $250 million loan for the construction of several dams in the state of Rondonia was interrupted because the projects encroached on Native lands. Second, state-owned Companhia de Electricidade Brasileira (ELETROBRAS) was asked to redesign its infrastructure program to include sound environmental assessment procedures. In 1987, under the pressure of American environmentalist groups joined in Congress by the Brazilian activist and ecologist Chico Mendes, who was to be assassinated shortly after by gunmen believed to be hired by powerful northeast landowners, ELETROBRAS rapidly set up a special department and hired experts with a mandate to review the firm's environmental practices (*Folha de São Paulo*, 03.10.94). In 1989, the IBRD again suspended a U.S. $500 million loan to projected power plants because they were to be built in the environmentally fragile Amazon area. In 1991, four main projects were therefore cancelled by Brazilian authorities while, at the Rio Summit of 1992, São Paulo governor Antonio Fleury announced that a thermal plant at Paulínia (one hundred kilometres from São Paulo) would not be built. In this last case, protests came from local residents and Brazilian environmentalist groups in association with U.S.-based ecologists. In the early 1990s, it was becoming clear that Brazil's energy policy was being closely monitored from Washington by international agencies through the principle of conditionality. Simultaneously, environmentalists both foreign and local would be keeping a close watch over the projects under construction (Mammana, 1994).

If the debate is still open on the extent to which international actors play a role in the adoption of reform policies, the literature is vague on the means by which they influence the course of policy implementation. We suggest they are likely to play a stronger role than expected. All authors agree that new democracies require some dividends from the market – such as the containment of the national debt, new investment in industry and technology, better performance of exports, and job creation – in order to pursue the deepening of structural transformation. Authors argue, however, over the usefulness of conditional aid as the appropriate form of support. Since such successes as those mentioned are highly dependent upon the cycles of expansion and recession – particularly erratic since the beginning of the 1980s – we feel justified in referring to 'appropriate timing' as a fundamental condition to the undertaking of a comprehensive economic policy. To borrow from Machiavelli's vocabulary, clever decisions can be made by leaders endowed with a high degree of *virtu*, but the success of their plans remains overly dependent on the unpredictable influence of *fortuna*.

We should remember that, in sharp contrast to earlier phases of liberalism in Latin America, when money was cheap and multinational firms competed to invest in Third World countries, liberal packages are now expected to achieve a high degree of consistency and success with very little help from the stagnating world market. There is no question that, quite independently from domestic factors, the implementation of liberal policies in Latin America is being undermined by contingencies such as recession on the world market and other international factors related to mounting regional competition among developed countries. Their outcome is dependent upon the unpredictable turns of world trade cycles. As early examples, Mexico and Brazil were in bad need of new money when interest rates ran high in 1982. Chile in 1991 was back in business and eager to export copper and fruit at a time when world demand reached all-time lows. From 1980 to 1992, as a result of unforeseeable trade cycles, Latin America's share on the unstable world market fell from 5 to less than 2 per cent.

Eight years had passed since the 1973 coup when, under sharply rising interest rates in Northern creditor countries, Chile experienced debt payment problems. Structural policies had been conducted so fiercely, in most sectors of the economy, that the Chilean negotiators had no problem in reaching an agreement with the IMF concerning a stabilization program by late 1982. Chile's recent monetarist policy was in itself a guarantee of a pragmatic approach to economic policy, under IMF prescriptions. As a consequence, postponement of payments and debt rescheduling were accepted, while the IMF channelled a new credit line of U.S. $1.3 billion, mainly to stimulate exports. This constituted an astonishing première: a Latin American dictatorship being rewarded for its strict compliance to the principle of aid conditionality.

By 1985, the positive consensus in the international business community over Chile's economic policy was so general that the IMF and the World Bank, as well as other financial institutions, offered the country a set of three credit lines, called 'Structural Adjustment Loans' or SALs. SAL 1, in October 1985, was intended to stabilize the balance of payments, develop exports, and create more job opportunities, mainly in the rapidly expanding export sector, given the 'comparative advantages' mentioned above (Ritter, 1990). The loan included U.S. $1 billion from the IMF Emergency Financing Facility Plan (an indication of the high priority attributed to Chile's economic recovery) and another U.S. $1.1 billion in new bank loans. SAL 2, in November 1985, was a U.S. $250 million extension of SAL 1, with an emphasis upon exports and social programs. Agriculture was to be the prime recipient of the new credit line. As for SAL 3, in December 1987, it allowed further investment and continuation of the reforms. As one can observe, only the first SAL, oriented towards an openness to world markets, is significant. In true liberal orthodox fashion, the whole package displayed far more interest in structural reforms than in income growth. Such was the package upon which creditors and a debt-crippled Chile agreed at this critical stage. Chile was to become the laboratory of IMF conservative philosophy. Foreign banks and enterprises would be free to take shares in the economy, even in the 'strategic' state sector undergoing privatization. For example, the Chase Manhattan Bank played an essential role in the privatization of communication firms, such as CTC and Intel, while Citibank had a strong presence in the mining and agricultural areas through its subsidiaries Citiforestry, Citicorp Woods, Citifishing, and Citimining.

All through the 1980s, Brazil encountered much the same problems in negotiating with its creditors that it met elsewhere in its various attempts to define a comprehensive policy. Contrary to expectations, its currency was never devalued, as has happened so many times in Mexico. Exchange rates were usually maintained in the 1980s, at least until the Cruzado reform (Dos Reis Velloso, 1990). Furthermore, not a single *plano*, especially the cruzado, was supported by international institutions, because they all displayed too much heterodoxy. As a consequence and in contrast to Chile, very little money was channelled into Brazil for structural adjustment purposes (Ffrench-Davis and Meller, 1990). In retaliation, debt payments were postponed, or sometimes interrupted under moratoria decrees, according to the availability of hard currency in the national treasury. Hard currency reserves were low in the 1980s, and this palliative policy helped to keep more money at home. High interest rates, consistent with the general policy, attracted new money, and reserves went up again in the early 1990s, to reach the impressive figure of U.S. $43 billion in 1995. Under such conditions, Brazil could more successfully resist pressure from international agencies.

One may question the willingness of Brazil to negotiate with foreign creditors under unfavourable circumstances. Whenever an agreement with the IMF was imminent on a specific package, negotiation teams under President Sarney Costa were regularly called back to Brasilia, where Congress invariably turned down the proposals on which they were about to agree. Tension was always evident between the Department of External Affairs or Itamaratí, more liberal and traditionalist in its approach to diplomacy, and the new technocrats actively engaged in reforms. This situation changed with the radical Plano Collor, which pleased the creditors and was interpreted as an indication of good will. Negotiations with the IMF resumed and finally resulted in a July 1992 general agreement on debt rescheduling, much on the same lines as that offered Mexico, under the strict conditions of such financial stabilization measures as reduction of the public deficit and a commitment to concluding the privatization of the industrial state sector. The Brazilians agreed to this but were lukewarm about a 'Brady package' on debt conversion which allowed foreign investors to take shares in Brazilian state firms. The 1988 nationalist constitution, it was alleged, prohibited such practices. The constitution could be amended, negotiators suggested, as soon as domestic conditions were favourable. As it turned out, however, it never was, until the election of Fernando Henrique Cardoso as president. Thus, the 1992 agreement was no more effective than the previous ones. By mid-1993, an old pattern repeated itself. With the constitutional revision process, featuring amendments favourable to foreign investment, about to be launched, a confident Cardoso sent his chief negotiator, Lara Resende, to Washington, and everybody met again around the negotiating table. IMF president Michel Camdessus commented dubiously that Brazilian ministers and staff changed so swiftly that he was not able to confirm that the present negotiation team even knew what the former one had agreed upon.

Far more complicated was the situation in Mexico, because the country was just emerging from a highly nationalistic, still expansionist, economic policy under President López Portillo. The 1982 nationalization of Mexican banks had further worsened relationships with foreign powers. At the same moment, the debt problem struck. To all appearances, the country was on the verge of bankruptcy. In near panic, the executive resorted to temporary palliative measures, such as an 80 per cent devaluation of the currency. Afterwards, negotiations with the IMF were pursued, albeit with frequent interruptions symptomatic of a weak consensus at home around the proposed IMF package. President de la Madrid's shrewd political strategy towards the Mexican media and the opposition consisted of implementing fiscal austerity while publicly marking his distance from the country's creditors. Exhibiting a sense of timing and strategy usually reserved for local elections, he was publicly denouncing IMF suggestions to do what he was in fact doing. Austerity had to be truly Mexican, not dictated by the IMF. How far could Mexican public opinion be lulled? The game proved only partially successful, and Cuauhtemoc Cárdenas's defection to the PRD could not be avoided.

There is no question that adhering to the GATT in 1986 played a decisive role in the restoration of Mexico's image abroad. The persistence, during just under five years, of structural adjustment policies in the country made it all the more credible and desirable to the First World. Although less mature than that of Chile, Mexico's reforms were sufficiently enduring to allow for a general, much-anticipated restructuring of its national debt. Negotiations with the IMF, the Club of Paris, and the World Bank were initiated in 1989. Favourable terms were agreed upon, although not as favourable as Chile's, with the support of the United States behind Mexican demands. Debt conversion was here again at the core of the proposed package. Accordingly, the opening of share-taking by foreign investors was immediately conducted by President Salinas de Gortari. Dialogue had been restored, and was further enhanced by the prospect of free-trade negotiations with the United States and Canada (Aspe Amella and Aguayo Mancera, 1989). The slow pace of the process in the first years, a result of the complexities of moving away from the nationalistic standpoint of earlier years, was, in this case, compensated by a rapid evolution during the last, crucial steps. A strong executive, coupled with rewards from the process of privatization and apparently sound structural adjustment policies, contributed to a favourable outcome of negotiations with foreign powers. In the case of Mexico, the sequencing was apparently satisfactory, and in fact proved more favourable than the performance of its economy could warrant.

By the mid-1990s, the swift deterioration of the Mexican economy created conditions for a wave of foreign aid of unprecedented magnitude. As it had done for Chile in 1982, the international community rushed to the support of 'liberal' Mexico, shaken by the late 1994 peso crisis. By December, the currency was devalued by 40 per cent, and Mexican hard currency reserves melted away from U.S. $26 billion to less than U.S. $5 billion in a matter of weeks. The Chiapas uprising was officially blamed for this sudden lack of confidence on the part of foreign investors, but other, more structural factors are likely to account for the Mexican difficulties. The trade deficit rose in 1994 to U.S. $28 billion, an indication of poor industrial competitiveness and over-dependency on imported technologies. Despite such unfavourable domestic conditions, Mexico's bargaining power with foreign powers proved so strong that the IMF, the United States, and other countries (both European and Latin American) swiftly designed a U.S. $49.8 billion package of assistance in emergency funds to the Mexican treasury, to avoid a much-feared repetition of the debt payment crisis of 1982. Surprisingly the IMF, while rapidly expanding its U.S. $17 billion credit line, never questioned the hastily engineered Mexican plan of action, which included the usual monetary policy measures and a reduction of the state deficit. President Clinton abandoned plans to gain legislative approval from Congress for his U.S. $40 billion rescue program, when it became clear that U.S. legislators intended to impose tight conditions on Mexico, such as reducing its support to Cuba, tightening enforcement of the American borders to stop illegal migrants, pledging oil revenues as collateral for the loan guarantees, and enacting legislation to guarantee the rights of workers (Latin American Data Bank, 02.01.95). In the midst of rumours and controversy, President Zedillo met with harsh criticism at home, which only added to his many difficulties. There are limits to enforcing aid conditionality, because too numerous conditions impinge upon the principle of sovereignty. Conditionality is likely to erode the credibility of reformist executives and strengthen opposition to reforms, and therefore becomes counter-productive. A U.S. $20 billion discretionary fund was instead offered to Mexico, with no special conditions attached. Many analysts believe, however, that President Zedillo's government has been asked to settle the Chiapas uprising quickly, in order to restore investors' confidence (Latin American Data Bank, 02.15.95). This is not to imply that Mexico was encouraged to use force against the armed peasants under Subcomandante Marcos.

10

Adjustment through Regional Integration

Aid packages, conditional or not, are only palliative measures in periods of adjustment. It could well be that an enduring solution to recurrent economic setbacks will only come from long-term regional projects which foster economic complementarity among neighbouring countries, assistance from the stronger economies for the weaker ones, and eventually the setting up of a regional industrial strategy under the umbrella of free-trade agreements or unions. The European experiment could provide an interesting precedent for such arrangements, possibly transposable to the Latin American context. François Perroux offers the following definition of integration:

Integration consists in creating tighter economic relationships among given zones. At the first level, it involves the free trade of products; at the second, the free circulation of production factors; at the third, the coordination of economic policies. The classic effects of integration have to do with allocation of resources, optimal size of firms, broadening of markets, greater circulation of factors, rationalised specialisation, terms of exchange and increases in production and income. The less classic arguments in favour of integration are an increased capacity to attract and absorb foreign capital, innovations and strong concentration through monopolies, and multinational centres for research and development. (Perroux, 1991: 677)

This detailed definition suggests a gradual process marked by quantitative and qualitative amplification of exchanges, of the modalities of such exchanges, and of their regulation by appropriate agencies. Perroux does not confuse integration with the unchecked influx of foreign capital, and neither does he attribute to international monopolies the key (and therefore decisive) role in the process.

The first step towards integration is the implementation of free trade; under the impetus of a marked increase in shared undertakings, institutional development will necessarily follow. Clashes between diverging traditions and practices soon make it imperative to coordinate the economic strategies of the partners. As a result of the newly arising supranational concerns, a predictable set of political consequences arises: the reduction of each state's power to direct its economic policies; some shrinking of the sovereignty principle; and a changing balance in the intimate links between political decision makers and local interest groups.

Integration brings major economic changes which in turn transform the potential areas of political intervention. Since decision makers are well aware of this reality, their adhering to the principle of integration can be ascribed to a desire to modify wherever possible the rules of the political regime, with an eye to furthering their own aims. We propose to identify these regimes and these aims, as well as the hoped-for repercussions. In exploring this unbeaten path, we will attempt to clarify the linkages between regional integration as an economic phenomenon and the political framework provided by the democratic system, in all its variations and possible modes of consolidation. Just as the European Community, in broadening to include three southern European democratizing nations (Spain, Portugal, and Greece), served as an instructive precedent concerning the ways in which an integrative framework can benefit democratic consolidation, there are lessons to be learned from the Latin American experiment.

The issue of regional integration has resurfaced in recent literature, with several new contributions examining the Latin American experiments. A few of these are descriptive in nature and provide an account of the various free-trade agreements (United Nations, ECLAC, 1991a, 1991b; Ferrer, 1991). The main body of contributions adopts a documentary and quantitative approach, tracing the growth of commercial exchanges and offering a chronology of liberalization of regional markets (Hirst, 1988, 1992; Chudnovsky, 1989; Camargo, 1989; Manzetti, 1990; Tavares de Araujo, 1990a, 1990b; Castro Escudero, 1991; Mármora and Mesner, 1991). A final, minute category is informed by a theoretical approach; it attempts to identify the dynamics which have given rise to the recent wave of trade liberalization (Rosenthal, 1990; Urías Brambila, 1991; Costa Vaz, 1992; Moneta, 1992; Davila-Villers, 1992; Petras and Vieux, 1992; Duquette, Turcotte, Soldevila, and Ancelovici, 1994). It is this last category which is of interest here.

Some theorists study this phenomenon in the context of a worldwide trend towards globalization which shows up the limitations of the traditional concepts of borders, sovereignty, and national identity. For Urías Brambila (1991), economic globalization is an agent of change; it tends to provoke structural reforms and gives birth to new varieties of regional models. In this view, integration is considered an attempt to increase an economy's competitiveness so that it might join the ranks of major financial, technological, and trading powers such as the United States, the EEC, and Japan. The precedents established by the EEC and by bilateral free-trade agreements (United States / Israel, United States / Canada) serve as guideposts for a growing number of interested nations. This is the 'diffusion hypothesis'; or, rather, the hypothesis of propagation – 'going global' – of the liberal model, from a single, original centre known as the developed world, whose dynamic power and capacity to inspire imitation are seen as unequalled. In this holistic scenario, it is the international market which plays the starring role.

Others point out the clear chronological parallels between regional integration and adjustment experiments, noting how such reforms adapt to the changes at the international level. The radical structural changes in developing countries are aimed at obtaining better access to international markets. Can high levels of growth occur without the adoption and the implementation of these reforms? The varying level of industrial maturity among the economies involved, and therefore the variations called for in their adjustment programs, will necessarily make the level and speed of integration dependent upon the compatibility they exhibit among themselves. Stabilization of the currencies of intended partners offers a fine example of an absolute prerequisite to the shaping of long-term commercial exchanges.

In this vein, Ramos (1986) explores the sharp contrast between the national-capitalist protectionist model of the 1950s, 1960s, and 1970s, with its industrial focus on import-substitution, and the neo-liberal model adopted in the 1980s by most Latin American nations. In this view, the recent wave of integration in Latin America is read as part of a neo-liberal package, with integration proper as the concluding chapter of the process. In this hypothesis, where a country is seen as converting to a new, liberal paradigm, the integration process figures as the dividend to be reaped from domestic-level structural adjustments. This simple causality approach has the main advantage of interpreting all formal free-trade agreements prior to regional integration as an indication of the efforts made by a given country according to its particular situation. Authors disagree about the nature of the correspondence between neo-liberalism and integration: is it a case of straight parallelism, or is causality at work? Theoretical conclusions will vary significantly according to whether integration is seen as simply accompanying structural reforms – and thus serve as a yardstick of domestic efforts at stabilization – or as providing conditions favourable to such stabilization; or as a reward for reforms.

According to Foxley (1983), liberalism and attempts at integration represent the major trend of the Latin American development model since the 1950s, increasing in step with the diversification of Latin America's share of world markets. Since some countries, such as Brazil and Mexico, have undertaken this process more dynamically than others, the already significant gaps between Latin American countries have widened. This, in turn, has given rise to protectionist moves and increasing bouts of economic nationalism on the part of the weaker nations, so that the move towards integration has been gradually paralysed. Economic nationalism may thus be seen as the result of the unequal development of the particular countries and of the various bottlenecks occurring on the path towards national industrialization within the paradigm of self-centred development.

Integration can sometimes occur as a contextual and defensive alliance of countries wishing to protect their economies against the destabilizing influence of 'globalization from the North.' Experience has taught them that industrial competition in a tariff-free market can inflict deadly damage to their production apparatus: deindustrialization, decreased national ownership, and increased dependency upon highly developed industrial centres. Such a defensive strategy has a fairly long history, beginning during 'national-capitalist' times and continuing even up to the recent past. The choice of more prudent and measured modes of integration has been inspired by the precedent of the EEC, and has been adopted by countries already partially liberalized but anxious to preserve their respective positions, and whose unfavourable domestic conditions have led them to undertake a cautious reform process marked by frequent interruptions.

While the sudden conversion of political executives to liberalism has been the subject of recent research, the phenomenon of Latin American entrepreneurs adhering to free trade has not yet been fully studied. Previous periods have been highly profitable to entrepreneurs, who remain well treated even in more recent times. The developmental undertakings of the authoritarian regimes have received ample attention, and are still, in Brazil, sufficiently alive to induce nostalgia in some parties. While it was a time of easy money and of princely budgets devoted to infrastructure projects, the majority's minimum needs went unmet, and the middle classes received an uneasy and unsatisfactory economic share. The short shrift they received was a ploy to depoliticize and to distance from the regime those who might have been the agents of its democratization.

The democratic exercise is predicated upon the restoration of free transactions among producers. Insofar as the authoritarian regime inspired the loyalty of entrepreneurs through policies of a reserved market and generous subsidies which made the private sector fully dependent upon the state, there can be no talk of free and spontaneous expression of particular interests establishing healthy competition among players in something akin to the logic of the marketplace, with benefits going to the most innovative producers rather than to those protected by cartel structures and a tight network of political backing.

Regional integration projects, like the democratic project itself, are based upon the premise that individual interests may be expressed outside of the logic of the incubator state, and would favour an opening of markets and of external initiatives. In some views, the appropriate source of such initiatives are the small and medium-sized businesses which, finding themselves faced with the domination of all-powerful oligopolies on their native soil, are on the lookout for areas of expansion which a stagnating demand and a protected market no longer afford them. This is a seductive hypothesis, which is only beginning to receive the attention of researchers (Manzetti, 1990; Montero, 1992). The situation seems to signal the existence, in several Latin American countries, of a new class of more individualistic entrepreneurs, less dependent upon state orders and subsidies, and whose horizons are wider than those of the preceding generation. The rise of this category of entrepreneur would count as one of the more spectacular consequences of structural reforms: more self-assured and aggressive in the marketplace because more 'innovative,' in Schumpeter's understanding of the term (Montero, 1992).

How to account for the attitude changes among the more traditional sectors made up of oligopolies, which are the main actors on the national economic stage? We may hypothesize that these sizeable groups, left to themselves by the state following the debt crisis and the dismantling of the import-substitution strategy, are also on the lookout for new markets. It must be kept in mind that the thirty largest firms are responsible for 76 per cent of the exports of Mexico, for 75 per cent of those of Argentina, for 65 per cent of those of Chile, and for 32 per cent of those of Brazil. This is the little-known sector of 'strategic alliances' wherein private players find a setting favourable to their conversion to economic regionalism. In this context, more than ninety joint ventures were arranged by large Brazilian and Argentinean corporations in the first eight months of 1992 (*Gazeta Mercantil*, 02.17.93).

'Conversion' is, in fact, an accurate term when one considers that the private sector viewed MERCOSUR, at least in its early days, as a purely governmental undertaking (Tavares de Araujo, 1988). It is pointless to look for its origins in hypothetical industrial or agro-industrial pressure groups; MERCOSUR was truly a child of the new democracies. It is true that the 1986 accord was enthusiastically received by the Argentinean private sector. The Brazilian entrepreneurs at that time, however, considered the Argentinean economy too modest and unsettled for their purposes, and continued to favour an economic expansion directed towards Europe and North America, both of which offered greater possibilities; they therefore pursued their previous strategy (Manzetti, 1990). Only six years later, according to a 1992 poll, these same entrepreneurs appeared so interested in MERCOSUR that 20 per cent of them were projecting some form or other of association with partners of the Southern Cone countries (*Latin American Weekly Report*, 04.09.92). The Federation of Industrialists of the State of São Paulo (Federacão Industrialista do Estado de São Paulo, or FIESP), easily the most powerful in Brazil, has declared that regional integration has become a necessity (Barthélémy, 1991). The states that support it are Rio Grande do Sul, which, sharing borders with the three other partners, is most likely to profit from it, and, for more obscure reasons, Rio de Janeiro and the *nordeste* states (Tavares de Araujo, 1990a).

This radical shift in position may be read as expressing the response of parties now confronted with cost-effectiveness problems on the markets which had previously assured their livelihood (a protected domestic market and a once-expanding, but now highly competitive, international market). They find themselves seeking out new byways in a reduced horizon. While these regional markets certainly hold less promise than the world markets which offer the potential of numerous well-developed consumer markets, they are (at least apparently) less threatening, given that world markets are in a position to impose their own rules. The advantage of Argentinean, Uruguayan, and Paraguayan markets, as far as Brazilian entrepreneurs are concerned, lies in the fact that each one by itself presents low risks of inordinate dependency or economic competition in the foreseeable future, while promising a cost-effective proposition for the short term.

It is reasonable to hypothesize that these players, when faced with a such a long-standing economic downturn, will prefer low-return, low-risk projects to high-return projects such as joint ventures with international firms, since new waves of foreign investment or strategic alliances with multinational companies carry with them quite substantial risks: market takeovers and mergers were rife in speculative-type industrial operations undertaken with developed countries during the whole of the 1980s. For some industries (the automotive industry in Brazil, for instance, linked as it was to European and American interests, and so susceptible to Japanese competition), the danger was imminent. The level of risk was made even less acceptable by the fact that the state's long-term commitment to an industrial policy outspokenly favouring national entrepreneurs was now a thing of the past.

We can hazard an analysis of how the corporate players reacted to regional integration, and how they came to transfer their priorities from the old strategy, which involved winning over developed markets, to the new, based on diversifying exports and setting up regional commercial structures which would afford them something like a substitute market for the one they could no longer preserve in its original form. Given the entrepreneurs (E), the state as a developmentalist variable (S), high-level risks (R^1), and minor risks (R^2), we can establish the following equation:

$$E * S = R^1 > R^2$$

The authoritarian framework provided an environment conducive to open competition on international markets, those of developed nations in particular, as can be gathered from South Korea's export strategy from the 1960s on. In the case of South Korea, however, the regulatory and competitive price structure was dictated by the hard market laws at work, whereas the apparently competitive prices of Brazilian products on the world market were in fact artificially shored up by government subsidies. The return on such products, lower than anticipated, proved insufficient to cover the costs of badly needed technological modernization. On the other hand, a restricted internal market and state-planned and -organized cartelization allowed firms to overcharge on the captive home market and thus make huge profits, at rates considerably above those of developed markets. Because of weak local competition, only a small percentage of such profits was ever reinvested in modernization, and thus the useful life of any given element had to be extended inordinately. The state took on responsibility for such modernization, through subsidies to graduate research and megaprojects, especially in the field of energy and armaments. The fact that low or unpaid corporate taxes did not cover these costs led to state deficits, and thus to state indebtedness.

State withdrawal from an investment role, whether early or late – swift, as in Argentina or Chile, or slow, as in Brazil – leaves entrepreneurs with no choice. They will certainly opt for regional competition, which will at least save a fraction of the advantages they are gradually losing on the domestic market. Although more gradual in Brazil, the liberalizing of imports and the subsidy cuts were correctly read by corporate players as decisive moves, which explains their delayed but firm commitment to MERCOSUR. Whence the equation:

$$E / S = R^2 > R^1$$

While the new framework is certainly less reassuring than the old, it is still better than a full-scale opening of the market to international competition, with no safeguards, which had brought such massive deindustrialization to Argentina and Chile in the 1970s. The memory of this costly mistake is painfully alive in both countries, and Brazil has no wish to tread the same path.

The above considerations hint at how MERCOSUR has come to acquire a 'familial' connotation for corporate players, who see it is as a transitional structure, Latin America being at present unprepared for the challenge of international market competition. Public policy in this area, applied differently in each country, must be aimed at raising market competitiveness. The entrepreneurial class is pushing for these reforms to consolidate the new regional market reserve. In their view, a certain number of preliminary reforms, aimed at a controlled liberalization of the economies of countries involved, are essential. These ardent supporters of structural adjustment are, for obvious reasons, in favour of measures aimed at supporting businesses.

11

Regional Integration in Support of Market-Oriented Policies

A long-standing and well-developed hypothesis describes regional integration as a shield against globalization, which is defined as worldwide deregulated free trade. The favoured model is that of the EEC, which uses the principle of 'community preference,' though this principle has recently been relaxed by the Maastricht Treaty. It has its origin in the political culture of various nations, and has found new support among nationalist circles in Brazil and Argentina which have denounced the Enterprise for the Americas Initiative (*Folha de São Paulo*, 07.07.90). The Economic Commission for Latin America and the Caribbean (ECLAC) was, in 1956, the first to propose such a model of regional integration, noting the existence of a bipolar world and perceiving the international market as a rigid system operating for the profit of industrialized countries (Castro Escudero, 1991). In 1960, following the ECLAC example, Argentina, Brazil, Chile, Mexico, Peru, Uruguay, and Paraguay signed the Montevideo Treaty, which gave birth to the Asociación Latino-Americana de Libre Comercio (ALALC). The treaty's main objective was to establish, over the next twelve years, a Latin American free-trade zone.

The first attempt at integration occurred *hacia adentro*, to use Urías Brambila's phrase (1991). Described as aggressive, this model was applied from the early 1950s to the second half of the 1970s, at a time when the dominant 'national-capitalist' development model was based on protectionism, import substitution, and a central role for the state in promoting business through infrastructure-development projects and government procurement. High customs tariffs were at the time justified by the necessity of protecting a fledgling national industry (Rosenthal, 1990). This view of development took the shape of modes of integration aimed at protecting Latin America from international competition, rather than at breaking into world markets. Though its objectives were ambitious, integration *hacia adentro* brought about nationalist-type withdrawals in a majority of Latin American countries, as a response to the disastrous commercial balance sheets arising from the energy crisis and high indebtedness; the achievements of the agreement were eaten away, and deadlines were pushed further and further into the future. Gradually, the model itself came under severe criticism. The Andean Pact, or Pacto Andino, is the best example of this nationalist reactive phase. It came closer to the principle of integration than ALALC insofar as it planned to implement a common customs tariff for all foreign countries and the abolition of interregional tariffs. It was an ambitious treaty, advocating a genuine industrial strategy, a common policy towards foreign investment (which brought about Chile's defection in 1976), and a harmonizing of macroeconomic processes among partners. These objectives were not fully realized. In 1983, participants agreed to redefine the Pact's terms and conditions; and in 1987, they signed the Protócolo Modificatorio del Acuerdo de Cartagena in Quito (Urías Brambila, 1991).

By 1980, the failure of the process initiated by ALALC had become obvious. Camargo (1989) attributes this failure to three factors: integration was slowed down by trade imbalances among members, who could not obtain access to the moneys necessary to wipe out their deficits; no mechanisms were available to facilitate reciprocal payments; and the lack of harmony between economic policies led to differences in productivity levels which prevented healthy development of export capacity. According to Tavares de Araujo (1990b), it is economic nationalism which is to blame for ALALC's failure. Shortly thereafter a new treaty was signed, giving birth to the Asociación Latino-Americana de Integración (ALADI), which aimed at greater flexibility and specified no fixed timetables. One of its objectives was the creation of a free-trade zone linked to the modernization of economic structures (Arnaud-Ameller, 1989). It saw integration as a means to stimulate growth on a market basis. In addition, it aimed at a less aggressive and less ideological approach (Castro Escudero, 1991). Unlike ALALC, which advocated multilaterality, it pushed for bilateral or partial accords between nations (Urías Brambila, 1991). The members of ALADI, anxious to preserve their autonomy in terms of national policy, had not insisted on harmonization of their respective economic policies (Tavares de Araujo, 1990a).

This second phase has been called 'revisionist' by some. Harmonization was all the more difficult to attain because some countries remained faithful to the national-capitalist model and to integration *hacia adentro*, while others were attracted by the monetarist-liberal model from the North. In the process of adopting more modest integration objectives, participants began to design a more informal, bilateral process in preference to a 'theoretical' multilateral approach, which was impossible to sustain in the face of increasingly diverse situations and diverging national strategies arising in response to the debt crisis.

This phase tolerated a greater range of objectives and deadlines from member countries. Even the original protectionist policy of curtailing foreign investment began to be loosened (Rosenthal, 1990).

It was in the mid-1980s that the effects of structural reforms undertaken by member countries (notably Mexico) made themselves felt. This period is referred to as the phase of growth through exportation *hacia fuera*. A greater convergence of economic policies was again called for, along with increased numbers and growing consolidation of democratic governments. Integration was to rest upon new development strategies, and protectionism was on the wane (Urías Brambila, 1991). The majority of authors (Urías Brambila, Arnaud-Ameller, Mármora and Mesner, Peña) are of the opinion that the concept of integration switched directions at this point, in an attempt to increase the Latin American share of the world market through its 'comparative advantages.' South Korea was everywhere cited as the model to be followed. For Mármora and Mesner (1991), it was a case of 'strengthening co-operation and regional integration to favour active insertion onto world markets.' The model was not without its ambiguities. Some countries, Brazil among them, were convinced that stimulating exports was not incompatible with gains to be made through import substitution. The new integration model was called upon to combine the various models in an attempt to reduce the commercial-balance deficit and reach for a currency surplus in order to finance the servicing of the debt (Arnaud-Ameller, 1989).

During the third meeting of ALADI's Council of Ministers in March 1987, a proposal for a 'normative' model of integration was put forward, containing the two following specifications: first, a strengthening of the Preferencia Arancelaria Regional (PAR) or Regional Tariff Preference (a major instrument of integration, it rose from 5 per cent in 1984 to 20 per cent in 1990 [Hirst, 1992]); second, a catch-up commercial program aiming for an average preference margin reaching 60 per cent, 'so as to divert to the regional market 30 per cent of the countries' imports from the rest of the world' (Gana and Bermúdez, 1989). Here again the aim was for an integrative institution representing a regional association to confront the dominance of developed areas.

While data indicate that intra-regional trade did in fact benefit, going from 8 per cent of overall trade in 1960 to 13 per cent in 1980 (Arnaud-Ameller, 1989), the most recent figures point to a noticeable decline of the intra-ALADI market share when compared to worldwide totals over the last decade. Certainly in absolute terms the recovery since 1985 has been significant, yet the fact remains that in the late 1980s, more than 70 per cent of regional Latin American trade was conducted exclusively between Brazil and Argentina. Foreign, non-regional countries remained dominant trading partners in each of our case studies (table 11). Faced with the existence of this obvious Brazil–Argentina axis, public decision makers sought to reinforce it through a formal agreement.

Remarkable changes have occurred over the years. For fifteen years, Brazil, under authoritarian regimes, sought economic complementarity with developed and developing countries by diversifying its export base of manufactured products (table 16). This was the probable cause of its being held responsible for the failure of ALADI. Obviously its industrial strategy was a slight to Brazil's 'official' Latin American partners. It aimed at significantly lowering Brazil's import ratio and was responsible for widening the gap between it and its neighbours as early as the late 1970s. The trend was most noticeable between 1980 and 1985; in those years, Brazil's annual trade with ALADI partners sank from U.S. $7.4 billion to $3.8 billion (Tavares de Araujo, 1988). ALADI was clearly the victim of a 'nationalist' reaction on the part of the three largest partners, Brazil, Argentina, and Mexico, in response to the worsening of the international economic situation. Argentina reduced its imports from U.S. $2.1 billion in 1980 to $1.3 billion in 1985. For the same period, Brazil's decreased from $3.5 billion to $1.7 billion. But it was Mexico whose decrease was most acute, going from U.S. $1.1. billion in 1981 to $291 million in 1987.

The civilian government, which came to power in 1985, brought a shift in Brazilian trade policy and led to the signing of trade agreements with its Southern Cone neighbours. Brazil responded to Argentinean advances dating back to 1983 under President Raúl Alfonsin. The political program inherited by the New Republic from President Tancredo Neves was anything but liberal. Brasilia wanted the restoration of democracy to be grounded in the affirmation of a regional solidarity both that was anti-conservative and anti-hegemonistic, as worked out by Itamaratí diplomats; in a word, through an alliance between a Centre-Left political coalition and a nationalistic bureaucracy.

The turning point occurred in July 1986 when Brazil and Argentina signed the Programa de Integração e Cooperação Econômica (PICE), which set out two distinct phases (Castro Escudero, 1991). The first was a phase of sectoral integration leading to the signing of a series of protocols pertaining to specific sectors, with the expectation of profiting from the reactivation of trade between the two countries. The areas covered by three of these protocols were particularly significant: equipment goods, wheat, and the automotive industry. For Chudnovsky and Porta (1989), it is clear that Brazil wished to profit from Argentina's agro-industrial potential as well as its qualified manpower, whereas Argentina considered its neighbour an important technological power and a good-sized market for a growing share of its fairly modest national production.

Twenty other protocols, signed between 1986 and 1989, covered co-operative agreements in such areas as biotechnology, energy, transport, and steel;

increased bilateral trade was not among the stated objectives. The main economic and political forces in the region were concentrated along the Brazil-Argentina axis. Their linking is geographically significant as well: together these countries occupy over 65 per cent of the subcontinent.

The second phase, scheduled to begin in November 1988, was intended to mark the beginning of a more advanced integration, in preparation for establishing a free-trade zone based upon better co-ordination of monetary and fiscal policies between the two countries, and fairly short deadlines for the abolition of customs tariffs – a mere ten years. This was the EEC model, with shorter deadlines.

The signing of the PICE in 1986 owes much to the strong similarities between the economic policies of Brazil and Argentina during the transition to democracy (Manzetti, 1990). Their respective stabilization plans exhibit revealing parallels: both the Cruzado and the Austral plans used a heterodox approach, and the Verão plan can be considered the main inspiration for the Argentinean plan launched in 1989. Severe economic problems occurring simultaneously in these countries forced them to postpone implementation. Hyper-inflation, with its destabilizing economic effects, and the loss of legitimacy of Presidents Sarney Costa and Raúl Alfonsin put the integration project temporarily both on the back burner and out of public favour (Ferrer, 1991).

The coming to power of Presidents Carlos Menem in Argentina and Collor de Mello in Brazil, each elected under a reform banner, gave new life to the 1986 agreement. There are striking parallels between the economic policies and practices of their respective governments. At the forefront came uncontrolled (that is, not fully charted judicially) privatization, along with deregulation and opening up to foreign investment. Simultaneously, and for the first time in their respective histories, these countries firmly undertook structural adjustments, yet without the minimal agenda necessary for laying down a set of ground rules and clear parameters which could be published for the benefit of the citizenry. This opened the door to auctioning off to the lowest bidder and to deregulated financial operations, with no consideration for the principle of public imputability which should normally guide such highly strategic transactions.

The renewal of bilateral negotiations were, however, the object of intense scrutiny in the Southern Cone; Paraguay and Uruguay immediately expressed their interest in participating in the second phase of PICE. In 1990, following several months of negotiations, representatives of the four countries signed the Asunción Treaty, which established MERCOSUR. Brazil at this point had already opened its doors wide to exports from its two small neighbours, thus setting an example for the region in adopting a leadership role backed by a solid industrial base.

MERCOSUR made provision for the free circulation of goods, for the adoption of a shared customs tariff and a common trade policy, for co-ordination of the macroeconomic policy of member countries, and for harmonization of their legislation. The transition phase which led to the signing of MERCOSUR displays many similarities with the measures adopted by the 1989 Canada–United States Free Trade Agreement (FTA). It planned a gradual reduction (over a five-year period) of customs tariffs applied to imports from third-party countries. This trade liberalization program also applied to non-tariff barriers and aimed at abolishing all barriers by the end of 1994. The influence of the FTA model, so obvious in the wording of the MERCOSUR agreement, indicates that the 'reactive' integration model may have reached its limits. This trend towards standardization of the parameters which marks the path of the American hemisphere's integration process underlines the permeability of the two concurrent actors: North America, on the one hand, and the Southern Cone, on the other.

The logic of trade liberalization leads naturally to opening negotiations with new partners. In June 1991, the MERCOSUR countries signed an agreement with the United States, leading to the establishment of the Advisory Council on Trade and Investment, with the mandate of identifying and abolishing obstacles to investment and to trade flow. If the creation of such a council came to be perceived as resulting from the Enterprise for the Americas Initiative, this might well signal a warming of relations between Brazil and Argentina, who had so far eyed the Initiative warily, and the United States. In November 1990, Brazil, as if to confirm this growing interest in North America, entered into an agreement with Mexico which aimed at tripling the volume of their bilateral trade within a two-year period. The reasons of this new trend are surely to be found in the profound internal changes which the economies of these countries have undergone in the course of the process of structural adjustment. Besides transforming the possible modes of economic association, these changes have brought the observable dynamics of southern Latin America closer to those of North America, thereby distinguishing, in the same measure, MERCOSUR from the previous model, which had been strongly marked by reactive protectionism.

Mexico, in the vanguard of Latin American countries, chose commercial liberalization as the spearhead of its economic strategy. As the 1994 peso crisis showed, Mexico is the best example of a conversion to a liberal paradigm and of the dividends such a conversion can bring. The North America Free Trade Agreement (NAFTA) can be considered the institutionalization of the economic reforms undertaken by President de la Madrid and pursued by President Salinas de Gortari. Had Mexico not gone forward with its adjustment and restructuring policies since 1982, it would not have been in a position to sign any such agreement with the United States and Canada. The strategy adopted by Mexico, as shown in the preceding chapter, took the shape of strict adjustment of public finances, privatization of the majority of the 1,155 state enterprises, deregulation of economic activity, and a remarkable tariff liberalization underscored by the July 1985 presidential decree altering tariff policy. Mexico's adhering to the GATT in 1986 also played a part. In 1985, fully 90 per cent of Mexican production was protected through a system of import licensing; ten years later, the proportion had dropped to 5 per cent. The maximum tariff first fell from 100 per cent to 20 per cent, and in 1992 stood at 6 per cent. This redefinition of the state role in the economy is a radical switch from the nationalist policies of President López Portillo, who had reacted to the 1981 liquidity crunch by applying an extremely strict policy of import reduction, which culminated shortly thereafter with the nationalization of private banks.

The strategy adopted by President de la Madrid and pursued by his successor Salinas de Gortari stimulated the development of the non-petroleum industrial export sector. Thanks to a favourable exchange rate and to the substantial development of *maquiladoras* (which rank second after petroleum among national industries), manufacturing-sector exports increased 17 per cent per year from 1983 to 1990, making up 52 per cent of total exports in 1990 against 14 per cent in 1982. Petroleum's share declined from 78 per cent of total exports in 1982 to 38 per cent nine years later (Banco de México, 1992). Its policy of opening up to exports led Mexico to sign trade agreements with Chile, Venezuela, and Colombia, as well as with some Central American countries.

While the economic reforms pursued by Mexico were crucial to the NAFTA initiative, strong economic complementarity with the United States remains a concern. Subcontracting to Mexico should make the United States more competitive internationally. The figures confirm the interdependent nature of their economies. The United States is Mexico's number one trading partner, accounting for over 70 per cent of its imports and exports, whereas Mexico ranks fourth for the United States, accounting for 18 per cent of imports and 23 per cent of exports. Over 80 per cent of private debt and 85 per cent of foreign debt is lodged with commercial banks, a third of which are American-owned.

Close to 50 per cent of non-petroleum trade between the two countries occurs through subsidiaries of American multinationals, and in 1985 U.S. funds accounted for two-thirds of foreign investment (Weintraub, 1990). Half of the intra-corporation trade, which goes through *maquiladoras*, is of American origin. The Mexican automotive industry, steadily expanding since 1977, has been exporting 83 per cent of its total output to the United States since 1989 (Hufbauer and Scott, 1992). For Canada, Mexico figures mainly as a competitor for the U.S. market, since both countries export textiles, vehicles, car parts, and heavy machinery.

In tune with the logic reigning when the Canada–U.S. FTA was signed, Mexico was granted a full ten years for progressively reducing its tariffs; it is noteworthy that corn and some types of bean were removed from free competition for a fifteen-year period. While NAFTA modifies none of the tariff agreements of the 1989 Canada–U.S. FTA, it does signal a move towards increased liberalization of services and harmonization of standards. Adjustments have been made to the process of dispute settlement and to the rules of origin applicable to specific sectors.

Chile offers convincing converse proof of the clear link between regional integration and structural reform: if reforms can lead to integration, their absence is sufficient to prevent integration. Chile backed out of the Andean Pact in 1976 because, alone among the other member countries (Peru, Ecuador, Colombia), it no longer wished to limit the influx of the foreign investments of which it was in such dire need. As we have seen, the country was at the time involved in a structural adjustment program, strongly orthodox in nature, masterminded by the then Minister of the economy, Sergio de Castro. This policy was felt to be incompatible with the strongly nationalist economic strategy in force at that time within the Andean Pact's countries, in particular in Peru under General Velasco Alvarado.

Chile has so far held back from the MERCOSUR alliance, setting as preconditions the lowering of customs tariffs by Southern Cone countries to levels matching its own markedly lower ones, as well as a commitment to general harmonization of their macroeconomic policies (United Nations, ECLAC, 1991b). In the vanguard of reformist trends, it had no choice but to be a lone fighter, at least until democracy was re-established in Santiago. With its low level of industrialization, it had little to hope for from neighbours barely better endowed in the way of new technology and capital. Only Brazil was in a position to make significant investments in the area. However, Brazil's internal difficulties, its indebtedness, its infamous inflationary trend, and, most of all, its uncertain economic strategy made it a low-credibility partner. Other Pacific neighbours, more distant but more prosperous, such as Canada, the United States, Japan, Australia, and New Zealand, seemed destined to play a more active role in this regard.

Throughout the period under study, dictatorship and democracy notwithstanding, Brazil has avoided agreements which would have subordinated it to the commercial momentum of a single industrially developed bloc. During the 1980s, it tried to keep faith with a commercial-diversification strategy which allowed it to maintain a balance between three main trading zones: approximately 26 per cent of its exports to North America; 24 per cent to the European Community; and another 25 per cent to a mix of swiftly expanding markets such as the Middle East and the newly industrialized Pacific countries. While the 'global market' was expanding during that period, Brazil's trade became more regional. In 1995, 19 per cent of its exports went to North America, almost 28 per cent to the European Union, 21 per cent to other Latin American countries, and 20 per cent to Asia (table 11). In each of these trading zones, it makes sure to maintain a positive trade balance, which allows it to remain solvable and ensure sufficient financial margins with its international creditors.

However, Brazil was forced to adapt to some constraints resulting from the international economic situation. Caught by surprise in the early 1980s by the strong protectionist trend in the United States, and faced with a mounting rivalry between trading blocs which threatened its diversification strategy, Brazil opened up to Latin America. The move towards regional integration was highly compatible with the convictions espoused by the democratic coalition carried to power in 1985. Southern Cone countries were not, in fact, among its major trading partners at the time, although their share was to undergo a spectacular expansion in the medium term. Rather, Brazil was, in this, obeying 'strategic' and gradualist imperatives, its objective being to weave closer political and economic links with its immediate neighbours in an attempt to thwart the growing influence of the United States in the region.

With a view to consolidating MERCOSUR, Brazil pushed the policy of a common external tariff that would create a regional reserve market, following a precedent set by the European Community. Chile, under President Patricio Aylwin, was opposed to such a defensive approach. Chile's unwillingness to join MERCOSUR and its desire to follow Mexico in adhering to NAFTA as soon as possible were a source of deep concern to Brazil, which has made no secret of its growing exasperation with the United States and Mexico, both of which are pushing for hemispheric integration in a framework of a so-called globalization. When U.S. president Bill Clinton asked for the collective support of Latin American heads of state for Mexico's application to join NAFTA, in the form of a letter he wished to present to Congress, Brazil rejected the proposed text, which referred to the initiative as a step towards hemispheric integration, in the middle term, of both American continents (*Gazeta Mercantil*, 10.16.93). Brazil has therefore been generous with diplomatic visits and invitations to Santiago to open negotiations, making it clear that it considers Chile as an important strategic ally, more important certainly than would be justified by trade considerations alone. The new flexibility shown by Brazil's trade practices, its pursuit of privatization in the sphere of national capital, and its questioning of its protectionist tradition are signs of a necessary adjustment to the present-day conditions of its immediate partners. Brazil nevertheless has remained faithful to its market-diversification strategy, and regional integration ranks only as a bonus, one element among others in an overall plan.

The coming to power of the Concertación government in Chile in the early 1990s, concurrently with the deepening of structural adjustments in several Latin American countries (among them, Mexico, Argentina, and Venezuela) has been an important factor in Chile's change of attitude. Its isolationist stance is being replaced by the establishment of tighter links, evidenced by the signing of various trade agreements. This is congruent with its export-based model, which forces Chile to gain access to new markets, given that its trade flows within the Americas have so far remained relatively modest. In its desire to change this situation, Chile has signed separate economic complementarity agreements with Mexico, Argentina, and Venezuela, and has agreed with the United States on the joint creation of the Advisory Council on Trade and Investment. But the key factor in this recent conversion to the principle of regional integration is the return of democracy to the palace of La Moneda.

Notable among these closer agreements is Chile's reconciliation with Mexico, which Santiago undertook as soon as it was restored to democracy. Subsequent to the breaking off of diplomatic relations, trade between these countries had fallen to almost nil during the crisis years of 1981–7. The revitalization was not felt until 1988, and suffered a slowdown as early as 1989 because of an exchange deficit which put Chile at a disadvantage. In 1989 Chilean exports to Mexico totalled U.S. $40 million; conversely, Mexico exported U.S. $80 million to Chile, mainly in the form of petroleum and petrochemicals; automobiles (Chile ranks second among Mexico's partners, after the United States, which in 1989 bought 83 per cent of Mexico's automotive production); and nylon and polyester textiles.

Chile's exports to Mexico have included fruit, forestry products, minerals, and textiles. In its attempt to develop non-traditional export sectors, it now also sells health products, mining engineering services, and mining equipment. In a 1991 bilateral accord, Chile and Mexico agreed to abolish their respective customs tariffs for most of these products by January 1996. A 1998 deadline was set for weaker sectors, which respond more slowly to restructuring. The main intent of this agreement was to boost trade between the two countries; a modest objective of U.S. $150 to $500 million has been set. These prudent deadlines and realistic figures are a sign of the times, and the accord is a good example of sound bilateral trade policy.

Exchanges with Argentina, while more considerable than those with Mexico, had suffered a sharp decline in the early 1980s. In spite of border conflicts in the late 1970s, economic exchanges remained significant, although, here again, uneven, as a result of Chile's relatively narrow export base. At the end of the 1980s, Chilean exports to Argentina had reached U.S. $120 million, and Argentinean exports to Chile, U.S. $350 million. This was the situation in

August 1990 when Presidents Carlos Menem and Patricio Aylwin signed a set of bilateral agreements aimed at establishing a wider market by late 1995, which included free circulation of goods, persons, and production factors; the total abolition of customs tariffs for bilateral exchanges; the building of gas and oil pipelines between the two countries; the opening of new border crossings; and research into possible new railways (Hirst, 1992). In August 1991, just a month before the Chilean-Mexican agreement, Chile and Argentina signed a free-trade treaty, the Acuerdo de Complementación Económica (ACE). Unlike the former, it did not include gradual reduction of customs tariffs (Gaete, 1991). Neither did it entail fixing a common external customs tariff, as MERCOSUR had done (Hirst, 1992).* Thus it is not marked by a reactive approach to the 'non-community international market,' as it is called by the Europeans. An aggressive strategy, it promotes common projects in various areas: industry, energy, mining, and tourism. Here again we have a commercial strategy established bilaterally and on extended deadlines.

Several Chilean mining companies responded enthusiastically to the signing of the accord. Shipping companies, electricity producers, harbour companies, banks, and insurance companies saw in it an opportunity to increase sales. A Chilean cardboard-and-paper manufacturing company acquired 51 per cent of shares in the Argentinean Química Estrella San Luis S.A., which produces chemicals; Bonafide, an Argentinean distributor of coffee, chocolate, and caramels, was purchased by a Chilean group, Costa S.A. (Spencer, 1991; Salman, 1992). There exists, however, an irritant which may lead to disputes: Chilean fruit producers will now be faced with competition from Argentina, which has free access to Chilean ports under the terms of the agreement. Since Argentina produces more fruit and wine than does Chile, while following a similar policy of promoting exports, it may be tempted to use the asymmetry of this accord to access the markets of North America and Asia.

The original phrasing of the Chilean-Argentinean agreement underscores the spirit of economic homogenization and the liberal logic of comparative advantages at work: the necessity of extending binational integration, thus establishing strong reciprocity of interests, to improve conditions for competitive insertion into the global economy. The agreement finally gave recognition to the fact that it was the similarities between the fundamental orientations of political economies which had allowed binational agreements compatible with the ALADI and GATT proposals. The agreement specifically referred to the

---

* The existence of MERCOSUR poses a problem to the commercial integration of Chile and Argentina. Brazil is in a position to set high tariffs for non-members, which would put Chile at a disadvantage *vis-à-vis* Argentina.

importance of full participation of entrepreneurs, and of the private sector in general, in the integration process.

Chile, inspired by the example set by Brazil and constrained by the narrow range of its marketable production, persistently pursued its aim of diversifying its export markets and of opening up to capital of whatever source. Its economy remains vulnerable to ever-possible decline in demand among its privileged customers. Seeking to reduce this dependency, it exports, in addition to nationally owned copper, forestry products, and frozen or modified sea products for human or animal consumption, some textiles, early winter fruit, and, thanks to the influx of European capital and technology, the products of a modernized wine industry. This range of exports, varied yet circumscribed, is unlikely to raise the mistrust of its more considerable partners.

While Brazil and Chile never abandoned their commitment to diversifying exports, Mexico undertook this process in the 1970s, having theretofore trusted its abundant and saleable petroleum resources. This mono-exportation was unfortunately subject to the fluctuations of a volatile market in a world with numerous petroleum-rich areas, the Middle East heading the list. Its diversification strategy rested on a basis more fragile than that of Brazil, which was able to count on the significant development of its agro-industrial and industrial sectors: automobiles, energy, mining equipment, and weaponry. In the 1970s, however, Mexico had undertaken, in marked contradiction to its nationalist-flavoured constitution, a process of improving its complementarity with the United States, thanks to the *maquiladora* system. Almost by default, this sector blossomed at a time when the petroleum-exporting strategy was collapsing in 1981. As this export base crumbled, and with it the dream of easy market diversification, the last ten years have confirmed that Mexico's economy is tied to that of the United States, all the more so because of the success of northern Mexico's complementary industry, the growth of which has become even more significant in the late 1980s, thanks to the gradual deregulation during that decade.

In the process of the structural reforms undertaken in Mexico, there appeared a gradual distancing from the ALADI regional integration strategy. The decline of the 'petroleum economy' had signalled the death of the dream of regional hegemony; the ambitious projects (to be backed by petroleum revenues) which President López Portillo had directed at the Caribbean and South America had to be abandoned; commercial flow with these two neighbouring zones has low priority, confirming Mexico's excessive dependency on its northern trading partner. Mexicans, though interested in NAFTA, are aware of the dangers of this dependency. The December 1994 peso crisis made it perfectly clear that the inevitable gap between two such different economies could cause a sizeable trade deficit detrimental to Mexico. This knowledge led Mexico to invite foreign investments from, and foster trade with, Europe, Japan, Canada, and a few privileged Latin American partners; this initiative has been quite significant since the early 1990s. Thus, although its liberalization led it to adopt a strategy of regional integration directed towards the North American bloc, Mexico intends to renew its traditional trade-diversification strategy, as evidenced by its reaching out to Chile and to the Pacific nations, and by the bilateral free-trade agreements signed in October 1993 with Venezuela and Colombia, which in several respects are similar to Portillo's initiatives in the Caribbean. Mexico has signalled a warm welcome to European investment in its banking institutions, now that their privatization is nearly completed. But will this come too late to an economy in which nearly 80 per cent of the exchanges are now occurring with the United States?

In the case of Chile, integration is clearly marching in step with trade diversification directed towards the Pacific Rim nations, Europe, and North and Latin America: in 1993, with exports totalling U.S. $10 billion, 31.5 per cent went to Asia, mainly to Japan, Chile's principal customer since 1989; 26.1 per cent to Western Europe; 13.2 per cent to North America; and 19.2 per cent to Latin America (table 11) (Guzman Organ, 1993).

Certainly its structural reforms have made Chile more competitive, particularly in the food industry. The cost to be paid was its withdrawal from the Pacto Andino in 1976. Chile, concerned about forfeiting the advantages of MERCO-SUR, has evinced a growing interest in tightening links with other Latin American countries: Mexico, Venezuela, Colombia, Argentina, and Brazil. It has also extended a welcome to capital investment from Japan, Australia, and New Zealand. These are clear signs of its desire to maintain a wide variety of trading partners in order to avoid for itself the excessive dependency suffered by Mexico.

The huge North American market presents a serious challenge and promises early rewards. For better and for worse, Chile is not Brazil. Small in size, with a clear advantage in a few areas of economic activity (notably mines and agriculture), it is in a position to carve out a space for itself in the 'globalized' market of the American hemisphere by adopting a 'niche approach,' made quite acceptable to U.S. protectionists by the fact that its export base, and thus the volume of its exchanges, will remain limited in the foreseeable future.

It is thus probable that the United States will soon extend NAFTA privileges to Chile, in recognition of its sustained efforts at structural adjustment. This explains why Chile is so reluctant to accept a defensive-type regional integration that would offer few advantages in relation to its long-term strategy; its free-trade agreement with Argentina and its shying away from MERCOSUR are eloquent testimony in this regard. Unsurprisingly, these reservations were directed towards Brazil, which enjoys significant advantages in the mining and agricultural sectors. The bone of contention was the current Brazilian practice of agricultural subsidies, which would allow the country unfair advantages in a free-trade context (Castro Escudero, 1991). Chile had abolished all such subsidies in the framework of its reforms, aiming for cost-effectiveness on the international market; the policy also made sense in terms of its national revenues, which were insufficient to allow for long-term subsidies to export agriculture, of the type enjoyed by Brazil, France, and the United States. The new regime was more concerned by the possibility of accumulating revenues from a potentially profitable niche in the market.

And thus it was not only on the basis of their own commercial traditions that Latin American countries redefined the parameters of present-day regional integration, with both neighbouring countries and those of the First World. Under pressure from their failed models, in a situation made worse by structural adjustments, and well aware of the immense potential of high-consumption markets, Mexico and Chile adjusted their orientation, while still keeping in mind the strong protectionist tendencies always at work in the United States.

What we have here is a shift in direction, a reform in terms of the preceding period. The problem of regional integration is a vast one, and it gives rise to unprecedented phenomena. Crucial issues are at stake, chief among them the question of 'supranationalism.' Decreased autonomy in the self-definition of one's model of development cannot be fully explained by the balancing of national interests. Democracy does not imply unanimity; it implies, rather, mechanisms for conflict resolution and for making choices which will become the middle way between gradualist programs and radical reformist moves.

12

Obstacles to Integration in
Partially Liberalized Markets

Any regional integration project constitutes *ipso facto* a shift from a self-centred national development paradigm, and leads to questioning the previous model of industrialization through import substitution; it is a natural successor to reforms aiming at opening up new markets. It is not, however, devoid of ambiguity. By establishing a common customs tariff, it aims to establish a reserved market which gives more breadth to local industry, redefined as regional, thanks to the agreements reached among partners, who in fact probably can exercise little choice in the matter. Such is the view proposed by Brazil and agreed to, at least for the moment, by the other members of MERCOSUR. For this reason, it is imperative to include in our analysis a control variable, to wit, the adoption of structural adjustments in each participating country, as a decisive condition to the extension of the MERCOSUR project. In our hypothesis, the economic reserve market will be compromised to the extent that participating countries put into effect structural adjustment practices which are incompatible or even contradictory.

The least industrialized partners, who stand to lose the least in the confrontation with international competition, were the first to initiate radical liberal reforms and to welcome productive foreign investment with its input of fresh capital and new technologies. Their industrial base is neither very diversified nor strongly competitive; this is true of Argentina, and even more so of Uruguay and Paraguay. The fact that Brazil chose to be prudent in the matter of an uncontrolled opening up of its industry to new investors increased the level of disparity among players. It was further evidence of Brazil's control over the regional integration process, and this in turn emphasized the defensive nature of MERCOSUR, making it appear as a regional market reserved for Brazilian products. This explains Brazil's insistence on enforcing rules of origin for MERCOSUR products, which are expected to be assembled in member countries from local components. Brazil's concerns thus echo those frequently raised by the United States since the Canada–U.S. FTA came into effect in 1989.

A careful reading of the MERCOSUR treaty sheds light on the difficulties faced by the various partners, notably Brazil, in getting the Asunción Treaty on its feet, and gives clear indications as to the motivations of each of the political and corporate players involved. The four founding countries of MERCOSUR make up 65 per cent of the surface of South America: Brazil, with a population of 157 million, with a strong and varied industrrial base, and a complex and highly regionalized political structure; Argentina, population 29 million, with a weak and segmented industrial sector, and its centralized political structure dominated by the huge Buenos Aires population basin; Uruguay, population 4 million, with an economy in stagnation since the 1960s, and an almost exclusively regional export market; and Paraguay, population 3 million, with its prosperous agricultural sector, a budding industrial base focused on food processing, and its totally deregulated trade. The diversity of their situations and their economies is striking. The situation is further complicated by the choices made in terms of industrial strategies, which were shaped, as we have seen in Part One, by the particular constraints of their political systems and the size, variety, and competitiveness of their economies. If everything sets them apart from each other, including their history, the Southern Cone countries now have something in common: all of them are recent democracies. There is, however, no guarantee that this shared trait will contribute to a harmonizing of their practices or even of their economic strategies.

The substance of the Asunción Treaty reveals two complementary, and to some extent contradictory, dimensions. As in the North America Free Trade Agreement, each country opted, at the outset, for a relatively swift reduction of customs tariffs, from 1990 to 1996. The possibility of establishing a common 20 per cent tariff on foreign products entering the regional zone was also discussed. North American influence, limited to trade and by nature more technical since it focuses on products rather than on political choices, was given priority at this first level of convergence, as was shown by the drawing up of an exception schedule listing various products considered ill-equipped to face immediate competition. Almost 700 products were listed, about 350 for Argentina and the same number for Brazil, which were to be protected until 1 January 1995.

These tariff reductions had two objectives: in the short term to boost local trade and its related industries; and also to allow and promote circulation, first of investment capitals and later of technology and know-how of the partners, which would bring higher rewards to the more diversified economies. This was attractive to Brazil, who understandably saw it as complementing its market-diversification strategy, as making room for joint ventures in which it could take the initiative, and also as allowing multinationalization of some of its most important industries in other member countries.

A major regional zone was thus being set up, which would make it possible in the long term to reach a level comparable to the rest of the emerging world market. There was, of course, the risk that the less favoured partners would slow down the integration process by attempting to curtail an uncontrolled influx of Brazilian products and investments onto their soil. This potential problem made it necessary to agree on mechanisms for the settling of disputes at every phase of this difficult transition process (Barthélémy, 1991: 146ff). Therefore, following the European example, the treaty also made provision, in the medium term, for the setting up of institutions for the settling of disputes; this phase was to precede the work of harmonizing and co-ordinating macro-economic policies, including a common trade policy. It becomes obvious that in this case, regional integration is both the organizing principle and a supporting factor for either radical or gradual reforms in each of the member countries.

Implementation of this second phase is likely to be far more complex because of its connection with constitutional and policy areas. It carries the implication that each country must undergo a far-reaching reorganization of the relationships among the state, the private sector, and civil society; it raises the question of supranationality; and, lastly, it puts an end to the old dream of creating a prosperous economy resting solely on the particular conditions and resources of each country. The sharing of the economic advantages of each country by all member countries will induce creative initiatives, in a spirit of complementarity, though some would say, of dependency. Backing out becomes next to impossible: the costs associated with withdrawing would be considerable for all the countries involved, and, most of all, for the country leaving. As Przeworski demonstrated in the case of the European experience, regional integration is a one-way street; in the medium term, it commits each of the participating economies, however reluctant it may be, to a path of either radical or gradual reform. If a given partner does not back out within a fairly short time, it is unlikely it will escape the necessity of reform, or be able to withdraw at a later date.

Even without reaching such extremes, the number of delays which have afflicted the 1986 sector-based agreements signed by Brazil and Argentina (dealing mostly with capital goods and wheat) are certainly symptomatic. Only a third of expected exchanges actually occurred (Tavares de Araujo, 1990b). Guido di Tella, Argentinean minister of foreign affairs, admitted in May 1993 that less than 80 per cent of products will be covered by a common external tariff by the 1 January 1995 deadline, rather than the expected 100 per cent (*Latin American Weekly Report*, 05.20.93). The smaller countries, which had requested an extra year's grace, are already going back on their commitment to the January 1996 date; Paraguay admits that it will probably not be ready until the year 2000. It is becoming clear to all involved that the recent agreements aimed at strengthening MERCOSUR are using deadlines which are far too soon; in fact, are quite unrealistic (Moneta, 1992: 35). A process which took thirty years to establish in Europe, a developed bloc in the First World, cannot be compressed into less than a decade, given the considerable disparities and asymmetries between the economies involved (Tavares de Araujo, 1988: 102). For this same reason, MERCOSUR could not come into effect before those involved had accepted delaying until the year 2001 the implementation of the common external tariff.

Two major problems have surfaced, and are worsening with the passage of time: the first is structural; the second, economic. Persistent problems arise in terms of the competitiveness of each of the economies, particularly the two larger ones. In the first place, there are severe wage discrepancies: wages for unskilled labourers are lower in Brazil than in Argentina, but the converse is true of skilled labour. The technological content of a given product will thus determine which nation is disadvantaged. Labour laws are also more stringent in Argentina, whose unions enjoy an influence and a proximity to circles of power dating back to the days of President Juan Perón's first mandates (1946–55); this situation increases its industrial production costs. Combined, these factors give Brazilian exports a competitive edge both in bilateral exchanges and international trade.

The Brazilian market is four times as large as the combined markets of its partners. Brazil produces 80 per cent of its own capital goods, compared to Argentina's 35 per cent, which low figure is one of the disastrous results of Argentina's previous deindustrialization phase. The severe differences in the availability, and thus of the cost, of energy sources (electricity, petroleum, biomass) give Brazil a clear advantage. The massive infrastructure program carried out from the 1960s through the 1980s provided the country with an extensive network of dams, thermal power stations, and continuous current transmission lines. Favoured by a more advanced road system, lower transportation rates give Brazilian industry an added advantage. Topographic particularities (a far longer coastline and the proximity of its larger industrial cities to the seacoast) as well as extensive infrastructures (a dense network of roads towards the interior and the Southern Cone) constitute the structural traits which are the finest inheritance of Brazil's developmentalist strategy envisioned by President Juscelino Kubitschek (1956–60).

There are economic problems related to trade and monetary policies as well: import taxes are higher in Brazil than in Argentina, in spite of a gradual reduction over the past ten years; and because of Brazil's monetary policy, since 1991 the effects of inflation on prices has been more severe there than in Argentina. Argentina decided in 1990 to align its currency on the U.S. dollar, which brought on a generalized price hike; this has simplified commercial bookkeeping and facilitated inflow of new investments, but it is also detrimental to the competitiveness of industrial production, already weakened on the export market.

The Unión Industrial Argentina, mouthpiece of the industrial sector, never misses an opportunity to point out that Brazilian entrepreneurs receive indirect export subsidies through artificially low prices on industrial necessities. They claim that the high inflation and subsequent devaluation of the cruzeiro were designed to create conditions strongly favouring Brazilian exports. This is no doubt why Argentina felt free to disregard the principle of a common customs tariff when importing, without the applicable restrictions, Danish food products marketed under European Community subsidies (*Gazeta Mercantil*, 10.29.93). It also imposed a growing number of quotas on Brazilian imports, such as electrical appliances and chemicals. A lengthening list of disputes thus opposes these two main partners, and negotiations concerning the implementation of a common customs tariff have been in difficulty since mid-1993.

These accumulated factors, whether structural or economic, whether dependent upon market conditions or official strategy, gradually become impediments to the satisfactory functioning of the integration process. Table 17 shows the persistent imbalance which has plagued Argentina, Paraguay, and Uruguay in recent trading with Brazil. This trade imbalance is, in fact, greater than that occurring with partners outside the MERCOSUR zone (table 18).

Measures can be taken to mitigate the more severe manifestations of this imbalance. Democratic governments make occasional gestures in the hopes of consolidating the fragile achievements of integration; this involves a hefty dose of interventionism and administrative planning. Brazil, for instance, under increasing pressure from Argentinean accusations of dumping (specifically in the mechanical metals sector, which led Argentina to raise its tariff from 4 to 10 per cent in late 1992), offered a purchasing package in compensation, valued at just under U.S. $500 million, mainly in petroleum, flour, and car parts (*Gazeta Mercantil*, 02.27.93). It is imperative that such measures be taken, as an admission of the necessity of government support for a project whose macroeconomic justification is not yet well established.

The fact that Brazil's investment flow towards MERCOSUR countries has remained substantially the same, although its government has made legal provision for increasing such transactions, is eloquent testimony to the level of uncertainty at work. Local investors still prefer to invest their international assets in the Caiman Island tax haven, the United States, the United Kingdom, or, more recently, Portugal, to make use of the 'European advantage' (table 19).

Those of MERCOSUR's structural problems which originate in the smaller countries are even more striking, given the weak economic differentiation of their respective industries. While Paraguayan businessmen, united under a national association called Feprinco, are demanding preferential treatment to ensure the survival of their fledgling furniture, clothing, and shoe manufacturing sectors, Uruguay, which already reserves more than a third of its trade to Brazil, is playing the card of attracting Brazilian investment and thus becoming the hub of the regional flow of trade. Thus, joint Brazilian and Uruguayan interests created, in early 1993, the Merco-Mineral consortium for the building of community harbour infrastructures for the handling of cargo loads of metals in Puerto Palmira (Uruguay) and in Porto Alegre (Brazil) (*Gazeta Mercantil*, 01.26.93).

There is no hiding from the fact that the main problem lies elsewhere. It has to do with the choice of structural adjustment strategies dictated by the situation in each of the countries involved. The foot-dragging exhibited by some of the partners, Brazil foremost, in the area of setting up the institutions which are planned as part of the second phase of MERCOSUR is indicative of a persistent malaise. The gradual nature of Brazilian reforms and the particular trade-diversification strategy it has adopted do not constitute fertile ground for an aggressive regionalist option. Brazil is not yet prepared to admit the principle of supranationality, which among other things would necessitate the setting up of regional institutions for settling trade disputes. It is even less receptive to discussing a joint currency, which would call for a common monetary policy and a common economic strategy (*Gazeta Mercantil*, 10.16.93). The number of economic teams succeeding each other in Brazília provided grist to the mill of the sceptics among MERCOSUR partners, particularly the Argentineans, concerning the possibility of a greater harmonization of their economies. It was only in late 1994, days before the treaty was to take effect, that the parties agreed to postpone till the year 2001 the implementation of a common customs tariff.

The escalation of negotiations concerning regional integration in Latin America is widely attributed to the Enterprise for the Americas Initiative launched by President George Bush in June 1990. His intention to establish a free-trade zone 'from Anchorage, Alaska, to Tierra del Fuego' accorded well with the worldwide trend towards economic globalization, while satisfying the present-day imperatives of the U.S. economy, whose markets are in need of expansion. The United States is hoping that the Initiative will allow it to reduce its huge trade deficit while strengthening the influence it already enjoys in the region. It is said that Brazil originally perceived the Initiative as a sincere American proposal aimed at settling the growing number of disputes between the two countries, through the creation of a bilateral framework for their settlement. This view was balanced by another, particularly strong in local business circles: the fear of a renewed U.S. hegemony in Latin America (Costa Vaz, 1992). Petras and Vieux (1992) express the same caution, pointing out that the Initiative is likely to increase Latin American dependency on the United States. These authors even draw a parallel between the policy put forward by President Bush and the reduction in trade restrictions applied by the Spanish Empire during its late-eighteenth-century revival, which were, in fact, an attempt at renewed domination of its colonies.

The Initiative is the first 'continental' plan launched by the United States since President Kennedy's early-1960s Alliance for Progress. For the United States, it is part of a plan to extend to the whole of the hemisphere the type of exchanges already ratified by the Canada–U.S. FTA, and to encourage the American model of market economy and liberal democracy already prevalent in most countries of the northern hemisphere. It includes three series of measures related to investment, the national debt, and external trade. In all cases, the co-ordinating role of the international agencies is underlined. It is stated that the mandate of the IDB and the World Bank is to support countries which reduce or abolish barriers to foreign investment (Castro Escudero, 1991). An endowment fund, to be managed by the IDB, would also be set up for the purpose of accelerating privatization programs, with an annual funding capacity of U.S. $300 million (United Nations, ECLAC, 1991a).

As far as indebtedness is concerned, various mechanisms were to be set up with the aim of reducing foreign debt incurred towards U.S. government agencies by Latin American countries, which totals some U.S. $12 billion overall for the region (United Nations, ECLAC, 1991a), amounting to just 3 per cent of the global Latin American debt. This is in line with the proposals put forward by Nicholas Brady, U.S. Treasury Secretary. It is, however, the measures concerning external trade which have the most far-reaching consequences. The recent signing of NAFTA, which created a three-way free-trade zone among Canada, the United States, and Mexico (a market of approximately the same importance as that of Western Europe), is the most spectacular manifestation of the Initiative. While it is, strictly speaking, no more than a trade agreement, observers point out that it will inevitably bring about an alignment of Mexican foreign policy with that of the United States, among other things on the Cuban question, and that it will confirm the dependency of the Mexican economy upon its northern neighbour (Petras and Vieux, 1992).

It is obvious that the Initiative provides a further argument for the hypothesis of globalization through a north-to-south diffusion 'or propagation' of the movement towards economic liberalization. Unlike its European precedent, the particular challenge of the hemispheric process in the Americas rests upon the considerable gap between the economies involved (income structures, concentration of property, entrepreneurial culture, role and efficiency of the state), which singularly complicates the formulation and the harmonization of their respective economic policies. It is widely recognized that the regulating and job-creating role of the state in Latin America is very different from that played by the U.S. government apparatus, especially as compared to the huge role of the private sector in the United States.

Can free trade overcome the flagrant disparities among the Canadian, the U.S., the Mexican, and the Chilean economies? To attempt to do so, the 'hemispheric leader' would have to turn its back on a ten-year history of increasingly protectionist practices. Will the United States do so by demanding that its partners adopt monetarist policies aimed at stabilization, within a strictly liberal orthodox framework? The globalization hypothesis cannot answer these questions if it fails to take into account the particularities of each of the economies and of the links each nation establishes between democratization and liberalization. These questions lie at the heart of present-day Latin American political economy. This hypothesis cannot adequately address the overall phenomenon of hemispheric integration. The Initiative is only one attempt among others to stimulate exchanges between partners by stating general principles and distant objectives.

The main interest of most countries in the Western Hemisphere is in free trade with the United States, since the United States is their largest trading partner and is also technologically their most challenging partner. (Wonnacott, 1991: 65)

It comes as no surprise that exporters of primary goods or economies welcoming complementary industries should wish to make their mark in a market as vast as that of the United States. The risk of dependency, however, remains high, and the most highly industrialized economies have chosen, rather, to diversify their markets, which is only possible if they have reached a certain level of financial autonomy, measured in the strictest sense by a trade balance surplus and in the wider sense by a current accounts surplus. Such autonomy makes servicing the debt an easier task and increases the negotiating power of those in power in the indebted countries.

13

Theoretical Linkages between Regional Determinants and Endogenous Variables

Our conclusions concerning the validity of hypotheses put forward in the current literature take into account the motivations of systems considered as wholes. These motivations appear at first sight to converge towards an integrative project, in spite of the variety of shapes taken by reform in the countries involved. It is time now to look further into the structure of these motivations, distinguishing between those of the public and the private sector. The motivations of the first group have to do with the issue of political action in new democracies, and may help identify the role and place of MERCOSUR in the attempt to consolidate democracy. Those of the second have to do with the issue, often raised in the literature, of real or potential economic complementarity. It might be in the interest of entrepreneurs to develop types of collaborative networks similar to those established by previous institutional initiatives, such as those of ALALC and ALADI; they would thus be building on the accomplishments of the previous generation.

To deal usefully with the multiple problems involved, it is appropriate here to call upon game theory, in order to explore the connection between liberal-type structural modifications and regional integration (RI). Regional integration is necessarily liberal, resulting as it does from the principle of each of the economies opening up to that of its partners. The desired economic anchoring is not precisely a domestic reform, but it does constitute an extension of the logic of structural reforms. It goes even further insofar as each of the participating economies seeks to find in the other an increasing fraction of the driving force of the economic growth which will sustain its own modernization efforts. New democracies may not have a perfectly clear idea of how RI will interact with the reforms they have undertaken at home, but they are aware that it will certainly exercise some level of influence. Their concerns can be classified under two complementary perspectives. The minimalist perspective leads countries to see RI as an economic project which will counter a temporary stagnation in their own markets, or as a means of prolonging a growth cycle prematurely interrupted by a situation of global recession. Such a perspective has already been suggested in our account of the export strategies of each of the countries under study. It is no accident that the end of the 1980s saw a blossoming of integration agreements, some bilateral (Chile, Argentina, Mexico, Colombia, Venezuela) and others multilateral (Argentina, Brazil, Uruguay, and Paraguay). Every one of these countries was seeking an alternative to what global recession had made an uncertain or, worse, interrupted lift-off of their respective economic reforms.

Regional integration, even when it deals exclusively with tariffs, can succeed in creating the equivalent of a reserved market. It allows participating countries to ensure – through occasional specific agreements – that their products will in fact find consenting purchasers in the reasonably short term. This constitutes an interesting and novel phenomenon, since it is an attempt to organize regional commerce, and even to submit it to 'rational planning,' in defiance of the *laissez-faire* approach which is the basic tenet of liberal economies.

The state's traditional area of intervention is thus noticeably modified. Rather than being confined to the usual interventionist mechanisms, such as boosting the domestic market or one of its industries (previously defined on the basis of ownership of capital), the neo-interventionist liberal state becomes, surprisingly, a regulating force in regional markets, making sure that its industries are in an advantageous position and ensuring some return on the hazardous and expensive investments it agreed to when committing itself to the path of structural reform. One has only to think of the extent of tax breaks accorded to the private sector in the hopes of ensuring its success during the difficult restructuring phase. Added to this are the transition costs associated with such rationalization: massive lay-offs, chronic anaemia of social policies, deterioration of the social fabric, and pauperization. In the short term, the liberal model requires an explicit market reward, which it finds within the dynamic of regional integration. For the newly elected democracies, this reward is the *sine qua non* condition of their survival.

Partners cannot agree to such a strategy unless it recognizes the principle of fair competition, and, therefore, of a selection, on the regional market, of the economic players best able to perform, whatever their nationality. This comes down to explicitly recognizing the complementarity of participating economies. This is the Achille's heel of a strategy which, in introducing the principle of supranationality, questions the capacity of each state to manage its economy according to locally defined concerns and according to its particular system of political representation. This is certainly why, in the long run, regional integration, pursued solely in line with the laws of the market, hits a plateau and is unable to go any further, as evidenced by the decline, after 1870, of the free-trade system set up under British hegemony, as well as by the growing difficulties of the more recent European Community. The dilemma between nation-state and supranational federalism has yet to be resolved.

This is not the situation facing Latin America, whose perspectives are still short-term ones. The assurance of access to a regional market has boosted industrial production significantly at the national level, while also giving – thanks to cross-border trading – a new lease on life to the economy of regions traditionally isolated or excluded from the central economy. It thus favours growth cycles and brings significant political dividends to the regimes promoting such access. This, in brief, is the minimalist or short-term perspective of most countries which subscribe to regional integration.

In the medium term, and this is the maximalist perspective, young democracies see regional integration as a global project capable of creating a unified and prosperous regional economy drawing its vitality from a market larger than that to which any given participant could aspire by itself. With riches held in common, the threat of an acute crisis of the economic model of one of its members, with all the possible political fallout, can more easily be averted; the danger is significantly reduced by the possibility of one-off support from a richer partner. Each of the democracies involved can expect to be in a position to avoid internal political upheaval and the much-feared return of dictatorship. In this connection, the literature makes clear the role played by the EEC in the 1980s during the difficult phase of democratic consolidation in Spain, Portugal, and Greece. There is no doubt at all that the new Latin American democracies are counting on the strength of this precedent.

In Spain, more than in Portugal or Greece, EEC support contributed to the implementation of the structural changes to which Felipe González's regime had committed itself in 1981, as well as to invigorating the trade economy. It also was instrumental in relieving the difficulties brought about by structural adjustments, which varied in intensity from sector to sector. In the case of Portugal and Greece, it allowed for occasional backtracking from a radical strategy to a more gradual one. One can see how strong the linkages are between, on the one hand, the consolidation of democratic regimes involved in the difficulties of structural adjustment with their attendant transition costs and, on the other, their commitment to regional integration, to the economic activities connected with it, and to the institutional support they can hope for. But, in our opinion, such consolidation manifests differently according to whether it uses an economic model born of a radical or gradual economic strategy. We would hypothesize that the interests and behaviour of governments having undertaken a

Figure 13.1

Anticipated growth

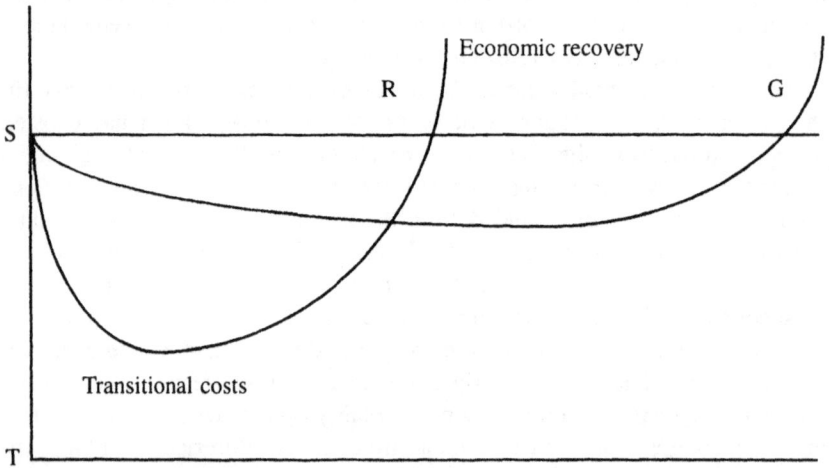

regional integration process will differ according to the nature and extent of the structural reforms which make up their agenda.

Przeworski has done a remarkable job of identifying the dynamic elements which govern political choices promoting structural reforms. His basic argument is as follows: given a level of consumption where S is the status quo, expressing a context, *ex ante*, of prolonged stagnation (caused by uncontrolled inflation, discontinuation of investment, decline of trade revenues, or a combination of two or more of these), a government undertakes economic reform. Given T = time on the abscissa, and the level of economic activity of a society on the ordinate, a horizontal line will represent S = the status quo. Two structural reform scenarios are possible, either R = the trajectory of a radical reform, or G = the trajectory of a gradual reform (figure 13.1).

If the situation is one of decisional coherence, the reform will be a radical one (R). By radical, Przeworski means a combination of fiscal and monetary reforms, whose first consequence is, naturally enough, a drastic plunge of economic activity. The advantage of a radical reform lies in the fact that its results are more quickly felt and the necessary sacrifices last for a shorter period. Conversely, its consequences are more brutal and are suffered by the majority: first, by the bureaucracy; then by enterprises and workers whose livelihood depends on government orders; and lastly, by the sectors providing basic consumables. Rural workers and those in the informal sector are less hard hit, as are companies working principally for the export market.

Przeworski admits that opting for structural adjustment is something like jumping into a well: no one knows how long the drop will be or when it will end. The value of Przeworski's model resides in its power of visualization. Working from a theorization of the experience of the European countries in the years of reconstruction (1945–55) as well as that of the 'Pacific Tigers,' his model uses a dynamic construction which refutes the 'structural overdeterminisms' of Barrington Moore's analyses, which allowed almost no room for the intervention of the various actors (Moore, 1966). Admittedly, the drop in consumption levels induced by R hits fast and hard, and its destabilizing effects are considerable, but popular acceptance of these difficulties will be on a level with the credibility of the government in power. This was the Spanish scenario during the early mandates of the socialist government of Felipe González (1982–96).

If the domestic situation is less favourable, as a consequence of political inexperience, incoherent decision making, lack of consensus over reform, or a swift rise of opposition, the reform will necessarily be gradual in nature (G). This is the Brazilian scenario. Yet even gradual reforms must show rapid results; otherwise, voters' confidence in the reform government may erode. While G will be less painful than R, the dividends will also materialize more slowly, exposing the government to a more prolonged period of low credibility. The G trajectory indicates the difficulty of mobilizing a society around the idea of reform. The sources of this difficulty are varied: fragility of the governing coalition; size and power of the industrial apparatus and its attachment to protectionism; or an unclear perception of the state of crisis among large marginalized segments of the population. In Brazil, a large minority living in the *Nordeste* and in underdeveloped areas have little sense of the structural crisis. Such situations give rise to political manipulation of the clientelist type by leaders who are at worst committed to the statusquo (S), and at best to gradual reform (G). Even in areas suffering from an economic crisis, such as the *Sudeste*, there is no full consensus over the necessity of reforms, because of due to the very strong corporatist traditions and the anti-liberal views of the opposition, whether among the Worker's Party (PT) or among the populist Partido Democrático Trabalhista (PDT).

Early in the process, be it radical or gradual, there is always the option of backtracking. We refer here to a specific event bringing into question a previous political choice. This is the time commitment $t = 1$. In the case of a coalition crisis, of widespread social movements, of rising opposition, or of an impeachment process such as that in Brazil, these factors can interrupt the dynamics of reforms and bring about a political decision to either opt for the status quo (from R to S, or G to S) or to fall back on a more gradual trajectory (from R to G).

It is wise to remember, however, that any 'return to normalcy' will take

Figure 13.2

Anticipated growth

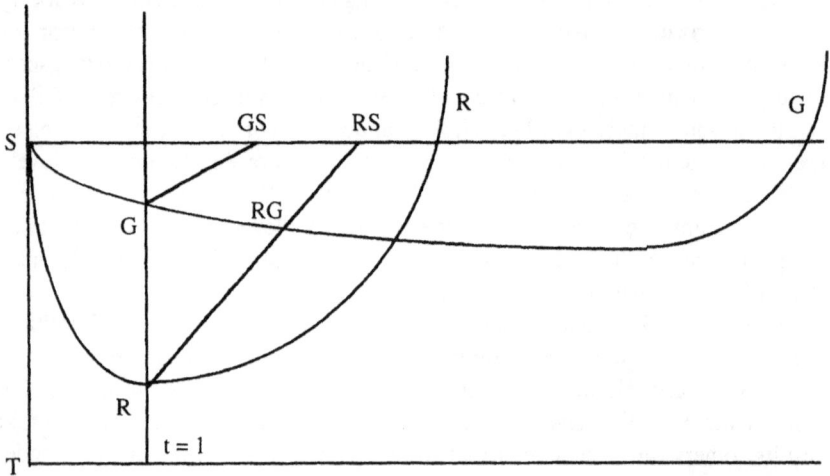

some time, the more so if the reforms were radical in nature and have modified the previous economic framework. A detailed exploration of the economic policies pursued by the new democracies indicates that reform trajectories are rarely totally abandoned. The passage from R to G, or even a temporary return to S, under the pressure of circumstances, is far more likely, especially, but not exclusively, in the case of new democracies. Some models appear to be more stable in this regard; while others, more erratic, testify to frequent rethinking of the global strategy and thus to occasional difficulties encountered by governments, to which, as we have seen, many factors can contribute. One can speak of recurring crisis situations of the type $t = 1$ (see figure 13.2).

Strategic retreat from R to G or from G to S is generally welcomed with a sense of relief, and helps to mollify the opposition. In Chile in 1982, it allowed a retreat from the orthodox model, caught in the grip of a difficult recession which had come close to bankrupting both a state seriously short of financial resources and a business sector which had rushed into a privatization process it could ill afford. Such a switch of policy, however, is often directly linked to electoral cycles. In Mexico, Miguel de la Madrid was able to retain his hold on the political evolution of the regime at the end of his seven-year mandate by introducing such heterodox measures as protecting the public nature of PEMEX, subsidizing staple goods, and slowing inflation-fighting measures. In Brazil, it made it possible for Itamar Franco to distance himself from the style of Collor de Mello and to offer some relief to a complaining public; thus, in 1993, several scheduled privatization projects were deferred, the fight against inflation was suspended, and subsidies were maintained. This, of course, is the attraction downgrading holds for politicians faced with electoral deadlines or with apparently insurmountable problems in the short term: it offers them a operating margin, which they will not hesitate to use if need be.

Unfortunately, its long-term dividends are fairly poor. Certainly, a move from G to S or from R to G is perceived as a temporary improvement by all: bureaucrats are relieved to be able to delay privatization of state enterprises; entrepreneurs enjoy the benefits of renewed government subsidies or get a boost from government purchasing; and the middle classes see their wages temporarily increasing after a decline. But none of this can be taken for true economic recovery. The reforms having been put off to a later date, essential investments and economic restructuring cannot take place. In the medium term, stagnation, represented here by a horizontal S line, will inevitably reappear.

On the political front, however, the ambiguity of such a situation can serve partisan and political objectives; for instance, in the context of an electoral campaign. Politicians in power will be tempted to present this apparent improvement to voters as evidence of the success of their previous choices and of their sensitivity to the needs of social groups bearing the brunt of transition costs. This type of rhetoric was sufficiently convincing in Mexico to allow Salinas de Gortari to come to power in 1988, although just barely; and, in Argentina, to provide Carlos Carlos Menem with a slim majority (48 per cent of votes) in the 1993 legislative elections, thus giving him access to a second mandate, after coming to political terms with the Radical Party (PR).

Such is the political hay that can be made from retreating from a reform to the status quo or to less stringent reforms. It is one reason politicians undertake radical reforms. It leaves them with a wider margin to manoeuvre, allowing them to retreat towards S, or to soften R into G, especially towards the end of their mandates. Przeworski gives convincing evidence that this expedient has its limits; there is, in effect, a point of no return, at $t = 2$, when the impetus of radical reform cannot reasonably be halted. Chile is a case in point, and to a lesser degree so is Mexico.

At this more advanced stage of structural change, the costs of retreating to G or to S are higher, and the time needed to reach G or S again will be longer than it would have been had R been maintained until the S trajectory had been crossed (figure 13.3). Not only has the country deprived itself in the meantime of the benefits of the completed reforms, but the return to G or to S will require a painful dismantling of the mitigating measures and take on an authoritarian flavour – renationalizing of privatized banks or companies, reintroducing price

Figure 13.3

Anticipated growth

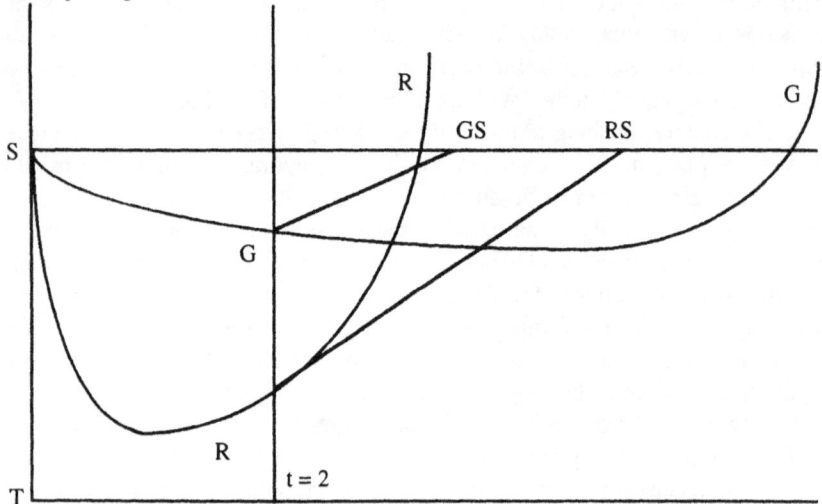

and wage controls, reintroducing a protectionist stance, and setting up new and higher customs tariffs – none of which are highly compatible with a more open market in which the economies of one's partners are also taking a more liberal direction.

Several cases illustrate this 'point of irreversibility.' When civil government was reinstated in Santiago in 1989, it soon became obvious that the level and extent of structural reforms undertaken under the military regime had made a major shift in economic strategy quite undesirable. Not only would it precipitate a legitimacy crisis, it would deprive the country of the dividends of R, which were only beginning to make themselves felt: significant levels of foreign investment, expansion of exports, stability of the banking sector, and, most valuable of all, a hard-won balance of public accounts. Such dividends are sorely needed by young democracies; the leftist parties understood this and joined the Concertación government in order to ensure a policy of continuity.

This use of Przeworski's model helps provide an explanation of the difficulties that new Latin American democracies meet on the path of structural change. Each country, in order to create wealth by making use of the comparative advantages afforded by its particular economy and by the strengths of its business sector, will be called upon to exercise both dexterity and transparency. It will have to make clear that the rules of the game have changed so drastically that it is henceforth ready to extend to entrepreneurs of other countries the advantages so far reserved for its own industrial sector. This can succeed only if the democratic government can convince its own business sector that what will be lost on the newly unprotected national market will be won back in the framework of a widened regional market. A business sector used to protectionism will necessarily be wary of such a shift, but the creation of a regional market reserve will serve to provide a transition strategy attractive in terms of prospective profits and reassuring in terms of immediate competition.

It is the complexity of such situations which leads us to add to Przeworski's model, in an attempt to visualize and understand the variety of possible trajectories to which the dynamics of RI will contribute in one way or another. At least four scenarios are plausible; three of these confirm the linkages between structural reforms and regional integration. The RI variable, in fact, compounds international factors. Radical reforms may be abandoned in favour of gradual reforms, or the opposite may occur. Przeworski's model could acquire a predictive power and might help anticipate changes in the economic strategy and general trajectory of new democracies in an environment conditioned by the regional variable.

1. A given government, engaged on a path of radical reform, may be seeking to accelerate its own restructuring through RI. In such a case, the post-reform recovery (R + RI) will accelerate as a function of the interplay of economic factors and will bring about an upward curve towards S and beyond the previous status quo more quickly than R by itself would have allowed. This government will naturally push for an extension of RI and of its mechanisms for settling disputes, to ensure that it will not be a victim of unfair competition from less liberal partners, who might attempt to export subsidized products. It will also insist on a greater level of harmonization of the economic strategies of all partners, which is to say, it will extol the virtues of its own (R) economic strategy (figure 13.4).

This is the situation in Chile, which is in the process of reaping the economic rewards of the structural reforms it has so far undertaken. In the mid-1970s, it was attempting to get its Latin American partners to follow its example, through such channels as ALALC and the Andino Pact. This attempt, as we have seen, met with failure. It is true also of Argentina, insofar as its industrial base became sufficiently competitive and diversified to allow it to increase its exports to Brazil and to accelerate the economic recovery of its ultra-liberal model.

Figure 13.4

Anticipated growth

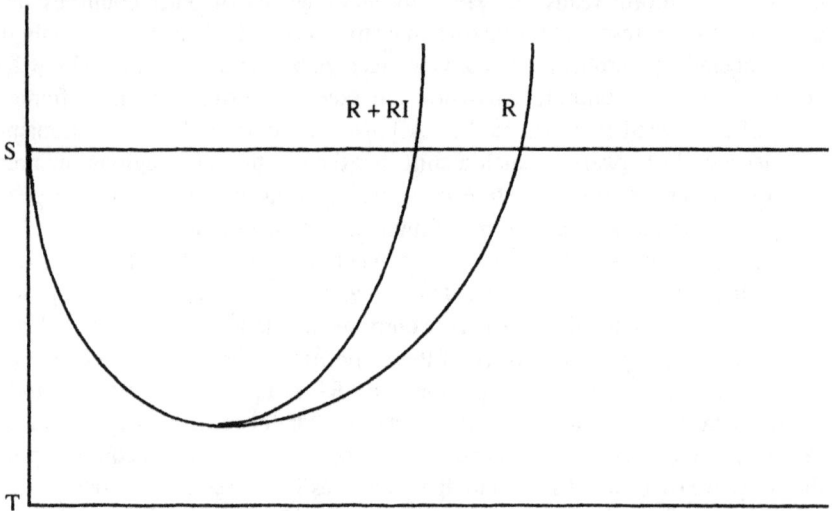

Buenos Aires repeatedly applied political pressure in Brasília in an attempt to balance their bilateral trade, because much of Argentina's regional successes depended on it. In 1993, it was able to access a protected market worth almost U.S. $5 billion, of which $1.5 billion had been negotiated at government level; excellent news for its economic recovery. Argentina hopes that in the space afforded by this reserve, joint ventures with high technological content will allow for a 'natural' specialization of the most dynamic sectors of both countries, which in turn will eventually allow them to face international competition. This is Argentina's very liberal interpretation of common external tariffs (which are generally intended to temporarily protect partners during the phase of selection of the fittest) and the basis of its abiding interest in MERCOSUR.

2. Another government, engaged on a *G* path, may be seeking to minimize, through integration, the negative effects of the extended wait for recovery (the major flaw of the *G* option) by accelerating the rate of gradual reform towards *S* and beyond. It will be careful, however, to avoid weakening, through adhering to the approach of partner countries engaged on an *R* path, the fairly conservative political coalition which agreed to *G* but clearly rejected *R*. Such a country will be in favour of RI, but not anxious to accelerate it since this could call for new *R*-type domestic reforms that, politically, it cannot afford. So for the moment, and in the absence of a viable alternative, it will be content with *G* +

Figure 13.5

Anticipated growth

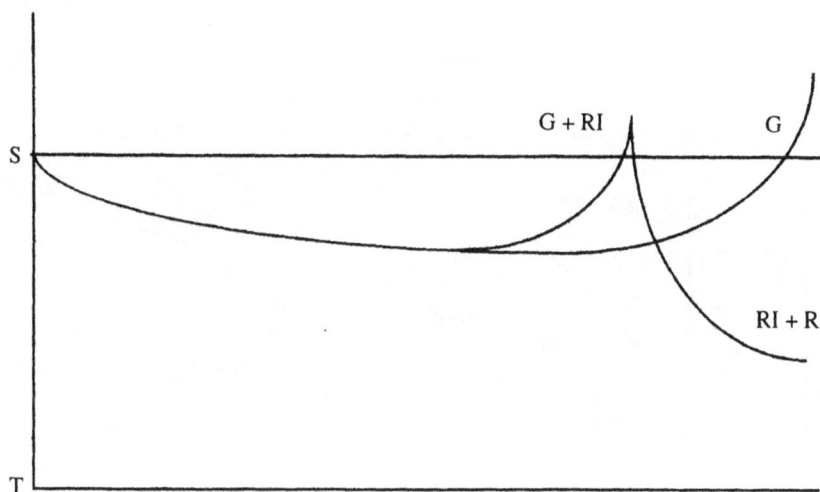

RI, holding its peace until RI's dividends have begun to accumulate and another electoral cycle begins.

If it is re-elected and current domestic conditions allow, it will be in a better position to defend a move to R, if this is the option it favours. In this way, RI can provide an environment favourable to the R option. This situation is indicated by the RI + R curve (figure 13.5). Such might be the trajectory of structural changes in Spain under Felipe González, who benefited from the sound support of the European Community.

3. A third government, originally committed to R, is forced by internal pressures to retreat to S. Unwilling to forsake all commitment to reform, it adopts a G path as a strategic compromise between R and S. In a situation such as this, RI will appear helpful in ensuring a swifter return to R than would be otherwise practicable. This gives an RS + RI type curve, which will connect with a G trajectory. Such a government will be favourable to RI. Its partners will soon push for 'harmonization of macroeconomic policies,' and this will provide it with the · leverage to prove to its constituency the inescapable nature of reform (figure 13.6). Paraguay followed this path, albeit unwillingly, when it became obvious that clientelist circles around General Stroessner were attempting to slow down the reform process. Neighbouring countries used the PICE platform to exert increasing political and economic pressure, with the objective of ousting the

Figure 13.6

Anticipated growth

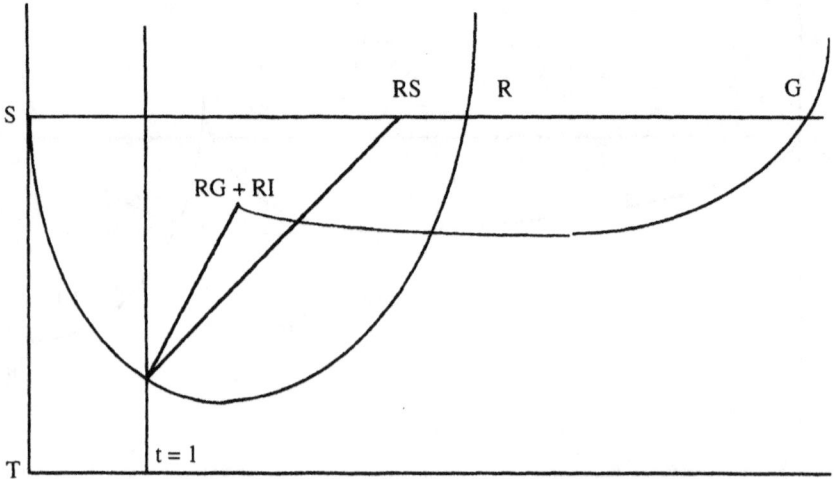

dictator. A liberal opening of the market through democratization thus appeared to Paraguayan business elites as the only possible option.

In such a case, it is the dynamics of the RI process itself, rather than internal power struggles or bilateral pressures, which guide a country's political and economic choices. The Paraguayan example shows that smaller countries are more subject to this dynamic because of their lack of strategic weight and credible alternatives (such as another type of economic alliance). Unfortunately for them, Latin America has no common market reserved for authoritarian regimes, as was made clear by the breakdown of the Pacto Andino in the days of Peruvian military president Velasco Alvarado and, more recently, in the days of the putschist president Alberto Fujimori.

The process of regional integration has extensive repercussions on the consolidation of democracies, and the reasons for this begin to be clear. Through the creation of a reserved market and the consequent intensification of economic activity, the RI process sets the partners on the path of a 'smoother' adjusment, which in turn gives credibility to new democracies faced with the threat of a possible return to military rule. This is a fair description of the present-day Brazilian democracy, which is looking to regional integration, among other strategies, to provide it with political successes which will help renew the credibility of the structural reforms undertaken by President Collor de Mello and subsequently put aside in the confusion which followed his pre-cipitate departure. It is a fact that over the last two years the main increase in Brazil's exports was made possible by new purchases within the MERCOSUR zone. It is also, as table 17 indicates, a promising market and could be, possibly in a near future, the most profitable portion of Brazil's overall trade.

14

Will MERCOSUR Support the Consolidation of Southern Cone Democracies?

To conclude Part Two, we consider the capacity of regional integration agreements to foster the rule of moderate democrats and to avoid any unwelcome return to authoritarian regimes, MERCOSUR being the main case in point. While it is fairly clear that it may act as a partly protected market and a transition to total market exposure in the middle term, the Southern Common Market must show solid dividends to its participants if it is to retain credibility in its pursuit of an upward trajectory. In this sense, MERCOSUR competes with other blocs committed to regional integration (the European Union and NAFTA). Its success is crucial for those public players who are in need of support for their chosen path of structural change; and, of course, for those economic players whose more straightforward objective is a long-lasting recovery of their businesses based upon the expansion of the domestic market. We have seen that MERCOSUR was created in response to the multiple and changing motivations of a variety of players, and that these motivations were less contradictory than one would have at first supposed. It remains true, nevertheless, that the participating countries display a diversity of national situations. Until recently, their political and economic regimes were quite divergent, and regional rivalries between them were accentuated by military regimes. Over the last thirty years, each of these countries has gone through phases of acute paranoia, comparable to the nationalistic frenzy under Franco in Spain or Salazar in Portugal. The 1982 war in the Falklands between Argentina and the United Kingdom, and the 1978 Beagle Straits incident between Chile and Argentina, were episodes pointing to the mutual mistrust between political systems marked by an exclusiveness whose only national justification was to accord a decisive advantage to a praetorian class linked to an entrepreneurial oligopoly. These groups are not at all encumbered with a social conscience; their sole concern is the profit to be drawn from any alliance, as pointed out by O'Donnell, Cardoso,

Evans, and other observers of the authoritarian regimes in Latin America. On a more general level, other authors state that one of the major causes of the failure of the ALALC and ALADI integration projects were the restrictions imposed on free expression of specific interests and the rejection of a democratic framework, particularly by the larger countries (Castro Escudero, 1991). This might be the explanation of the undeniable turning away from regional trade in the 1970s and early 1980s of Mexico, Argentina, and Brazil, in favour of a strategy of trade diversification which did not threaten the isolationist practices of the region.

New bridges ought to be built. There are important theoretical and practical repercussions to the fact that the efforts undertaken in the field of regional integration in Southern Cone countries run parallel with the restoring of formal democracy. These are agrarian countries, dominated by more or less modernized *latifundista* models, by cartelized banking and an industrial oligopoly, which, in political terms, has translated into a protectionist industrial strategy with a prewar flavour, reminiscent of authoritarian corporatism, or even of Mussolini's Italy. While democracy is still 'protected against itself' by a praetorian guard (as is the case in Chile), the process of consolidation is nevertheless in progress. It is reinforced by the simple fact of its continued existence, in spite of its indecisiveness, blundering, and the sometimes flagrant amateurism of the new elites involved in the definition of its policies. It survives because it is the only possible avenue forward, in these times of global crisis when the crumbling of the socialist model leaves no viable alternative to liberalism.

In times of crisis, any backtracking is bound to be very expensive; the ex–Soviet Union is still paying these immense economic costs. One cannot imagine the United States being patient with any backward movement of the liberal democratic model. The same is true of the European Community, who has seen the excesses of authoritarianism up close, from within and from without. We have recently had proof that liberal democracies have both the political and the economic clout to make their displeasure felt: the treatment inflicted on Iraq's leader, Saddam Hussein, and on the unconstitutional regime of General Cedras in Haiti are cases in point. This tendency is in fact gaining strength under the administration of President Bill Clinton, who has not shown the tolerance towards conservative dictatorships in the Third World evidenced by conservative Presidents Ronald Reagan and George Bush, who were first and foremost preoccupied by the fight against communism. It is the large capitalist countries who exercise control over the international aid agencies; as it happens, they are also committed to the principles of liberal democracy. Such control gives considerable power to their normative concerns; the various players ignore this at their peril. Indebted countries are subject to the standards of conditional aid, and can only free themselves by consolidating their financial independence through lasting reorganization of their institutions. The strength and extent of this reorganization are the sole guarantees of their democratic consolidation. In such cases, the idea of democracy is made manifest in the restoration of an open market for capital and labour: for capital, through the practice of open competition on a previously protected market that had brought inordinate riches to a capitalist class, one with mafia overtones; and for labour, more job opportunities through an expansion of the market-place, such as exists in developed countries. The latter condition implies consolidation of middle and labouring classes that are educated and competent, and have attained a standard of living and a level of political representation allowing them to play a significant role in the democratic process. Reformist agendas are expected to fill a very tall order.

Consolidation is dependent upon the broadening of democratic institutions. It is also dependent on the implementation of public policies marked by the opening up to competition of previously restricted markets. This is to be undertaken first with immediate neighbours, which – and this is particularly true of Southern Cone countries – appear less threatening to regional players than more developed countries.

The case of Brazil is the most theoretically significant in the context of regional collaboration; it alone in the southern hemisphere is in a position to protect highly sophisticated production facilities whose inception and growth would have been impossible without the impetus given by an industrial strategy marked by strong continuity. This policy was set up under the governments of Presidents Getulio Vargas (1930–45, 1951–4) and Juscelino Kubitschek (1956–60), and taken further under the interventionist authoritarian regime, particularly under President Ernesto Geisel (1974–1980). In the present context, the new Brazilian democracy has inherited a heavy responsibility. It is called upon to consolidate credible representative institutions in order to maintain as best it can the gains of an aggressive and sophisticated industrial strategy which offers decisive advantages in times of budget constraints. At first glance, this objective appears incompatible with the neo-liberal tenets of economic *laissez-faire* and state withdrawal, which are being promoted by international aid agencies such as the IMF. This is confirmation that Brazil is in a class of its own, which makes it all the more interesting to scientists studying the process of democratic consolidation in a context of the opening up of large markets. Argentina is not afflicted with the same problems: its industrial complex, which was fairly modest in the first place, was further reduced in the days of ultra-liberal opening up, which occurred under the later military *caudillos*, whose grotesque odyssey met its tragic end in the Falkland crisis.

It is no accident that one of President Raúl Alfonsin's first moves after coming to power in 1983 was to reach out to Brazil, inviting it to open negotiations with a view to establishing integration. It is significant that Brazil did not respond to this proposal until after the military was ousted in 1985. The 1986 integration agreement was thus among the first moves towards democratic consolidation undertaken by the two signatories; it occurred in the context of generalized political change (Manzetti, 1990). The simultaneous switch to new political regimes in Brazil and in Argentina brought an important change to the logic of their political decision-making processes. Long-standing geopolitical rivalries were set aside, and preference given to issues such as market integration and high-level regional co-operation involving governments (Chudnovsky and Porta, 1989). Some authors identify the economic collapse of Argentina and the strengthening of the Brazilian economy as the main factors of the dissolution of this long-term rivalry (Ferrer, 1991). According to Hirst (1992), integration projects are furthered by the process of democratization and the progress towards consolidation, in which case it would make sense to link recent efforts at integration to the recent political pluralism in the area. The vast numbers of players participating in decision making in new democracies multiply the possibilities for friction and the need for negotiation. Creating conditions favourable to the diversification of interests is the cornerstone of regional integration strategies. Next, the opposition process, which is an integral part of the democratic system – especially in its infancy, when opposition and demagogy are easily confused – gives a further boost to the change in attitudes. Democracy is judged on its results; it has no army to enforce its legitimacy. Quite the contrary, in fact; democracy itself can easily become a target of opposition. This curious situation inspires daring improvisations in democratic leaders, who must search for original solutions to problems never before resolved and which threaten the fragile edifice under construction.

There is no doubt that the present-day democratic governments of Latin America have put much effort into the process of regional integration (Hirst, 1992). This is natural enough: new governments planning economic reforms take integration as an indication that they are, collectively, on the right track. MERCOSUR has even called for a ruling which would exclude from the alliance any country forsaking its democratic structures. Even the problems raised by the departure of President Collor de Mello delayed validation of this clause (*Infobrazil*, 5 Dec. 1992: 11).

As further proof of the link between integration and democracy, it can be noted that Chile and Paraguay were excluded from the negotiations leading to the setting up of MERCOSUR as long as the military was in power. During the meetings held in Montevideo in 1987, Presidents Alfonsin, Sarney, and Sanguinetti reaffirmed their intention to co-operate exclusively with democratic governments. As early as 1986, they began to pressure Paraguay to shift local business circles away from the ageing dictator-president Stroessner, as is evidenced by a drop in trade with the Guarani republic between 1986 and 1989. The moment General Stroessner was ousted, Paraguay was invited to join negotiations and participate in the design of the future MERCOSUR.

The Iguaçu Act states explicitly the causes which led to the integration process in Paraguay. Consolidation of newly democratic governments was essential, because if any one of the countries backslid towards authoritarianism, its neighbours were in danger of suffering immediate negative consequences. The swift loss of a partner, in the case of a military coup, unbalances the complementary relationships built up between partners and forces each one to return to a starting position, that is, to an economic model where decisions are taken in closed circuit and under a bureaucratic-authoritarian logic. An authoritarian coup is like the proverbial worm in the apple: it corrupts all it touches, casting doubt on the difficult choices all new democracies must make, and on which their survival depends. This knowledge is at the bottom of the marked aversion felt by new democracies towards the hidden power of the military class. Better for all concerned to simply expel the delinquent country. To avoid a situation perceived as intolerable, the Iguaçu Act states that any political coup will cause loss of all privileges attached to co-operation and integration within MERCO-SUR (Davila-Villers, 1992).

Within MERCOSUR, the linkages between democracy and integration go both ways. On the one hand, democracy is considered an essential prerequisite to integration. On the other, integration facilitates the consolidation of democratic elites. Both Presidents Sarney Costa and Raúl Alfonsin have several times stated that the creation of a free-trade zone had helped consolidate their new regimes. Of course, official declarations are declarations, and not facts. It is true however, that economic growth strengthens the practice of democracy through a resulting increase in the standard of living, and thus allows for the entry of new social groups into the system of political representation. As we have seen, there were at least two paths leading to reforms: the gradual path followed by Brazil, and the radical one adopted by Argentina (Mota Menezes, 1990).

The problem is made more complex by the fact that MERCOSUR covers an area with a long tradition of authoritarianism and military coups, which are self-defence mechanisms on the part of traditional powers, set off at intervals in response to the entry onto the field of new political players, often arising from the urban middle classes. This is why these countries, with their very recent commitment to democracy, will look to each other to ensure the cohesiveness of their own approach. And it is also why they are often tempted to undertake radical reforms, which serve as a demarcation from the past, and which they hope will prove an insurmountable barrier to the forces of the old order.

PART THREE: DETERMINANTS OF SOCIAL REFORMS

15

Adjustment against Justice

Two years after the United Nations' 1995 Social Development Summit in
Copenhagen, persistent poverty is still widespread in Latin America, while
greater access to communications has only increased people's frustrated expectations, according to a recent report prepared by the Santiago-based UN Economic Commission for Latin America and the Caribbean (ECLAC) (*Chronicle
of Latin American Economic Affairs*, 02.09.95; 23.03.95). The UN agency estimates that an annual economic growth rate of at least 6 per cent is needed for
the region to catch up in technological and social development. Nevertheless, in
the first five years of this decade, regional growth averaged about 3 per cent
annually. Growth alone will not guarantee more equitable distribution of wealth
if it does not generate productive employment and better salaries, and if it is not
linked to more efficient social policies:

An effective reduction in the equity gap demands an approach that integrates economic
and social policy in a mutually supportive relationship and permits complementarity
between measures to encourage competitiveness and measures to promote social cohesion. Although they may seem in conflict in the short run, public policy can benefit from
the many points of complementarity between economic and social measures. (ECLAC,
1997: 4)

The persistently skewed income distribution has largely favoured the top
levels of the socio-economic pyramid. The share of total wealth of the 10 per
cent of homes with the highest incomes rose from 1990 to 1994, while that of
the poorest 40 per cent slighty dropped. One of Latin America's main problems
is that 84 per cent of jobs remain in the informal market, which does not contribute to social security or other tax income. Legalizing the informal economy,
which encompasses 56 per cent of Latin American urban workers, could signif-

icantly increase the number of jobs available in the region. Unfortunately, many small and medium-sized enterprises exist on the margins of the law. Lines of credit would need to be made available so that they can modernize and acquire appropriate technology; they also require government programs offering training and assistance.

Although regional poverty dropped from 41 to 39 per cent of the total population between 1990 and 1994, it rose in absolute terms from 197.2 million people to 209.3 million in the period. Before the debt crisis of the 1980s, Latin America sheltered 135.9 million poor, equivalent to 35 per cent of its total population. Extreme poverty, or indigence, which affected 15 per cent of the regional population in 1980, rose to 18 per cent by 1990, but then dropped by only one percentage point between 1990 and 1994. According to international criteria, homes unable to afford the cost of two basic consumer baskets of food are considered poor, and those that cannot afford even one are indigent. In Latin America, one out of six homes is still unable to satisfy its basic dietary needs, even if it dedicates all its scarce income to that end. The scant progress in fighting poverty confirms ECLAC's warnings that the region has not recovered the social development trend seen prior to the 1980s (Spanish News Service [EFE], 08.05.97, 09.09.97; Inter Press Service, 01.03.97, 04.04.97, 07.04.97, 10.04.97; *Chicago Tribune*, 04.12.97).

How can transitional democracies make social progress on their way to achieving economic inclusion under such adverse conditions? Unfortunately, classical models which invite comparison between new Southern constitutions and institutions and their counterparts, the Northern democratic 'ideal-types,' are likely to be of limited interest since classical democratic transitions of the modern era have had few if any social concerns at all. From the nineteenth century onwards, social policies were essentially incremental in nature. In the Cold War period, when prosperity reigned, they marched decisively under Keynesian principles. Unfortunately, Keynesianism is foreign to the developing world. Many authors argue on moral grounds that in new democracies, social policies are a necessity to the very consolidation of the new regime, even before growth has resumed. Bresser Pereira, Maravall, and Przeworski (1993) are prominent advocates of a social democratic alternative to ten years of stringent liberal economics. To meet with success, they argue, governments must couple structural adjustment reforms with social measures aimed at easing the transitional costs which are so threatening to democracies. Economic reforms must be explicitly oriented towards the resumption of growth. They must protect the welfare of those hardest hit by market reforms (the lower middle classes in urban areas) and should, in this endeavour, make full use of representative institutions. In doing so, these regimes could defuse social conflicts, survive the worst years of adjustment, and consolidate. Therefore, the premises of social policies pursued under these new democracies would be useful indicators of the degree to which policy makers distance themselves from liberal economics, from the traditional Latin American legacy of political exclusion and economic inequality, and from clientelist practices that characterized the early phase of democratic transition. Social policies would shed some light on the reformers' personal motivations.

Bresser Pereira, Maravall, and Przeworski's hypothesis is seductive. It moves away from the systemic view that envisions social downstream reforms as an almost automatic output of adjustment, and endows the political actors' behaviour with defining attributes. By advocating a major change in the whole philosophy of reforms, it is not satisfied with shallow accomplishments in the social area. In their view, only decisive social policies can give an accurate indication of the change of the guard. Nevertheless, there are important theoretical problems in relating social policies to the rise of new elites in the context of a transition. One must not overlook the fact that sincere reformers have innumerable enemies among traditional elites and face resistance from the military caste. Their space to manoeuvre is very narrow, no matter what their own assessment might be. Also, as far as social progress is concerned, appearances can prove deceptive. Available data are scarce, and their release is totally under the control of politicized state agencies, and therefore subject to over-interpretation. In a word, they lack minimal accuracy.

Many half-authoritarian regimes experiment with anti-poverty programs aimed at making structural adjustment more bearable to their impoverished populations. Mexico's National Solidarity program (PRONASOL) comes to mind. If we consider countries such as Guatemala, Ghana, Peru, Thailand, and the Philippines to be far short of a democratic threshold, while at the same time they engage in apparently bold social initiatives, is it accurate to consider socially minded reformers as the sole engineers of social policy?

In Latin America, researchers are facing paradoxical situations in which true democracies attempt to sort out neo-liberal economics but remain shy on social issues, while decadent semi-democratic regimes seem to be boldly engaging in social policies in what amounts to a desperate effort at capturing popular support from impoverished urban outskirts and the countryside. For instance, consider the Mexican countryside of Morelos, Guerrero, Oaxaca, and Yucatan (the main recipients of central state subsidies under PRONASOL), regions that provide so many migrants to the United States. Where is the boundary between social policy as the accomplishment of political visionaries, and social policy as an instrument of political control and regional clientelism? Obviously, in Tocquevillian terms, we ought to draw the line where there is an autonomous and organized civil society, and recognition, on the part of the state apparatus, of independent, non-partisan leadership and associations. If these organizations are properly structured, their demands will be channelled to the state apparatus one way or another. Some demands should therefore find their way into the decision-making process and, despite whatever difficult times, be to some degree reflected in the framework of public policy. This situation does not necessarily ask for political actors to shift their individual preferences from one philosophical school to another, from neo-liberalism, say, to social democracy. It only asks for some form of representative mechanism to work effectively, even if that means direct, simple – almost primitive – modes of dialogue between state and civil society, as in Chiapas. Classical labels borrowed from the Northern tradition and alien to local conditions are of little use in the jungles of Southern Mexico or the Brazilian heartland. They may have more to do with electoral discourse than with the true dynamics of institutional consolidation, and therefore with reforms themselves.

There is no question that the challenges are many. In Brazil, poverty and social indicators display a net deficit, in terms of public investment in health, housing, sewage, and educational infrastructures (tables 21–3). Minimum wages vary considerably in accordance with monetary policies, which often include wage freezes and cuts in public services, already anaemic by developed countries' standards. Unemployment rates, though, have only been slightly affected by massive lay-offs in the public sector; figures remained stable for most of the period under study (table 24). Finally, the number of physicians per thousand patients, infant mortality rates (table 25), and life expectancy (table 26) are representative of a middle-income developing country, although just slightly below general averages for that category.

In recent years, if social development has become an explicit priority of the Chilean democracy, the numbers hardly substantiate it: public-health expenditures rose from 7.5 per cent of total expenditures during 1981–90 to 11.4 per cent in the 1991–5 period, but social security and welfare expenditures declined from 37.7 to 33.5 per cent (table 27). Indeed, Chile's classification among the lower middle-income economies, with a GDP per capita income in 1992 of U.S. $2,786, belies significant progress in improving general conditions. Nevertheless, key social indicators, including average life expectancy at birth, infant mortality rate, malnutrition, educational attainment, and adult literacy rate, are getting closer to those of higher-income societies endowed with many more economic advantages, than for any of our other case countries (tables 22–3 and 25–6). Marginality remains a significant problem, with an estimated 4 million Chileans annually earning less than the poverty-line income of U.S. $450.

If social spending has not increased since 1990, data point to other interesting developents. Authorities have engaged in extensive administrative reorganization and taken measures to enhance the quality of social-service delivery; to strengthen the process of bureaucratic devolution to the regions and cities; as well as to encourage public participation. They have fostered collaboration between public and private health-care providers, and devised limited subsidies to enhance educational opportunities for low-income children. Social investment in Chile has been more in the form of reorganizing its long-neglected and decaying institutions, than of investing new money ino them. We should therefore not be surprised if existing programs display tougher rules and restricted criteria for accessibility, and discourage unconventional, 'socialist-inspired' projects and demands.

Our reservations about Mexican reforms are confirmed by the rather poor showing of social indicators, relative to the considerable amount of money invested in the area under PRONASOL and other related programs. The outcomes are closer to those of Brazil than of Chile. Housing facilities and sanitation, in particular, are deficient; as a consequence, infant mortality remains high (table 25). However, access to education shows steady progress (tables 22–3). Data point to a middle-income developing country slighty below general Latin American averages.

In all three of our case countries, agrarian reform and the modernization of land tenure (a problem of considerable magnitude in many areas of Latin America), publicly monitored job-creation programs, basic and higher public education, a national science-and-technology policy, and other socially oriented policies are challenging the status quo, so that clashes with conservatives can be expected. These issues are exposing reformers and collective actors to the risk of serious confrontation with traditional entrepreneurs, possibly foreign creditors, and ultimately the military (Stallings and Kaufman, 1989). At the same time, such possible conflicts are indicators of a deepening process of structural change arising from open political competition. If social programs are put forward, the voluntarist action-theory view will read them as indications that the reformers are acting boldly on their own in a long-term perspective, beyond and obviously outside their own institutionalized parties. If they are solely devoted to changing those structural conditions which have, in their mind, traditionally prevented the consolidation of democracy in Latin American history, they must distance themselves from party politics, even at the risk of losing their supporters and clienteles. Hence that 'imperial' style for which the Mexican and Brazilian press criticized Presidents Zedillo and Cardoso. The 'continuity' view suggests that it is the uneven system of resource allocation, beginning with the access to economic power, that makes all actors moderate in their respective programs. Politicians dedicated to acting at the centre of an already polarized spectrum will retain their initial advantage over hard-liners and radicals.

Cautiously keeping away from the ethics of adjustment, which many deem unavoidable, comparative analysts who remain first of all empiricists agree that 'working for an egalitarian world' does not constitute a sound starting point for the investigation of actors' motivations and behaviour. Following Aristotle's suggestion, they envision actors as *zôon politikon*, or political animals, eager to survive the hardships of adjustment in the jungle of power competition. The implementation of social policies, they insist, is related to the immediate containment of transition costs resulting from adjustment. New democratic actors face short electoral deadlines and, in the meantime, mounting social unrest which undermines their popularity and lowers their capacity to conduct further reforms. Simply put, 'buying peace' may be their only practicable answer to the threat of retaliation from an increasingly hostile civil society. This concern goes beyond electoral cycles and may engulf the whole democratic debate, especially if the bargaining process becomes perennial. Social pacts with the major components of civil society have a preventive nature. To echo Fox's view (1994), the politics of social policy tell us much about the non-electoral dimensions of democracy. They tell us about the mobilization of civil society in times of austerity and disarray; about the capacity of leaders to reach compromises with popular organizations; and ultimately about the ways compromises are made.

At this point, Smith, Acuña, and Gamarra's provocative hypothesis is helpful, suggesting that contrary to what was conventionally agreed upon, economic hard times associated with adjustment policies do not necessarily aggravate socio-political conflicts (Smith, Acuña, and Gamarra, 1993: 2 ff). Worsening economic conditions, they allege, create a destabilizing shock throughout civil society and, in most cases, weaken the response of minority groups to governmental initiatives. Neither Mexico under President Salinas de Gortari nor Brazil under President Collor de Mello experienced social unrest that can be related to monetarist, market-friendly programs during the first years of adjustment. Nor did the number of strikes or lock-outs increase. However, both social mobilization and labour uprisings skyrocketed in periods of respite, or when general conditions began to improve. If this hypothesis is sound, it would mean that transition costs are not so much to be feared by governments in the crucial launching period of reforms, but rather in their aftermath. Economic improvement achieved by the reforms would provide further resources to opponents in their efforts to organize collective action and militancy against a deepening of these same liberal reforms. While, at first glance, this hypothesis tends to weaken the systemic view, it may also provide useful insights into the passage from the upstream to the downstream side of reforms. It supports the optimistic view that economic improvement will favourably affect and therefore strengthen all potentially militant interest groups, organized labour and local associations alike.

Each country has characteristics of its own when it comes to organizing collective action in local conditions. Brazil may run opposite to Smith, Acuña, and Gamarra's hypothesis. Nowhere more than in this country did social mobilization gather momentum in the early transition era. At the outset of the New Republic, the rising influence of mobilized public opinion and organized social groups was fostered by an oversized territory with marked regional cleavages, by the rising militancy of unions in a significantly industrialized economy faced by foreign competition, and by highly uneven patterns of income distribution. We can easily envisage how much this last feature served as a powerful brake on reform, since transitional costs could be expected to widen the already considerable gaps between social groups, thus sharpening labour dissatisfaction and other types of opposition. Furthermore, these forms of opposition were not counterbalanced by solid institutions or by solid political traditions at the national level. As a result of twenty years of authoritarianism and power concentration, emerging political parties were weak, and poorly structured and disciplined. Such conditions allowed for opportunism on the part of manipulative leaders, whose programs were vague and contradictory, as was the case in post-Franco Spain during the Unión del Centro Democrático (UCD) years (1975–81).

Powerful groups, not only the marginal, can also mobilize. The reformers may not be strong enough to impose a new vision of their own; for example, to allow open foreign competition with local oligopolies in order to enhance national productivity among the surviving firms. The entrenched power of local oligopolies is a consequence of protectionist policies under the late military presidents, and full exposure to the global market is detrimental to these traditional entrepreneurs. Transitional costs being unacceptable to a highly protected local industry still very influential in politics, it is likely that the costs of any type of liberal reform will fall on the shoulders of less-protected social groups. Hence the intensity of political opposition to structural reform in Brazil. Credibility runs low, when there is no space left for a minimally equitable policy in times of transition. In such a case, Maravall and Santamaria's (1989) primary condition – observed in the case of democratizing Spain – to wit, strong popular support for a government devoted to reform, is hard to obtain.

Given the conditions observed in our case studies, the systemic explanation suggests that Chile's more effective 'marketization' of the economy under the military dictatorship would give democrats the means they need to undertake reform and engage in programs targeted on wage redistribution. In support of this scenario, we can point to the stimulating impact of Chile's entry into the thriving regional Southern Cone market, leading to full MERCOSUR member-ship, and possibly inclusion in NAFTA in the near future. Most observers agree that Chile is among the few Latin American countries that had solved its main economic problems prior to the democratic experiment. In support of this opin-ion, the timing of the adoption of social policies in the final phase of adjustment suggests that market successes achieved in the previous era played a major part, although other domestic determinants were at work (Nelson, 1994a; Diamond and Plattner, 1995; Przeworski, 1995). The tax burden ratio to GDP is consider-ably higher than in Brazil and Mexico, giving Chilean reformers an enhanced capacity to spend on social improvements (table 28). Recently released research (Hunter, 1997: 456ff) fails to demonstrate that the two Concertación govern-ments of Patricio Aylwin and Eduardo Frei Ruiz-Tagle managed to influence the composition of the military high command, and to thereby weaken both military prerogatives and the military's role in internal security, all the while making the electoral system fairer to the majority of voters. This argument would be more convincing if former self-proclaimed president Augusto Pinochet and some of his followers were put on trial over accusations of human-rights abuses. Furthermore, no survey has to this day substantiated the view that Chilean democrats have succeeded in imposing a package of constitu-tional amendments that would allow them to go forward with the implementa-tion of decisive social reforms. On the contrary, it seems, government efforts to change the constitution were blocked by right-wing opposition in May 1996, creating a Gordian knot for the uneasy process of democratic transition. Despite strong popular support, it is generally acknowledged that Chilean reformers have not been able to confine the military to the apolitical, professional role that it occupied before the 1973 *golpe*. But what is also becoming clear is that the earlier orthodox and market-oriented policies have produced all they can in terms of the stabilization and restructuring of the Chilean economy, and that they can no longer meet the mounting expectations of civil society. The Chilean reform process, which has gone forward so boldly until recently, is now stalled.

Neither the systemic nor the continuity theory accounts for the whole range of phenomena associated with this case on the issue of social policy. Other determinants of evolving social policies may also be at work. Social and politi-cal actors may come to play a defining role that proves more important than anticipated. Social groups are freeing themselves from the previous corporatist model, as in Mexico, or are engaging in organized opposition to market reforms, as in Brazil. In Chile, new coalitions are emerging, proposing pro-grams for agrarian reform, the sharing of authority, new housing, and the improvement of health and education, as well as measures against absolute pov-erty and marginality, and, less convincingly, for protection of the environment.

Comparative analysis is not comfortable with social movements, which evoke negative memories of street confrontations, radicalism, and *golpes*.

Social movements in the post-adjustment era can be seen themselves as a product of reforms, and as an organized public response to the rise of poverty amid the ruins of the previous corporatist order. They do not necessarily mean the return of 'radicals' of a generation ago. Conditions have changed and, with them, the rules of the game. For social movements to influence decisions, their leadership must move to the centre and renounce the use of violence. It is difficult in this context to subscribe, as the maximalist outcome to be expected from the process of transition, to Smith, Acuña, and Gamarra's best-scenario hypothesis, in which dominant interest groups and state-controlled labour organizations will actively restore traditional political linkages with the state and its bureaucracy. We believe, rather, that collective actors tend to forge new coalitions, as we have suggested in the preceding section. These new compromises and arrangements between distinct, autonomous loci of power indicate the strengthening of the political centre and the expansion of a moderate coalition.

Various authors agree that full institutional independence of the organizations of civil society will not be achieved for many years. We suggest that, in order to carry out downstream structural reforms, democratizing elites are compelled to respond to certain social demands simply because they wish to widen their political base. In the process of co-option, they will likely integrate a number of political influences that were repressed under the authoritarian era. As is to be expected from a poorly defined institutional system, their commitment to socially oriented policies will be dependent upon the intensity of political mobilization around each issue, and the process of decision making will reflect the participation of affluent interest groups. It will remain to the president and his close team of advisers to intervene directly in the process of mediation, and to take final decisions that reflect a talent for compromise. Henceforth, social reforms will not be sectoral issues that can be processed on a case-by-case basis and channelled to a particular public department. Social issues will be far-reaching, possibly overwhelming. This is why only central authorities are capable of designing social reforms in such a limited context.

This way of understanding social policy is not consistent with the classical view. First, social improvements in developing countries are usually not provided by the state; rather, they depend on the characteristics and quality of community life, and then on the capacity of various communities to politically reorganize. Second, how could radical reformers ever make their way to the top of Latin American democracies by advocating swift social changes, without being opposed by conservatives allied to more moderate reformers, and to the corporate establishment? As an example, consider the 1994 Brazilian scenario that saw candidate Cardoso's PSDB and the right-wing PFL rise against Lula's PT candidacy. There is no question that Presidents Ernesto Zedillo, Patricio Aylwin, and Fernando Henrique Cardoso, as well as their presidential contenders, Cuauhtemoc Cárdenas and Luis Inacio da Silva (Lula), are all sincere democrats with high social aspirations for their people. However, as hostages of a power system that will never allow advantages to the poor to be taken on the back of entrepreneurs, they are bound to keep a very distant relationship with radicals, who are still influential among various associations within civil society. There is an implicit agreement behind the transition to democracy in all these countries, that future redistribution will essentially come from sustainable growth and prosperity. In order to achieve this middle-term goal, we can expect moderates to give priority to market-friendly adjustment programs, and to pursue them thoroughly to their end. We should not be overly surprised if this means postponing for a time socially oriented public expenditures. Therefore, the unsteady transitional conditions offered by the political system are likely to affect the social agenda more than the preferences of individual actors, quite independently from the fact that the country may have benefited from the economic successes of adjustment. This brings us back to the structural determinants implicit in the continuity thesis. It is against the background of such constraints that social movements and collective actions come to acquire all of their historical importance.

16

Agrarian Reform and the
Modernization of Agriculture

Several factors are responsible for political change in Latin America, many of which can be traced back to the authoritarian period, and many more to post-colonial times. With the active support of nationally organized and independent information networks in Brazil, non-governmental organizations (NGOs) in marginal regions and union solidarity movements were involved in rural mobilization operations. They called repeatedly for agrarian reform and political participation. They fostered a high degree of social awareness concerning the people's basic rights. It happened that government reformers were not in a political or financial position to fulfil all legitimate demands. However, they were interested in establishing institutionalized linkages with the more moderate elements of these groups, to challenge the influence of radicals over mobilized opinion, on the one hand, and to convince traditionalists and hard-liners, on the other, of the necessity of restricting their influence over the vulnerable and less-politicized fringes of the population. Was this agreement a covenant upon which the 'Tucano' PSDB, leader Fernando Cardoso, and the PFL agreed, with a view to the 1994 general election? The bone of contention here was agrarian reform. Fortunately, Chilean reformers did not face this dilemma.

Chilean authors confirm that the policy of the military towards agriculture in Chile did not entail a return to *latifundista* principles, which had carried with them clientelist and paternalist practices of an earlier age (Echenique, 1989; Silva, 1992). Echenique suggests that the agrarian reform conducted under Christian Democrat president Eduardo Frei the elder, from 1966 to 1970, paved the way for a modern capitalism in agriculture, which can be equated with an agrarian reform. We identify two phases in the Chilean program. At first, as was to be expected, the articulation of liberal political tenets in this sector was fairly crude, since the military had thoroughly crushed unions and rural peasant organizations. The consequence was a dispersion of mobilized workers. The regime's goal was to depoliticize the issue of agrarian reform and avoid the so-called communist rural movement that was then gaining ground. The same phenomenon occurred in the mid-1970s in Portugal and in neighbouring Andean countries such as Peru. Contrary to a widespread belief, the military did not simply return public land to its former owners. They opened up a significant space for cooperatives and individual farmers, which supports our hypothesis that modernization of land tenure was carried out independently from the restoration of the previous order (table 29).

The Pinochet regime cleverly justified the drastic reduction of subsidies to producers by budget constraints. It wished to ease market adaptation, much in line with other monetary measures discussed above. A liberal, all-out openness to imported agricultural goods through tariff suppression was intended to trigger adjustment and submit the sector to the laws of the market. However, the state introduced no transitional programs which might have avoided some of the ensuing disruption. Wages were depressed in the late 1970s because the unemployed workforce remained large. To use neoclassical terminology, these factors turned to 'comparative advantages' for Chilean export agriculture. Nevertheless, production showed a steady decline for eight years, and numerous bankruptcies of non-competitive rural entrepreneurs accelerated the concentration of tenure in fewer hands. The level of orthodoxy evidenced by the agricultural policy in Chile has no equivalent in other Latin American countries or even in developed countries, such as the United States or the United Kingdom, which have followed consistently liberal policies. In these two countries, considerable subsidies aimed at fostering the modernization of selected entrepreneurs have been an enduring feature of state intervention in agriculture, under Presidents Ronald Reagan and George Bush and under Prime Minister Margaret Thatcher.

After this initial period, the clumsy Chilean agricultural policy fuelled harsh criticism from all sides. Social groups which had supported the 1973 coup voiced their concerns clearly at the highest executive level. They made state subsidies an essential condition for their future support of the regime (Echenique, 1989). Rising discontent brought changes in policy, an unexpected sign of flexibility on the part of the regime. During the second phase, from 1983 onwards, state intervention resumed through a series of rectification measures more heterodox in nature than the rest of the economic policy. Higher tariffs for imports, a fiscal policy based upon expected instead of actual producers' income, and minimal prices for goods helped to reactivate agriculture. Thus the sector was given considerable attention by the authorities, who expected agriculture to give Chile the initial push towards a general recovery, in the absence of a significant industrial base. Since the country had achieved financial stabilization, agricultural exports could eventually play the important role they had assumed by the beginning of this century in Brazil, where they accelerated the process of capital accumulation and fostered industrialization. In a country with climatic advantages, a population of 13 million, and medium to low wages, such a prospect seemed fairly realistic. A new class of entrepreneurs could then thrive in the fertile valleys that had been neglected for centuries.

Decision makers were seeking an enduring solution to the backwardness of the Chilean countryside. They made it plain that they would not accept an agrarian reform on a socialist blueprint, including land redistribution and collective management. Nevertheless, fresh money awarded to producers in the form of subsidies and incentives, along with the presence of state agencies in rural areas, made an interesting although only partially satisfactory, contribution to the centuries-old Latin American debate over land use. Hundreds of thousands of low-wage workers and the marginal still wander in the deserted Chilean valleys in search of temporary work and affordable land on which to build their dwellings. Structural change only became an issue in the countryside when the *Concertación* came to power.

Early state involvement in the modernization of agriculture in favour of a crop-exporting economy characterized Brazil at the time of the military regime. The 1971 Plano Nacional do Açucar (PLANALSUCAR) and the 1975 Programa Nacional do Álcool (PROÁLCOOL) are evidence of such interest. PROÁLCOOL was aimed at reducing energy imports by alcohol-fuel production. Both programs had their heyday during the 1980s (Duquette, 1989). The state also gave impetus to exports of orange and other fruit juices, and of soy beans, of which Brazil became the world's second largest exporter. Brazil came into open competition with the United States with respect to this important product, as well as with chicken meat. A backing away from an ambitious policy of subsidies to large producers was noticeable from 1980 to 1985, as a result of budget constraints. Surprisingly, growth in the sector was not much affected, showing instead high levels of productivity. A 7 per cent increase from 1980 to 1983 rewarded investments and state incentives.

The New Republic was, in its first years, openly committed to the decisive growth of basic food products, under the social tenets expressed by President Tancredo Neves's political program. This was very much in contrast to Mexico's path. Wishing to distinguish itself from the military regime, the central government in Brasília provided generous subsidies to producers, so that planted areas could be greatly increased. Three consecutive good harvests, from 1987 to 1989, were all encouraging signs of the evolution of agriculture in Brazil during the difficult transition years. Interestingly enough, given an increasingly restrictive access to public financing parallel to the reduction of public spending in the early 1990s, the performance of agriculture went far beyond what was experienced in the industrial sector during the same period. It makes clear that agriculture more effectively responded to adjustment measures than did industry.

As early as 1986, a debate arose in the Constituent Assembly concerning the sensitive issue of agrarian reform. The picture is eloquent: *latifundistas*, or large landowners, comprised 2 per cent of all landowners and had control over 60 per cent of the country's total cultivated land, which amounts to 245 million hectares (Latin American Data Bank, 11.13.91). Five million *minifundistas*, or small farmers, enjoyed property titles over small tenures, amounting to 34 per cent of total cultivated land. The remaining land, 6 per cent, was left to millions of squatter families and yielded meagre unsubsidized crops to these indigent, semi-nomadic residents (*Folha de São Paulo*, 12.16.97). Incidents between squatters and private militia became frequent in the 1980s, particularly in the southern part of the state of Pará, and resulted in casualties. Later on, in the early 1990s, rural mobilization extended to the southeastern states (São Paulo and Paraná), following the migration of rural workers to these rich sugar- and coffee-producing areas, and sparked similar incidents.

Agrarian reform seemed a priority, at least in words, to President Sarney Costa, himself son of a wealthy landlord from the northeast state of Maranhão. The constitution stated that rural workers could claim property from an area of neglected or abandoned land of considerable size. Among Latin American countries, Brazil displayed perhaps the most shocking inequalities in land distribution, and was badly in need of public action on this issue. The Institute for Colonisation and Agrarian Reform (Instituto Nacional da Colonização e Reforma Agraria, INCRA) began to review cases of land mismanagement. However, the class of landowners, an enduring feature of Brazil's postcolonial history, proved to be more influential in the politics of the New Republic than the reformers had expected. This may explain why the shaky transitional governments under President Sarney Costa usually retreated on most cases of dispossession. In the first democratic years, very little progress was recorded on this sensitive, highly symbolic issue. In the meantime, Brazil's inequitable land distribution remained a central source of violence between landless *camponeses* and large landowners (Latin American Data Bank, 06.10.95).

President Collor de Mello opened the road to a pro-market strategy in support of large-scale production over smaller operations. The collapse of production in 1990–1 only added to the difficulties that appeared elsewhere in the economy. It remained to be seen if the countless bankruptcies among smaller producers had opened the way to a new wave of land concentration, mainly in the states bordering the Amazon Basin, or if President Itamar Franco's fragile, thus more conciliatory, administration was open to giving more impetus to agrarian reform. Reformers were to be disapppointed, as the president postponed the whole process, under considerable pressures from the lobby of wealthy landowners.

By the mid-1990s, Brazil was still capitalizing on its earlier successes and had become a major trading country and a world leader in agricultural exports such as sugar, orange juice, poultry, and beef products. Unlike in Chile, however, there is little hope that agriculture in Brazil can provide a push to recovery, given the size and population of the country and its already advanced patterns of industrial diversification. Brazil still faces in the countryside primitive patterns of labour-to-capital relationship, fostered by technological backwardness. Indifference to the poor and indecisiveness, under President Itamar Franco, signal a shameful tendency on the part of the New Republic to harvest the fruits of a lengthy tradition of conservatism in this critical sector of the economy: not quite in the *continuismo* fashion, yet not making any effective departure from the previous model favouring large state-supported estates devoted to export crops. As we know, the main challenge this sector is likely to face for some time is, simply said, self-sufficiency in food.

Because they are fragile, new democracies are sensitive to popular mobilization, the more so when it becomes politically structured. As resentment was growing among the rural workers and the marginal, a social movement of considerable significance came into the open by late 1993, to be later encouraged by the Chiapas uprising. Numerous groups began mobilizing around actions conducted under the leadership of the Movement without Land (Movimento sem Terra, MST), and began raising as well far-reaching ethical questions. Established in 1980, the MST is one of Latin America's largest and most active grassroots organizations, with half a million member families. Among its first spectacular actions, three thousand MST rural workers occupied in November 1993 the 6,000-hectare Fazenda Ribeirão dos Bugres, in the *municipio* of Getulina, state of São Paulo. This land met all the conditions specified in the constitution for repossession, and the workers asked for the enforcement of a recent INCRA decree made under the new agrarian reform law. An armed force of two thousand men, under São Paulo authority, attacked and dispersed the crowd, destroying its settlement. Local newspapers reported dozens of casualties, among them children (*Gazeta Mercantil*, 11.20.93). A few days later, President Itamar Franco, keeping faith with the INCRA rule, issued a decree in favour of land claims, thereby rejecting the owner's arguments. This action was to become a precedent.

Was President Itamar Franco's government more receptive than his predecessors' to social demands on the issue of agrarian reform? Franco was prone to yield to popular mobilization when it materialized around sensitive issues such as agrarian reform. Slow progress was noticeable at fifty-two large estates, totalling 415,000 hectares. This land was retrieved from absentee landowners and handed over to twelve thousand families. Presenting it as an initial success for the MST movement and in total contrast to the way the authoritarian regime dealt with agrarian reform, the Brazilian reformers ostensibly distanced themselves from the authoritarian regime.

This attitude was clearly fostered by an increasing level of social mobilization. In 1996, the MST carried out 176 land occupations, involving more than forty-five thousand families in twenty-one of Brazil's twenty-seven states. Tension in the countryside rose in early 1997, following passage of measures to promote limited agrarian reform. These included the new Rural Lands Tax (a 20 per cent annual tax on large unproductive estates) and the authorization to expropriate idle lands. With these laws, and under considerable pressure, the Cardoso administration was speeding up agrarian reform to fulfil a commitment to give land to 280,000 families before the end of his mandate in 1998. Landowners were quick to reorganize, as they were in Mexico, under the banner of União Ruralista Democrática (UDR), which had been recently disbanded. Fifty peasants were slain in land disputes, including twenty in the state of Para by police forces. The plan was to block the MST by arming security forces to guard land susceptible to occupation. Following these events, the MST was among the most vocal and militant critics of the Cardoso government; its struggle was gaining political overtones. According to MST leader Gilmar Mauro, its agenda 'goes beyond the contryside and simply obtaining land ... The MST is the most important social movement this century in Brazil' (interview, 12.15.97). In fact, when addressing social issues, it even moved ahead of labour unions and opposition parties such as the PT, speaking out in protest of economic exclusion, unemployement, and privatization of public firms (Latin American Data Bank, 03.14.97). An open clash with government was becoming inevitable.

When he empowered Justice Minister Nelson Jobim to end rural violence by any means deemed necessary, President Cardoso reluctantly recognized that in fact MST leaders were acting as leftist 'radicals' facing rightist 'hard-liners.' The states would authorize additional powers for the judiciary and the police to arrest and process MST activists and counteract rural violence and land invasions in the areas of greatest conflict. Special forces of the army, the federal as well as the military police, would participate in cautious, media-covered operations to disarm both landless peasants (*camponeses*) and landowners. In this highly visible way, the moderates in government sought to distance themselves from extremists on both sides, and to avoid an unwelcome repetition of the

Mexican scenario. Very much in tune with Schmitter's 'systemic view' (see O'Donnell, Whitehead, and Schmitter, 1986, vol. 1), which emphasizes the role of moderates over the threat of radicalism, this operation offers no guarantee that such a strategy will succeed in the long term. In April 1997, a massive demonstration of twenty-five thousand peasants, joined by human rights activists, union workers, church representatives, and leaders of opposition parties, gathered in Brasília to denounce impunity regarding human rights abuses. This peaceful demonstration opened the way to the institutionalization of the rural movement. A public poll conducted by the *Folha de São Paulo* indicated that the MST had the support of more than 68 per cent of the population. This is probably why the minister of agrarian reform, Raul Jungmann, proposed broadening the donation program, if only the MST would agree to put an end to its occupation of private land and government offices, a condition that was later met. Active networks of communication between moderate reformers and mobilized groups are being restored, and they are coming forward with *pactos*, giving further corroboration of Schmitter's 'systemic view.'

In Brazil, NGOs are always active on the issue of hunger and marginality. In September 1993, a nationally organized campaign against hunger (Campanha nacional contra a fome), supported by prestigious artists and other public personalities,[*] political parties of many stripes, non-governmental organizations, and the media, released to the public a dramatic figure: out of 156 million Brazilians, 32 million experienced hunger and faced starvation on a daily basis. There were reports that many hundreds of thousands of children under the age of two had died of malnutrition in recent years. Brazil was no better than, say, Ethiopia in the mid-1980s, or present-day war-stricken countries such as Mozambique or Somalia. The campaign undoubtedly gave credibility to the MST radical program and harmed the image of the moderates, because it was asking for urgent public actions that went far beyond the actual capability of the government, both in terms of available financing and organizational capacity.

It is a shame that despite its early and sincere social commitment, the New Republic has achieved so little on the whole issue of food and technical assistance to poor rural farmers. Millions are mere squatters surviving on frontier lands. The new regime has never channelled sufficient investment through technical assistance agencies. In the late 1980s, it even went so far as to suppress several such agencies, Empresa Brasileira da Terra (EMBRATER) among them. It also remains unclear whether Brazilian agriculture is coming any closer to offering a solution to the immense problem of hunger; in spite of its vast

---

[*] Including the prominent sociologist Betinho, who died of AIDS, contracted from a blood transfusion, in 1997.

potential, it remains backward and almost feudal in nature. However, as political mobilization rapidly develops in this area, as it has over the issue of corruption, the whole agricultural sector shows some signs of moving towards a comprehensive framework of social reform.

Mexico is our only case study that features a long and genuine agricultural tradition, and it offers an interesting case of explicit peasant politics emerging from the turmoil of a revolution (a defining characteristic shared with China and Vietnam). Barrington Moore was the first to establish a comparison between Mexico and China, who both endowed their peasantry with a revolutionary role. The traditional *hacienda* system was overhauled and almost entirely destroyed between 1910 and 1917. Then came the institutionalization phase of the revolution, but Emiliano Zapata's memory and the fierce *campesino* revolt against landowners were never forgotten. From 1934 to 1940, President Lázaro Cárdenas, the son of a peasant himself, established the *ejido* communal land system in the first decade of the PRI regime. However, because of its historical and geographic isolation from the Mexican mainstream, the state of Chiapas did not benefit from this agrarian reform, which became the cornerstone of Mexico's post-revolutionary constitution. The *finqueros* (estate holders) in Chiapas had banded together to battle the 1911 Carranza government's land distribution edicts. They eventually forced the federal government into a tacit agreement that institutionalized the status quo. In the following decades, the entire area was regularly patrolled by private militia, which the Zapatista movement only began to challenge in the early 1980s, through this resistance would come dramatically into the open by the mid-1990s (Ross, 12.16.1996).

The turning point away from the agrarian reform of the late 1930s, which had been furthered by President Luis Echeverria in the early 1970s, occurred under President Lopez Portillo, who, in an attempt to curb, on macroeconomic grounds, the structural tendency to low levels of production and dependency upon imports of basic goods, put forward a policy something like Brazil's. This was a necessary consequence of the extreme fragmentation of the *ejido* system arising from uncontrolled demographic growth and overpopulation of the countryside. It is important to note that the significant investments in infrastructure modernization (an estimated U.S. $4 billion between 1978 and 1982) in the period of the oil bonanza occurred prior to any adjustment reforms. Enhanced productivity, increased exports of selected products, and a stronger balance of payments offered the Prista reformers a modest margin within which to manoeuvre, and preserved minimal consensus among a strategic segment of the population that would manifest political support to the PRI in later, harder times. Authorities were fully aware that, as had been the case ten years earlier in

Southern Europe, transition costs had to be kept lower in the countryside to avoid social dislocation, migration to the cities, and peasant activism. The PRI–dominated Mexican regime would respond to these threats in the same way the European Community had, with ample regional subsidies.

When oil money dried up, the move towards liberalism accelerated significantly. The Mexican adjustment package was characterized by lowering the priority given to agriculture, which had been a main concern of earlier nationalist PRI politics. President de la Madrid's mandate was marked by austerity and a gradual phasing out of subsidies to prepare for market integration of the Mexican agricultural sector, in much the same fashion as the first phase of Chile's reforms. In 1986 Mexico also joined the GATT, thus promising to abide by its rules. Newly elected President Salinas de Gortari had no hesitation in putting forward a complete reform of the *ejido* system, to do away with its communal, allegedly inefficient structure. The reform made possible a full privatization of land in favour of individual residents and, through incentives such as PRONA-SOL, encouraged the regrouping of producers in larger, more modern estates (*Comercio Exterior*, 1991). The *ejido* system was expected to play a less significant role in sustaining self-sufficiency in food production than it had during the previous period. The public interest was in the proliferation of irrigated modern estates on favourable lands that would provide winter crops (fruits and vegetables) to the North American consumer market. Under NAFTA, many Mexican entrepreneurs began thriving on export-driven modern estates, which, in addition to tomatoes, strawberries, and eggplants, were producing illicit cannabis and opium. A consequence of inexperienced decision making under President Salinas, this poorly regulated and undesirable orientation of the Mexican export economy bore consequences of importance. Self-sufficiency in basic goods steadily yielded ground in the 1980s, thus worsening conditions in the countryside and weakening the position of the ruling party on this issue. With fresh money pouring in from the black market, regionally defined and clientelist powers were poised to exert a strong influence over local constituencies, where financial resources remained scarce. They would dream of eventually influencing national politics.

The 1991 reform may have weakened the rights of indigenous communities, particularly in the backward states of southern Mexico. The steady decline of production in the *ejido* system explains, in large part, the acceleration of rural exodus, partly to Mexican cities but mainly to the United States. It is clear that Mexico has not made a priority of the modernization of agriculture and the communities it supports, except for a series of winter products to be exported to the North American market. The problem of income distribution in the countryside remains untouched, contrary to other areas where the state has more successfully intervened. Mexico is behind Chile in this respect, as millions of rural Mexicans still constitute the bulk of the poor and the marginal.

This situation sparked the Chiapas uprising, which contributed to weakening the central government and the process of adjustment, and thus slowed down the Mexican transition. International actors and NGOs began establishing linkages with local organizations; this proved insufficient. In January 1994, the Zapatista movement or Ejército Zapatista de Liberación Nacional (EZLN), known to have 2,500 fighters under arms and training in the Lacandón jungle, helped land-poor Maya-speaking *campesinos** to seize two hundred thousand hectares from landowners. Taken by surprise, the regime reacted by sending a considerable military force, but then yielded to strong suggestions by NGO negotiators from neighbouring countries to call a truce and engage in discussions with sub-comandante Marcos, a mediator figure, not from Chiapas, but from an educated family of the Mexico City area. Eager to defuse immediate tensions, the government also created a special fund to purchase occupied lands from ranchers and absentee owners, amounting to thirty-one thousand hectares of disputed lands. Simultaneously, the local church (taking the side of the indigenous groups) sponsored a mediating group (Comisión Nacional de Intermediación, CONAI), which began negotiations with EZLN. Support for the insurgents was voiced from Mexico City by the PRD leader Cuauhtemoc Cárdenas and by the human-rights NGOs. However, differences between landlords and the local hierarchy of the PRI, on one side, and peasant organizations, on the other, proved impossible to bridge. The peace process came to a standstill for more than a year because of the government's refusal to recognize some of the agreements reached by its own mediators, particularly the prominent Mexico City mayor, Manuel Camacho Solís, with leaders of EZLN (Latin American Data Bank, 11.12.96). In late 1997, the peace process received further setbacks when a paramilitary group attacked two bishops in San Cristobal de las Casas, while, shortly before Christmas, a mass grave of forty-five slain peasants was discovered in Actéal, in the vicinity of San Cristobal de las Casas.

Despite its adamant appeals for peace and reconciliation, the Zedillo government has until now been unable to challenge the power of local landowners in Chiapas. By late 1997, the situation had gradually reverted to a condition of rampant civil war. This development point to the impracticability of reconciling in the short term the macroeconomic opportunities offered to wealthy *latifundistas* with indigenous rights and the immediate needs of self-supporting,

---

*Mainly Tzotzil and Tzetzal Maya-speaking communities in the outskirts of San Cristobal de Las Casas, and Choles around Tila and Ocosingo in the northeast end of Chiapas.

marginalized communities that survive on arid or poorly irrigated communal lands.

In Chiapas, it is becoming clear that the moderates cannot build on a local basis a viable coalition conducive to compromises and practicable reforms. The political scene is crowded with wealthy landowners, a local *camarilla* of 'hard-liners' closely associated with the ruling PRI and strongly opposed to agrarian reform, and paramilitary groups swiftly mobilizing against the EZLN, who are equated with 'radicals' leading a so-called 'Marxist guerilla' war. The EZLN contends that the administration of President Ernesto Zedillo has not only failed to control the paramilitary organizations but is tacitly supporting such groups (Latin American Data Bank, 11.12.97). This situation is obviously not compatible with the 'systemic view,' but rather is part of a well-documented tradition of polarized politics, common to Latin American peripheral enclaves. As we have seen, this situation has its almost exact parallel in Brazil's São Paulo countryside.

17

The Issue of Science and Education

What of public policies aimed at fostering quality rather than quantity? What of enhancing human resources, which are plentiful and under-used in Latin America, rather than only crops and shipments of commodity goods? Everywhere in Latin America there is growing interest in national (or even regional) systems of higher education, and in public support to science and technological innovation. Investment in science and technology, higher education, and in skill training, along with a new concern for creative human input, are favourite issues for social reformers, and therefore they are at the forefront of the ongoing political agenda. All Latin American nations now share a common perception that little has been achieved so far in terms of a policy area which is of paramount importance. With the possible exception of Brazil, they must admit to inadequacy in this area; no other government has displayed a significant and enduring commitment to these issues.

Orthodox liberalism, especially the local Latin American variety, has made no secret of its absolute indifference towards the enhancement of basic education. As a rule, authoritarian regimes simply do not invest in policies which foster social mobility. The military, sharing no common language with scholars or with educated public opinion, had little interest in enhancing the prestige of the intellectual and scientific communities. However, they knew the importance of fundamental and applied sciences for economic development. For example, the military regime in Brazil maintained a limited scientific community to proceed with its nuclear research program, which had begun in the 1950s. Mexico, though, relied on technological transfers from the United States or other industrialized countries through foreign investment and the *maquiladora* system, and set up no national scientific system of its own. In Chile, scientists fared even worse as General Pinochet's regime depopulated university campuses and physically destroyed humanities and social science faculties. Scholars and teachers were often murdered, dispersed, or forced into exile.

Recent years have seen concerns emerging which exceed the narrow limits of classical market-oriented policies. While these policies have been responsible for some significant successes in the areas of financial stabilization, state budget equilibrium, and debt negotiation, they nonetheless are of no avail in the face of structural problems such as an anaemic research sector, unqualified manpower, weaknesses in the industrial sector, and technological obsolescence. These unresolved problems, worsened by the debt crisis and lack of money, give a fairly good picture of Latin America in the late-1990s. Backward science, an unskilled workforce, primitive Taylorism, and aging industries – even in such a large, industrialized country as Brazil – are among the main problems and may account for the steady decline of these countries on the global market. They may also explain the low economic return on international trade, thus providing a sharp contrast to many East Asian economies.

At this point, our discussion shifts to qualitative development, technological innovation, and human resource enhancement. On this issue, given the level of performance of their respective adjustment programs, Chile, Mexico, and Brazil display three distinct paths to the furthering of their economic model. The case of Chile may be more indicative of changes to come in the field of social policy, since it meets several of the prerequisites for policy consistency in this area. The data gathered so far allow us to establish a sound correlation between the type of political regime and the economic policy pursued in recent years. Let us begin with the so-called Latin American Tiger.

As early as 1987, Chile was experiencing the limits of its liberal stabilization policy as a general philosophy of development. It is true that the overall macroeconomic situation had markedly improved. However, Chilean exports suffered from a weak industrial export base and competition from other copper- or fish-exporting countries. No enduring solution was in sight, even after the strengthening of relationships with selected partners such as Mexico and the United States. Unfair tactics used by U.S. farmers against Chilean products blocked for some time the export of fruit to that country. The extent of poverty was intolerable, mainly in the countryside but also in Santiago's neighbourhoods or *poblaciones*. The relationship between labour and capital was becoming increasingly conflict-ridden as strikes and riots intensified. The usual authoritarian methods could no longer silence the mounting opposition of the majority. Political parties restructured, and a new leadership, drawn mainly from the Christian Democrats, began to challenge the regime. The entire liberal model came to a standstill; the authoritarian regime was going out of fashion.

The electoral defeat of the ultra-right forces in October 1988 made the crisis of the military regime plain to all. In spite of their different political outlooks, the main opposition parties – Christian Democrats, Socialists, the Party for Democracy, and the Radical Party – managed to build a common front at the centre of a highly polarized political spectrum and issued a common political program: the Programa de Concertación, featuring bold policies which they put forward in their respective departments (Hojman, 1990). It came as no surprise that the coalition defeated the military in the December 1989 general election. It has been a surprise, however, to see how faithfully the coalition has adhered to its principles in the implementation of the long-awaited policy. In the context of a multiparty coalition, we are thus entitled to talk of stability and of a strong executive in the new Chilean democracy. It is quite interesting to see that all but two ministers of the Concertación were still in office at the end of President Patricio Aylwin's mandate in December 1993.

The financial and technical aid which this government has been providing to small and medium-sized companies shows a more sophisticated model of development than under the military regime. State agencies like Corporación de Fomento (CORFO) were given momentum for this very purpose. A reform of the professional, technical, and higher educational systems is under discussion. This reform, coupled with a program that offers attractive positions to researchers and scientific personnel returning to the country, may well bring positive returns within a few years. This incipient policy points to a renewed interest on the part of the state in educational matters. However, given the state of decay of infrastructure facilities, from roads and sewage to medical and educational facilities for both basic and higher education, Chile has a long way to go before it reaches developed world standards.

In the mid-1990s, state activism on educational matters is still unfocused in Chile. Lacking prestige, scientific research in universities is poorly funded and expected to establish immediate and direct linkages with private enterprises, in order to enhance the export capacity of the country. This stipulation is not likely to foster independent academic research. As can be seen, the economic model is still overwhelmingly influenced by liberal tenets. It is more interested in achieving some sort of economic performance than in seed investment in fundamental research. It is convenient but insufficient to say that heavy foreign debt payments, under tight deadlines, and poor productivity probably offer the reformers no alternative, well intentioned as they may be. In the absence of a nationally defined blueprint, Chile is likely to encourage indiscriminate private initiatives and seek foreign aid to foster education and rebuild its scientific community, which had been dispersed under the military. The repatriation of local scientists and intellectuals acts as a stimulus to a 'freelance' approach. But the monies allocated to technological modernization have remained insufficient. The creation of the Fondo Nacional de Desarrollo Tecnológico y Productivo (National Development Fund for Technology and Production) is a promising initiative, as is the Fund for Scientific and Technological Development (Fondo de Fomento del Desarrollo Científico y Tecnológico), which divides its budget among the research projects and the scientific and technological services in universities and research institutes. Unfortunately, its budget in 1997 was limited to U.S. $65 million (Chile, Comité Interministerial de Desarrollo Productivo, 1992; Marquez, 1993).

There is no question that the overall Chilean policy is overly characterized by *continuismo*. This policy devotes marked attention to strict budgetary equilibrium, support of local enterprises, and incentives to exports and foreign investment. We must remember that the Chilean democracy is slowly extricating itself from the still over-powerful influence of the military, on one side, and the local oligarchy, on the other; its education policy is witness to this. As an example, the 1980 constitution still channels 2 per cent of the income generated by copper exports into the military complex. The executive has no choice but to accept the so far indefinite postponement of payments due to the state (about U.S. $35 billion) for the 1983 purchase, by private local investors, of the public banking system. In this case, a serious breach of behaviour is at stake in the relationship between state and the private sector. The Chilean Tiger is tamer than a house cat when it comes to bringing some discipline to its own corporate sector. In the meantime, it allows public expenditures in education to only very gradually rise to 13.5 per cent of total spending during the Concertación, from an average of 13.2 per cent in the 1981–90 period (table 27). Not an impressive performance for the Latin American leader in structural adjustment.

As we stated earlier, Mexico, playing the *maquiladora* card from the 1970s on, has been relatively well rewarded in the economic sphere, and intends to reinforce market integration within the North American region. It resorted mainly to market-active measures to stimulate technological innovation. Foreign capital presently plays a large role in its economy, being responsible for monetary as well as technological investments, even in the formerly state-controlled strategic oil and gas sector. Modernized assembly lines in Mexican branches of multinational firms (mainly in electronics and in the automotive industry) have been geared up for full operation since the implementation of NAFTA.

Brazil, as reluctant as ever to fulfil the promises made in the 1988 constitution, remains unresolved on the issue of science and technology. It still questions the validity of a state policy, formulated quite recently, that would enhance the importance of state labs and subsidize technological innovations.

The mediocre results achieved by the state-protected local computer industry are often cited as an example of state non-effectiveness. Strategic concerns inspired the military to protect the local computer industry against foreign competition. Nevertheless, after U.S. threats of further trade retaliation, the relinquishing in the early 1990s of all tariff protection for this sensitive area of local scientific innovation against international (mainly American) competition proved to be a painful and humiliating decision. It left deep scars in the local research community and deepened the feeling that little had survived in the realm of public policy under adjustment for this important area of industrial strategy.

In public, Brazilian corporate associations formally support what they call 'market-oriented' practices, but they are never critical of government support to industry through the national network of state-controlled universities, labs, and local small and medium-sized industries. Given tight budget constraints, the resources allotted to the scientific community are slowly dwindling. Universities rely more heavily on aid from the World Bank (IBRD), the Inter-American Development Bank (IDB), and other international agencies. The market has not sufficiently rewarded the Brazilian economy; few significant players are investing money and technology to stimulate innovation outside the rather thin network of collaboration between state labs and the industrial sector; policy is far from mature in this area. New investments in the country, following the deregulation of the São Paulo stock exchange or Bovespa, are taking what action there is in scientific and technological innovation outside the public education system.

Several factors have led to a redefinition of science and technology policies, which has brought about important structural and institutional changes. Among the main factors are a constant reduction of government investment in R and D in the shape of direct federal allocation of budgets, the withdrawal of federal interventionist practices, and a transfer of decision making to the state level, as foreseen by the 1988 constitution; the decreased productivity of Brazilian industry, the effects of which began to be felt from 1990 on, when protectionist practices were set aside; and, finally, the policy which brought about the privatization of large state enterprises, whose R and D infrastructures had for two decades ensured the diffusion of new technologies for the benefit of a locally owned industry.

There has been, moreover, a weakening of the links between the scientific community and the upper echelons of public administration. The traditional bureaucracy has given way to officials nominated by the political parties themselves, which are not necessarily strong advocates of governmental investment in science and technology. In 1990, President Collor de Mello's government announced its intention to devote 1 to 2 per cent of GDP in the area, but no follow-up occurred, as the budgets passed by Congress since the president's dismissal testify. Brazil, which in 1985 had 52,863 scientists and engineers working as researchers (to South Korea's approximately 77,000 and Mexico's 46,000), is in danger of witnessing the dismantling of its entire national research network, which had been built up at great cost over the last twenty years. While the links between R and D investment, responsibility for innovation, and competitiveness are increasingly placed at the door of private enterprise, the setting up of favourable conditions for collaboration between the research and the production sectors (definition of the legal aspects of contracting, tax incentives, and modes of subsidy) appears increasingly difficult, given the continuing trend of government withdrawal from this previously state-dominated strategic field (Delaunay, 1993).

The 1988 constitution is possibly the main culprit here. In an understandable desire to constrain the power of a potentially authoritarian political centre, the political reformers (of whatever party) insisted on a basic shift in revenues and responsibilities from Brasília to the state governments.

State governments continued to spend freely, partly because they were less exposed to international censure, while more prone to yield to the pressing demands of their political clienteles: the scientific community, labour, landless workers of the MST, and many others defined merely as 'constituencies.' Whereas the federal government has pared back its spending on staff, that of local governments has nearly doubled over the past eight years (*The Economist*, 02.23.93). Under a reformist rule, such spending has resulted in the establishment of significant educational programs. A recent study on the state of Bahia reveals that, in the mid-1980s, two state universities were founded under state governor Waldir Pires, a demonstration of sincere commitment on the part of local reformers to foster higher education. In contrast, the federal government cut its own public funding for science and technology programs in half over the transition period (Carvalho Nunes, 1993).

18

Public Intervention against Marginality

The history of social policy in Chile precedes adjustment. It is worth remembering that the political program put forward by the Unidad Popular government (1970–3) aimed at making profound changes in Chile's economy that would achieve key improvements in redistribution and growth. In the first year of his mandate, President Salvador Allende allowed credit from the central bank to the public sector to increase by 110 per cent. A sharp growth in real wages of 22 per cent and ongoing efforts to keep pace with price inflation, which abruptly rose from 152 per cent in 1972 to 363 per cent in 1973, were made possible by a state-controlled system of wage fixing, in which the United Confederation of Workers (Confederación Unida de la Trabajadores, CUT) became a major partner of state authorities. The president and a close team of advisers were left to achieve this ambitious project themselves, since international actors (lending institutions and the United States alike) made no secret of their aversion for a 'socialist' experiment which was alien to their traditions and which they only wished to undermine. For tactical reasons associated with ideological preferences and the logic of the Cold War, they played against the Chilean redistributive model.

The administration of Salvador Allende devoted considerable energy to job creation. As a result of a significant increase in public sector employment, which grew by 38 per cent in three years, unemployment rates reached their lowest historical level in 1972 (3.1 per cent) and remained well under the 5.0 per cent mark, despite the significant drop in production and export figures which ultimately led to the collapse of the regime in September 1973 (Horton, Ranbar, and Mazundar, 1994: 171–3). In the twilight of the military regime, concern for the poor and action against underdevelopment became avowed priorities of the incoming democratic Concertación government. In the immediate aftermath of its 1989 electoral victory, the coalition government made public an agreement it had managed to secure with the industrial elites concerning a reform of social policy. It issued a blueprint on a whole array of programs, intending to channel money into them from a concurrent reform of the corporate sector, which was expected to yield approximately U.S. $600 million in new funds on a yearly basis. It succeeded in gathering U.S. $788 million in 1992. Reform was overdue: figures showed that, between 1978 and 1988, 80 per cent of the population was impoverished, while only 20 per cent were acknowledging progress in their consumption patterns (Hurtado, 1991: 131–4).

The first steps of the new policy were nevertheless cautious. The Concertación set up two new institutions devoted to carrying out their respective tasks in complementary fashion: the National Fund for Regional Development (Fondo Nacional de Desarrollo Regional, FNDR) and the Solidarity and Social Investment Fund (Fondo de Solidaridad e Inversión Social, FOSIS). From the beginning of talks among the political players, it was out of the question to establish a full-fledged social-coverage policy reminiscent of those in social democratic countries like Scandinavia, France, or Canada. Nonetheless, all parties agreed that something had to be offered up as a tribute to democracy.

Under the terms of this reform, the corporate sector agreed to contribute to the solving of several social problems related to the rise in marginality and indigence. It firmly stated it would not fund assistance and social dependency upon the state. Thus, entrepreneurs rejected universal unemployment insurance or social security coverage in the form of subsidies to workers and needy families. Instead, they favoured the liberal approach because, after so many years of market-oriented policies, it obviously had strong roots in Chile, and even found adamant supporters among the new political elite.

Both FNDR and FOSIS would act as independent semi-private agencies reviewing projects from self-organizing groups who wished to enhance their economic situation and engage in small-scale agricultural production or other types of semi–industrial activities. FOSIS would work directly with local groups, communities, and non-governmental organizations. It would channel financial help to these groups to insure short-term self-sufficiency. The aid would involve municipal and regional governments (there are eleven regions in Chile) and be conditional on significant achievements within tight deadlines. Two priorities would be set for investment: first, access to irrigation for dry underproductive land (Programa de Fomento al Riego Campesino); and, second, a skills-improvement program for marginal younger workers (Concurso de Proyectos de Capacitación y Formación para el Trabajo Destinados à Jóvenes de Sectores Marginales). The state entity CORFO would provide technical support, but the peasants would have to provide their own labour and begin cultivation according to the general principles of the national agriculture policy. Its rules were not particularly stringent. The expected output was to provide accessible and cheap food for rural labourers, thereby providing a partial solution to the enduring problem of manpower scarcity and high prices in most regions of Chile (Flaño, 1991: 154ff). Conscious of the difficulties associated with rural self-organization, FOSIS committed itself to stimulating community participation, fostering local leadership, and providing encouragement to groups. It would also help in formalizing their particular projects. Project proposals would be handled through a competition (*concurso*) process, thus providing individual grants rather than subsidies. One can see how cautious and market-oriented was the new proposed public framework that the Chilean reformers designed for their social intervention program.

For the first year, foreign countries such as Canada, Norway, Holland, and Spain provided, through the network of local Chilean NGOs, the seed money needed to launch the initiative. As early as 1991, however, the program was domestically funded, and the central government supplied money directly to both FNDR and FOSIS. Initial sums were surprisingly small: U.S. $9 million in 1990, U.S. $25 million in 1991, U.S. $30 million in 1992. The authorities made it clear that the program would develop on the basis of its own sound results, and not as a result of some sort of 'socially oriented' ideology.

The year 1992 proved to be more fertile in the area of social policy. The central government devoted 25 per cent of its spending to the health system, followed by education and social housing, with 23 per cent and 12 per cent respectively (Yañez, 1993: 14). Official sources went so far as to state that absolute poverty was almost eradicated in Chile, with more than a million minimal-income households (one out of four) having reached a lower-middle-class standard of living, a statement that has to be independently confirmed (data remain scarce and the sector is poorly surveyed).

Notwithstanding financial limitations, the Concertación was building new hospitals to attend to the needy. It emphasized basic care as well as the development of backward regions. In November 1992, Finance minister Foxley declared that social spending would henceforth represent 30 per cent of total government spending, a figure it never managed to achieve (table 27). However, Chilean reformers paid more than lip-service to the social cause; they did what the general conditions imposed by the constitution allowed them to do. Based on the democratic government's economic strategy, called Crecimiento con equidad, the main features of social liberalism are discernible in Chile. The systemic and the continuity theses are almost compatible in this case. The cautious and gradual inclusion of social concerns and the gradual implementation of social programs, beginning with education, already noticeable in the 1980s, is certainly a result of adjustment strategies achieved before President Aylwin's

Figure 18.1 Income distribution, in per cent, by quintiles (city and suburbs of
Santiago, 1957–93)

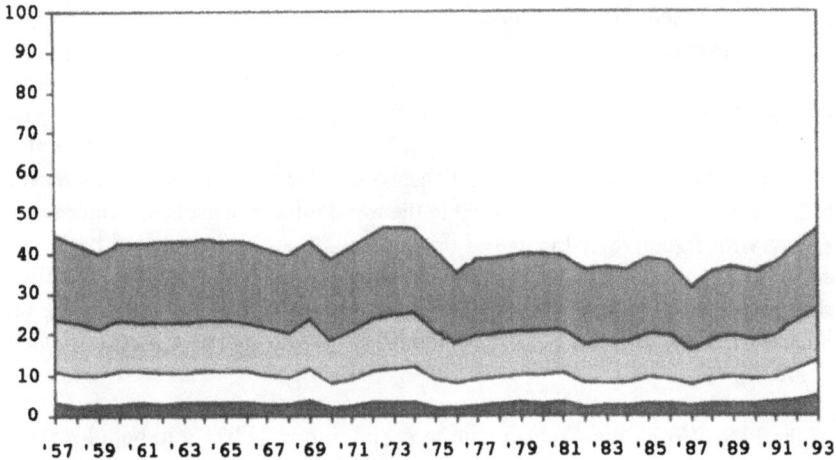

election, and of the rewards provided by these reforms and an active diplomacy.
The combination of these favourable conditions stabilized inflation, strengthened the currency, and liberated more money into the economy. Pressing
demands from civil society, channelled through the state apparatus by party
representatives, could therefore be attended to.

Political mobilization is still low in Chile, as a consequence of prolonged
military repression, and also because the Concertación is itself acting as an
inhibitor of social struggle. Self-discipline being the implicit motto of the new
regime, participating political parties are more interested in securing a significant role in the executive for their respective leaders than in mobilizing their
supporters and militants around sensitive and conflict-ridden issues. In this
sense, Chile exhibits strong indications of extricating itself from the previous
authoritarian regime. Still its recent social policies are a demonstration of the
narrow limits which dominant forces continue to impose upon democratic policy makers. Social and political actors do not seem to play the same active role
as they do in Mexico, and the social agenda suffers from a lack of *rapport de
force*. As a consequence, political action on social issues is remarkably timid,
given the challenges which Chile faces.

Figure 18.1 (data for which were gathered by researchers of the University
of Chile in Santiago) shows that significant changes are taking place in the very
uneven structure of income distribution (Balmaceda and Olguín, 1993): since

1990, a pattern of income distribution is noticeable which parallels the efforts of the Unidad Popular regime (1970–3), and which is in total contrast to the previous military regime (1974–89). More encouraging still are the results of research released by the Instituto Nacional de Estatísticas (INE) in August 1994. Considering that Chile's economy has grown at an average rate of 6 per cent a year in the early 1990s, the INE data show that household incomes increased by 94.9 per cent in nominal terms against cumulative inflation of 51.8 per cent in the same period. The survey points to a real growth of 8.7 per cent in the overall net income received by households. The highest nominal increases, of 86 to 93 per cent, were registered in the middle-income groups, a figure consistent with figure 18.1. Income of the poorest 20 per cent increased by 81 per cent; that of the richest 20 per cent increased by 74 per cent. These findings strengthen the argument that Chile's anti-poverty program may be among the most successful of Latin American countries (*Latin American Weekly Report*, 11.08.94).

Nevertheless, if it is to reach patterns of income distribution similar to those of the First World, the Chilean path to social reform is likely to be a long and thorny one. The first quintile of wealthiest households of the greater Santiago area still controls a little over half of total income, while the three last quintile, with 60 per cent of total households, do not control a quarter of it. Nevertheless, in these last four years, the Concertación has exhibited an ability to play its hand both quietly and boldly. Thus it has achieved some degree of success under its own terms. The Chileans may have something to teach other Latin American countries in the way of designing genuine social policies – a way that encourages democratic participation and politial inclusion, not necessarily economic retribution.

In Mexico, the systemic thesis, which establishes clear connections between structural adjustment policies and the containment of transitional costs, is fully substantiated. Central government expenditures for health, education, and social welfare more than doubled between the 1980s and the 1990s (table 27). Social and political movements may also have played a major role, giving grounds to the 'actionist theory.' Opposition grew throughout the transition period. Both the social democratic PRD and the conservative PAN openly fought for dominance among the shambles of the former one-party system. Civil society mobilized, and state-dominated corporatism slowly dwindled away. Now faced with powerful challengers, the PRI was so determined to stay in power that it resorted to socially oriented policies. Launched in 1989 by President Salinas de Gortari, PRONASOL, which had a budget of U.S. $1.7 billion in 1991 and almost U.S. $2.4 billion in 1992, and which grew steadily until the peso crisis of late 1994, can be interpreted as an attempt to add a social dimension to the Mexican liberal model; as a political antidote to the harsher consequences of rural decay and urban marginality; but also as a desperate response of the PRI to the mounting competition from opposition parties in all states of the nation. In any case, it allowed social policies to come to the forefront of the political agenda.

In the general elections of 1994, the ruling party felt it could not rely on its contentious tactics of the 1988 elections. Thus, the PRONASOL was considered a national 'emergency program' and given considerable attention by PRI authorities. In order to accelerate the selection process of heavily funded infrastructure and social projects to be implemented in backward and overpopulated areas of the country, local task forces, linked directly to the political executive, were sent to marginalized rural and urban communities. This intervention could be helpful in both alleviating extreme poverty and slowing down the current exodus of dispossessed Mexicans to the United States – a pressing demand from Washington. But, with the 1994 electoral deadline looming on the horizon, it is clear that PRONASOL was implemented to rebuild broken bridges between the PRI and an increasingly dissatisfied and autonomous civil society:

As a strategy of governance PRONASOL's fundamental objective is to lay the ground rules for renewed clientelist policies at all levels of government, and especially with popular sectors sympathetic to the left-wing PRD. (Dresser, 1991: 19)

In Brazil, the liberal model put forward by President Collor de Mello was obviously not socially oriented, even if the president had a style of his own that relied heavily on populist rhetoric to influence the people (*povo*) and the marginal (*descamisados*). The extreme polarization between a president formally committed to liberalism, but lacking credibility to achieve this program, and a well-organized opposition, did not offer favourable conditions to deepen the process of adjustment, much less of redistribution. Recent empirical research makes it clear that the conservative forces manipulated the reformist agenda put forward by the new constitution of 1988 in the field of social policy. Their successful action led to an indefinite postponing of reforms. This is possibly the worst manifestation of the impotence of the New Republic (Schneider, 1992; De Melo, 1993). The 'social mobilization' thesis suggests that, contrary to the rural movement that found political expression with the MST and gathered numerous adherents, the urban poor in Brazil were unable to coalesce their many regional interests and set up a national movement. They were left in a situation of political marginality, from which they never succeeded in escaping during the transition period. Public action would be taken over by local entrepreneurs.

Reformers were calling for a drastic change from the previous model. The system had been characterized by excessive bureaucracy, centralization of decision making, the exclusion of the needier, and excessive permeability to corporate interests. The reformers set two general goals: income redistribution and reduction of absolute poverty. They selected three immediate fields of action in Congress: public health, housing, and social security. They set up a department of urban development (Ministerio do Desenvolvimento Urbano, MDU) in the very first years of the new regime, to work in close relationship with the National Housing Bank (BNH) and the local communities. However, the objectives of the Plano Cruzado, the Plano Bresser, and afterwards the Plano Verão of reducing the public debt were not compatible with the mounting demands of reformers for more spending in the area. The whole issue fuelled harsh criticism on the part of the ultra-conservative Right. President Sarney Costa, whom came to be known as a very moderately reformist figure, encouraged this opposition. The extinction of the BNH made housing policy a secondary issue on the political agenda, and President Sarney Costa's close advisers became solely responsible for housing projects. The public was yielding ground to the private, leaving the path open to traditional clientelist practices and political manipulation. President Sarney Costa was not long in building a clientele of his own outside his party, the Brazilian Democratic Movement (PMDB). His network was set up through the allocation of contracts to selected urban developers.

Faced with growing opposition from manipulative leaders and corporate groups (numerous in the early days of the New Republic) favouring personal political strategies in the secure environment of status quo *ex ante*, the reformers were unable to present a unified front. They did not succeed either in building a viable political coalition around the issue of urban poverty. This was particularly clear in the debate which surrounded the reform of the health-care system. Clashes occurred between the representatives of a group of reformist physicians devoted to carrying out the principles of preventive medicine in low-income suburbs and rural areas, on the one side, and the national Association of Hospitals allied with the Brazilian Association for Collective and Work Care (Associação Brasileira de Medecina de Grupo e Empresarial, ABRAMGE) on the other. Both had strong influence in Congress and even with the presidency. The reformers' proposal to secure popular and general access to a new decentralized health system with fresh federal funding antagonized the corporate state agencies. They were simply turned down in Congress, in spite of heavy debate.

The reform of social security was facing a special dilemma. With scarce resources available, universal coverage could be achieved only through the reduction of the monthly payments made to the already retired public employees, obviously a tiny minority among the workforce. Many more retired workers from the private sector already enjoyed special plans and were not affected by a projected policy aimed at providing some sort of coverage to ordinary workers in the informal sector, including, for example, domestic employees, the bulk of agricultural workers, and countless petty traders.

Given the magnitude of this challenge, reformers understandably gathered around what they believed to be a realistic strategy. They fought in Congress for the gradual indexing of social security budgets, and agreed that such budgets should reflect the level of global national wealth, and would depend upon the future successes of the economy. Hence they adhered to a liberal vision which foresaw social security as a long-term dividend derived from a thriving market economy. This concession on their part was of no avail to the cause. To achieve rapid progress on the issue, they either had to accept reducing the already conceded privileges to the majority of pensioners, or downsizing their original goals. Reformers now in office at the Welfare and Social Assistance Institute (Instituto de Administração Financeira da Previdência e Assistência Social, or IAFPAS), the main public agency responsible for social security, suggested a radical reorganization, involving the restructuring of the IAFPAS financial base and the reshaping of its impotent bureaucracy. On this important issue, radicals were rapidly gaining ground over moderates.

Irresolute on this sensitive issue, and reluctant as ever to engage in initiatives that could undermine his thriving political clienteles, President Sarney Costa simply forwarded the whole project to the Constituent Assembly. In this arena, marked by ferocious debates on a whole array of political issues, the project was attacked by influential lobbies such as the powerful national association of Brazilian pensioners (Confederação dos Pensionistas e Aposentados Brasileiros, COPAB), which is 10 million members strong. The entrepreneurs, fearing new taxes on their profits at the outset of foreign competition, also joined the opposition. The social security policy which was finally agreed upon in 1988 was much watered down in comparison to the initial proposal. It still featured some interesting areas of progress in universal access to benefits and greater extent of coverage, basic health services. It is worth remembering that both reforms were inscribed in the new constitution (De Melo, 1993: 119ff).

19

In Search of Political Conditions to Pursue Social Policies

The Brazilian reforms in the area of social policy, symbolic as they may appear to citizens of the First World, are highly illustrative of the main obstacles new democracies meet on the path to structural change. Social reforms require considerable money and must be seen as long-term investments. Chile's Concertación regime was able to undertake a temporary tributary reform that became permanent. This was obviously the price to be paid, for a peaceful transition to democracy, by a delinquent corporate sector too closely acquainted with the military. In return, local industrialists expected to cash in abroad on the enhanced image of their isolated country. Negotiations with the United States and Canada were begun as early as 1995 on the issue of extending NAFTA to South America. Slow progress was achieved on a sensitive issue likely to affect the fragile equilibrium of power between a tiny elite of the wealthier, and the majority of impoverished Chileans. This progress meant a modest although significant reallocation of national revenue in favour of new and less traditional areas of economic activity, and therefore a new wave of state intervention, to which reformers were at first reluctant to commit themselves.

In the case of Chile, what remains of the systemic thesis on democratic transition leading to social policy? Is this country an example of liberal economics spontaneously giving rise to another model of development, often referred to by international agencies as 'development with a human face'? This new orientation will not appear for philanthropic reasons. It will stem from the very necessity for moderate reformers to mobilize long-neglected segments of public opinion around the principles of political inclusion and institutional participation. Its economic rationale is to stimulate an underdeveloped domestic market, expected to participate in the growth of a thriving Chilean consumer goods industry. For the state, the strengthening of a consumer market in the less-favoured and elder strata of the population is not a decisive shift from the previous model based upon income concentration and economic exclusion, but a widening in scope of the earlier adjustment program, aimed at expanding state capacity through tax collection.

It is becoming clear that, to be accepted by a political system still largely dominated by conservative elites (particularly in the case of Chile) and eventually to be carried out with the support of the bureaucracy and other interest groups, this bolder type of reform needs all the power of the political executive acting consistently in the long term under realistic social tenets. The commitment to social development becomes as much a necessary condition to complete and correct the effects of adjustment reforms as was, a decade ago, the determination of politial reformers to undertake them. The cohesion and the credibility of the democratic team are the main premises of any long-lasting political action in the conflict-ridden social arena. The political power of a particular country may stem from economic stability, but the subtle public domain of credibility is related to the executives' behaviour and dexterity. Among states already profiting to a certain extent from earlier reforms and popular sacrifices, Chile makes an interesting case, with its thriving civil organizations, although the overbearing presence of the military certainly accounts for the excessive self-discipline of the decision makers. It is notable that Chilean leaders accepted this discipline independently from the influence of their respective political backgrounds, whether Christian, Centrist, or Socialist.

Self-restrained reformers may end up making endless circles in the political arena. In consequence of the Chilean deadlock on social issues at the outset of Eduardo Frei Ruiz-Tagle's mandate in 1994, political action gradually shifted to matters of constitutional reform, with Christian Democrat and Socialist reformers competing for dominance in Parliament. Christian Democrats have taken a lead in struggling for the removal from the senate and the powerful constitutional tribunal of eight senators and other military representatives appointed by General Pinochet. These individuals, who voted in line with opposition rightist parties – the Partido de Renovación Nacional (PRN), led by deputy Andres Allamand, and the conservative Unión Democrata Independiente (UDI) – have been the major obstacle to passage of much of the social legislation proposed by the two Concertación governments.

The fragile *modus vivendi* between political reformers and unions that had characterized the early phase of the Concertación began to break apart. The unsettled times created mounting polarization. The first victims of the ill-defined *continuismo* were to be the democrats themselves. In addition to the right-wing opposition, problems within the Concertación were now straining the coalition. In April 1996, a power struggle between the Socialists and the Christian Democrats erupted over leadership of the United Confederation of

Workers (CUT), main partner in social policy under Allende. An alliance between Socialists and Communists, a premiere of the Chilean democratic era, resulted in the election of Socialist Roberto Alarcón as CUT president (Latin American Data Bank, 1996). As a result, street demonstrations multiplied in the following months, culminating by late October in a major riot at La Moneda presidential palace that involved the military against thirty thousand municipal employees. The late October municipal elections took place with few problems. However, a shift occurred within the coalition, strengthening the leftist parties and slightly weakening the Christian Democrats.

What is at stake in this conflict is the capacity of reformers of diverging allegiance to intervene in social policy, through their control over the CUT and other state-related institutions. Previously, there had been little evidence from Chile to substantiate the hypothesis that envisions social policy as a response to social unrest. Under the military and during the first Concertación years, the prime intention of what seems to have been a set of preventive measures was to avoid such disturbances by co-opting moderate reformers of the Left and alleviating immediate transition costs. But it is now clear that conditions are rapidly changing. Therefore, our Chilean case reveals that conditions which play a part in the adoption of social policies vary in accordance with the timing of economic adjustment. The process bears with it unpredictable ups and downs, which influence agenda setting and the selection of measures. Under the military, agriculture was the first goal of palliative policies aimed at reducing the impact of transition costs while enhancing competitiveness in a highly strategic sector. To policy makers of the time, redistribution and adjustment were incompatible, while some palliative measures were deemed tolerable. Data show that in the greater Santiago area, and even in the countryside, poverty rose steadily. Redistribution took place, however, from traditional large landowners to thriving middle-class entrepreneurs. Conflict around social demands was postponed for a time, under the strict rules of authoritarianism, to finally break out in 1989 with democratization. At the outset of democracy, an uneasy transition was negotiated between political forces of the moderate Right and Left, thus triggering further compromises around mild social reforms built over former adjustment policies. This was called *continuismo* by local analysts. It is unlikely that such moves were triggered by social mobilization, thus confirming Smith, Acuña, and Gamarra's (1993) hypothesis. They came from a process of inter-elite bargaining, whose momentum was now increasingly difficult to maintain. A mounting competition between the two dominant political forces within the Concertación (Christian Democrats and Socialists) forecasted hard times ahead for a now strained 'social pact' system, meaning slower progress in social policy. To a growing majority of Chileans, with polarization on the rise, the improvements achieved in social policy under President Aylwin remain the more insufficient given that their pace is expected to slow down under President Frei-Tagle. They pale in comparison to the remarkable performance of the economy on regional and world markets. Therefore, it is fair to say that, if 'trickle-down effects' do not spontaneously manifest themselves in the broader social arena, they have to be engineered by actors committed to social development. Is it foreseeable that Chile's social reforms will accelerate in the coming years because social activism associated with the dividends of adjustment is on the rise? The reformers would have to successfully extricate themselves from the authoritarian legacy, so evident in the political institutions inherited from the 1980 constitution. More troublesome is that reformers are now stalled at a crossroads. Mounting expectations may either spur endless political unrest detrimental to economic stability and therefore to redistribution, or contribute to a new social-pact system reminiscent of Northern social democratic countries.

While they have displayed a high level of policy consistency and dedication to liberalizing their economy and investing in social programs, Mexican policy makers have usually lacked political legitimacy. Either too dependent upon powerful PRI party politics, which have developed into even greater confusion with the assassinations of official candidate Luis Donaldo Colosio and party president Francisco Luis Massieu in 1994, and the self-imposed exile of the incumbent leader Salinas de Gortari in 1996; or challenged in their efforts by a slow-acting, partly corrupt bureaucracy, Presidents de la Madrid and Salinas de Gortari remained, in a single-party political arena, closely scrutinized hostages, endowed, it would seem, with the image of apprentice-sorcerers. Both leaders knew all too well that, while it was engaged in the bold adjustment program common to all Latin American countries, Mexico was likely to experience the worst transition costs of all because of its regional unbalances. Civil society, although still in part manipulated by the state apparatus, was on the verge of repudiating the ruling party through which the Mexican revolution's principles were kept alive under the national motto: domestic stability and independence from the United States.

How difficult it was to pursue this program further with makeshift solutions is evidenced by the sharp changes in policy which occurred following the 1982 crisis. These reforms were aimed at redefining the seventy-year-old relationship between the party-state system and civil society. These changes, however, did not propose a credible alternative. It was clear, in the executive's mind, that the fossilized clientelist network was unworthy of trust. The executive expected these worn-out institutions to give way to new, more modern mechanisms of political control. It is unfair to pretend that, in this case, reformist leaders intended to rely solely upon populist politics through a barrage of media, advertising campaigns, and sponsored polls. Presenting an impeccable public image, and with the help of market rewards, they intended to create a new political momentum that would favour a 'controlled process of democratization.' Their use of social policy towards that goal is patent. Throughout the adjustment period, they were granted full control over press and media, where they personalized their respective approaches. Both presidents endlessly sought public support for their reform policies from the active memberships of public institutions, and rewarded accordingly those who gave it.

In Mexico, social policy was essentially state-controlled. So supple was the consecutive presidents' approach to adjustment policies that heterodoxy gradually made its way into the Mexican model. With heterodoxy, social spending was allowed for political reasons, and to keep together the coalition upon which the PRI-dominated national system was based. On the one hand, President de la Madrid more than once yielded to popular calls for food subsidies, and postponed adjustment measures when it became clear that transition costs would seriously weaken his grip over the state apparatus. On the other, President Salinas de Gortari was cautious not to overuse the state's control institutions and thus stir up political opposition. While remaining distant from the PRI network, he and his economic team engineered a shrewd plan to counteract the worst transitional costs associated with adjustment in the countryside, keeping in mind that rural emigration was a main bone of contention between Mexico and the United States. Understandably, his socially oriented Programa Nacional de Solidaridad (PRONASOL) attracted considerable attention and favourable comments from economic reform teams all over Latin America.

Between 1990 and 1994, PRONASOL channelled U.S. $6 billion to rural communities and residents of urban slums, for purposes ranging from sports facilities to infrastructures (sewage, hospitals, and schools) to food distribution (table 27). This rather improvised, although substantial wave of public investment was apparently successful in gaining the PRI political support from the marginal in the 1994 national polls. However, not all regions of Mexico would enjoy this special attention. Far more threatening was the Chiapas situation, which went out of control in January 1994, thus shaking the entire system. The rebellion was to worsen in the months ahead. High PRI officials, such as Manuel Camacho Solis, special envoy, wished to counteract the influence of reactionary PRI *corrigidores** in the region. These local leaders relentlessly resisted the trend towards democratization in the 1980s. Interviews with PRI-related high officials and academics confirmed one of our early hypotheses, that state control under a truly independent economic team is paramount to the success of

---

*Historical term for political affiliates or local rulers.

structural reform, here as in any country. In the rural Chiapas region, the ruling party should have taken decisive steps towards agrarian reform in favour of marginal indigenous communities. When state control over an entire area fails and public decision making is kept in check by regionally defined and clientelist petty powers, reforms are neither proclaimed nor fully implemented. Indigenous activism being on the rise in the 1990s throughout the American hemisphere, clashes were bound to occur. Not surprisingly, they burst out of control in Chiapas and Central America.

When no favourable conditions are in sight, as in the case of Brazil, social reformers can achieve little progress in spite of considerable efforts. President Sarney Costa's administration featured a 'non-decision' strategy, aimed at preventing decisive choices and defusing social conflicts, to achieve short-term personal and electoral objectives. Ultra-conservative lobbies entrenched in defiant business circles still managed to influence politics and manipulate decision making. Under President Sarney Costa, many national leaders were in fact leaders of clienteles representing all regions of the country. Brazil's new republic, poorly rewarded in the area of economic policy, was particularly sensitive to such influences, and therefore impotent on the mounting issues surrounding social policy.

Is Brazil a unique case, hardly comparable to the others? Farther south and away from the United States, its intellectual elites being influenced by Europe, where many refugees found haven from the military regime, this country displays features not found elsewhere in Latin America. As a consequence, radical liberalism never became a major reference for its economic policy or for any of its technical teams, in particular when a challenge to state intervention was raised. Brazil had a strong and enduring tradition in the area of state involvement in the economy, which began under the Brazilian Empire (1822–89) and whose objective was to unify an immense and diverse territory – a tradition that, to a certain extent, brings Brazil into the same category as countries such as Canada, China, or India. As we know, the military regime ordered infrastructure mega-projects. Under the umbrella of an industrial strategy aimed at fostering local capitalism, the business oligopoly was in the habit of diverting revenues, including state revenues, for its own purposes. This tradition left little room for social programs because it throve on low-paid manpower with no social-security coverage or benefits. State subsidies to business remained considerable until the mid-1980s, and declined only recently under President Collor de Mello and afterwards. At the same time, however, market adjustment was making slow progress. Genuine policies were designed, in accordance with the complexities of regional Brazilian politics. Because the power of local oligopolies remained untouched, although increasingly challenged by civil society, conflicts arose between hard-liners and radicals in the countryside. The intensity and influence of an autonomous and vocal opposition to liberal reforms reached high levels. Under these circumstances, the New Republic remained undecided over the need for social policies. Rewards, generated both internally and from opportunities provided by the global market, need to be provided if this nation is to cross the fuzzy border that separates social from traditional capitalism. Brazil has enjoyed no such rewards so far.

Turning back at domestic determinants, the Brazilian constitution of 1988 is the Gordian knot within which one can find all the political influences that arose at the onset of the democratic transition. The constitution stratifies and, to a certain extent, neutralizes conflicting influences. Its text has opened the political system to constant conflicts between Congress and the Presidency, to clientelist practices on the part of the leaders and ill-defined parties, to increasing impotence of the central bureaucracy, and to devolution of power into the hands of local states endowed with very uneven capacities. On the one hand, there is no question that the constitution was nationalist in nature. Integrating some of the features of the nationalist Centre-Left program of President Tancredo Neves (who incidentally died one month after becoming president in 1984), it reduced the role of the federal government to that of a mere coordinator of the economy, and decentralized power in favour of states and cities. It nonetheless protected the bulk of the public sector against privatization, advocating 'national ownership' of the nation's industry, particularly in the strategic sectors of energy and computing. It imposed formal barriers against foreign capital, and tariffs against imports. It formally prohibited the take-over of national assets, public or private, by multinational corporations or through the conversion of parts of the foreign debt into market shares. It adhered to the principle of tariff protection against competition in sensitive areas, such as the burgeoning armament and computer industries. On the other hand, the constitution harked back to older times. It managed to secure the over-representation of the backward *nordeste* to the detriment of the industrialized, more progressive *sudeste*, to foster the network of influence of many political figures of the New Republic: first the president, a native of Maranhão, with a core of new deputies who joined the Partido do Movimento Democrático Brasileiro (PMDB) in the mid-1980s and made it a party of the Centre-Right; second, the leaders of the conservative Frente Liberal (PFL), made up of *nordestino* political leaders prone to clientelist practices. The road was wide open to the worst consequences of periphery politics and regionally defined electoral blocs. These forces, all strongly opposed to the Left, overwhelmed the fragile equilibrium of representation in Congress. They managed to build a common front against the moderate reformers, gathered mainly in the Workers' party (PT) and among 'Tucano' social democrats of the Partido

Social-Democrata Brasileiro (PSDB). This cleavage among the Left certainly explains, in good part, the unpredictable context in which President Collor de Mello, an almost unknown personality from the small state of Alagoas, managed to attract a majority vote in the *nordeste* and unexpectedly came to power in 1989.

If the constitution opened the way to electoral manipulation, the practice of new democratic leaders in office in Brasília frequently conflicted openly with its basic principles. Privatization, debt conversion, new foreign investments, and the phasing out of tariff protection were all, at one time or another, important issues on the local political agenda, in spite of mounting and understandable criticism from the opposition for such constitutional breaches. In time, political conflict became exacerbated, and President Sarney relied increasingly on decrees, which fuelled accusations of *presidencialismo*. By 1992, the conflict between the Presidency and the Congress reached intolerable levels, leading to a procedure of impeachment. President Collor de Mello was later cleared of these accusations for lack of evidence, but the opposition that swiftly gathered against him during his presidency was aimed at terminating a liberal economic policy considered contrary to the principles of the 1988 constitution.

The confusion was not limited to economic issues, but rapidly engulfed the whole area of social policy. The constitution was, on paper, very generous to the underprivileged. It spoke of agrarian reform, of universal social security, of social housing, and a global reform of the health system. Here again, as could be expected from a president and a majority of political figures taken directly from the traditional elites, which are characterized by low party mobilization and personalist politics, reformers faced heavy opposition from conservative politicians present in almost every party in the Constituent Assembly. Taken by surprise and unable to unite, they saw all their efforts sabotaged, and the social concerns which were embedded in the constitution, betrayed. The new policies meant that fresh money would be needed. With the federal state and the regional states facing near-bankruptcy, with the exception of São Paulo, Rio de Janeiro, and Rio Grande do Sul, only the corporate elites were in a position to provide it. In contrast to their Chilean counterparts at the outset of the Concertación, they agreed among themselves that they would not do so.

The goal of the traditional Brazilian elites was, simply put, to avoid a deep tributary reform that would reduce their economic power and make them sponsors of new social policies monitored by socially activist local states; reforms that might lead to new patterns of income distribution detrimental to their hegemonic status in the political system. And so they have fought, successfully so far, to prevent the tributary reform that was to become the main policy and political achievement of the Concertación government in Chile. Under such conditions, it comes as no surprise that, without a tributary reform, many of Brazil's unforeseen woes and public deficits were a result of irresponsible spending by local governments.

Our first observation at this point is that domestic political consistency, including a majority of those conditions expounded in Part One of this book, is a prerequisite to the deepening of the whole process of change. But change is no match for continuity when a given economy is faced with economic stagnation and poor market performance. In a globalized context, successful adjustment is the introductory phase of a deeper process, to which social policies may contribute both at the macroeconomic and local levels. At the same time, educational and social policies are testimonies to a democracy that has achieved a fair degree of internal and institutional stability at the national level. Our second observation is that several, inescapable conditions have to be met to achieve such a level of stability, both economic and institutional. On the one hand, upstream economic reforms are a necessity. They need not be liberal, orthodox, or heterodox, only coherent and feasible, and, most importantly, adapted to local conditions, so that they are practicable in the field. On the other hand, significant successes on the market and a noticeable economic recovery are what make new types of investment possible. Furthermore, in purely political terms, for the survival of a dominant coalition composed of moderates, social investment is a definite priority, to widen the ranks of supporters and voters. Thus, the sufficient conditions for social policy point to institutional coherence within the constitutional framework, a sound party system channelling the behaviour of both leaders and rank and file, and a civil society structured in acceptable, representative associations. A sustainable balance must be established between business and labour or marginal groups competing for influence. Since, in the aftermath of authoritarianism, the representation system remains fairly embryonic, reformers may have found a practicable solution in the form of formalized 'socio-economic pacts' that gather representatives of the state, business organizations, and civil society into *planos* built around precise, rather incremental social goals dependent upon macroeconomic conditions. These pacts would involve fiscal reform, much in line with the Chilean precedent.

In the Latin American context more than anywhere else in the developing world, we envision social policies as acting as a precondition to democratic consolidation, because their main task is to defuse the harsher forms of class conflict that may give impetus to hard-liners and radicals, and to authoritarian alternatives. Mexico and Chile are clear examples of this rule. As an alternative to alleged 'clientelism,' democratic institutions and their collective actors must come to work more independently than before from particular interests, moving from state-controlled 'clientelism' to autonomous 'citizenship.' Social pacts around acceptable compromises may do just that, in the absence of other practicable means to achieve social equilibrium. This option in itself should justify an ample role for reformers acting within the state apparatus, and provide stimulating jobs to a new generation of able democrats, managers, and social visionaries.

Conclusions

Are Democracies Able Policy Makers?

Most authors set the power of the political executive as a strictly necessary condition for successful structural reforms. Nevertheless, the nature and the boundaries of such power have never been made explicit in their writings. Is there sufficient power when there is authoritarian or semi-authoritarian methods of making public decisions? Authoritarianism is only moderately reformist, if at all. Who will dare to affirm that General Pinochet wished to restore a free-network of producer-to-consumer relationships or that he was devoted to freeing both society and the economy from state controls and ideological preferences? We doubt that the principles of a free market economy are even minimally compatible with an authoritarian rule. Some structural reforms may appear liberal because they bear some resemblance to, or converge with, our view of such a policy in a free-market economy. We have seen that, in Latin America, appearances can be deceptive.

Democracies are the only true bearers of a genuine process of structural change. But is democratic rule weak and paralysed by nature? At first glance, new democracies may seem weak and even shaky. However, Remmer (1990) has made an interesting point in stressing that new democracies are not as fragile as common wisdom believes. Using data taken from studies of twenty countries, she has shown that implementation of policies is by no means beyond their capacity, at least as far as stabilization measures are concerned (Remmer, 1990). Nevertheless, democracy as a political process has also to be distinguished from the rule of its transitional leaders, as we have seen in the cases of Brazil and Mexico. During the late 1980s and early 1990s, newly elected presidents all around the world have pretended to undertake liberal reforms. How real and deep is their commitment to structural change? By what means do they convey their beliefs to their party, to the opposition, and to the state apparatus? Are they committed only to stabilization measures aimed at defusing immediate conflict, or do they hold to bolder liberal reforms?

Economic reformers claim that democracies need strong leaders. We have shown that while the commitment of new elites to change has been essential to policy adoption, political reformers had no choice but to compete for dominance against powerful influences that favoured continuity. The more reform leaders are exposed to the forces of reaction, the more they are in urgent need of competent, honest personnel, and the more important it is that they display a fair degree of coherence all through the decision-making process, as was discussed in Part One. In the heat of political debate, new leaders inevitably distance themselves from previous ones. Some may be thoroughly corrupt, many more are less so, and others not at all.

A number of new leaders and their followers in democratic parties are coming together in a shared aversion for a traditional bureaucracy that is both corrupt and authoritarian. New coalitions emerge from 'proto-parties,' such as the Party of the Brazilian Democratic Movement (PMDB), the Chilean Concertación, which unites Christian Democrats and the Socialist party as main players, or the Mexican PRD, reminiscent of the Spanish Unión del Centro Democrático (UCD) or the Partido Socialista Español (PSE). This process may prove arduous and slow since 'proto-parties,' much like Noah's Ark, are by nature transitional structures where the survivors of many distinct political families, united mainly by their opposition to authoritarianism, take refuge for a time while seeking political action. The UCD was in power in Spain from 1977 to 1981, and succumbed to internal dissension among members of the fourteen smaller parties which composed it. The Chilean Concertación, by contrast, although of a similar composition, is a model of internal discipline and fidelity to its initial pragmatic commitments, all the while under intermittent threat of a return to military rule. The Brazilian PSDB, too small to obtain a majority, has had to make a coalition with the right-wing PFL, an unlikely alliance that may account for much of its impotence on social issues.

New parties, in their process of institutionalization, eventually issue political programs. These may be ambiguous and confusing, but they gradually assume distinctive characteristics and come to be known as conservative, liberal, or social democratic programs. When in office, new political leaders are bound to follow a different path from that of their adversaries. New rules are the engines of change, and new parties are the engineers of such rules. In total contrast to traditional Latin American studies, characterized by the blend of Augustinian pessimism and determinist historicism known as 'dependencia' theory, we emphasize the dynamics of change over the weight of tradition. To compound the idea of parties, leaders, and social and other organized groups (whether corporate or labour) marking their distance from corporatism and coming to the forefront of the political arena to express their economic and social demands, we introduced the concept of political mobilization. First, we suggested that political mobilization is an indication that a system of free expression is being restored. Without it, groups could not organize and therefore would not mobilize. However, we expressed concern that such mobilization should be effectively channelled through representative institutions, to ensure that the state remains as autonomous as possible; hence, decision making can resist pressures from particular interests. This is a decisive step towards democratic institutionalization. Secondly, if such representative institutions are more than merely nominal, then socially organized demands should be reflected in the way parties and authorities design political programs and public policies. Findings in Mexico have shown a democracy in transition that is still some distance away from the free expression of social demands. Political programs, whether from the Left or the Right, do not differ drastically, except in their electoral rhetoric. Przeworski accurately observed that, once in power, Justicialista leader Carlos Carlos Menem pursued the same neo-liberal policy as had (less successfully) his conservative Radical party predecessor Raúl Alfonsin.

Policies may differ less in the goals they pursue than in the specific means through which they are conveyed to civil society. Why the means and not the goals themselves? Simply because goals are not always what is at stake. There is a chasm between democratic ideals and day-to-day politics, especially in developing countries. Severe economic conditions, such as inflation, recession, foreign and domestic debt, and many other unfavourable factors, have imposed direct limitations upon new Latin American democracies and therefore on the policies they were about to design. Economic conditions apart, public policy is by no means mechanically predetermined by a concealed and permanent alliance of bureaucrats and entrepreneurs. Domestic opposition from one side or another may bring about either a slowdown or an acceleration of structural reforms. If we can accept the plain fact that new democracies show their difference from authoritarian regimes in the way they engineer and pursue an economic, and eventually a social, policy, notwithstanding all the constraints listed above, then the study of particular policies is of great interest, offering a final indication of what a democracy and its actors really are, and what it can do on its own during the transition process.

As examples of new democracies pursuing their own peculiar paths to structural change, our three cases provide interesting evidence about four closely interconnected phenomena. First, Mexico reveals in considerable detail the grey zone which lies between the logic of an authoritarian rule and that of a democracy. Second, Brazil offers evidence for the fact that a considerable margin of interpretation is open to countries engaged in adjustment policies, if they enjoy a strong international bargaining position. This is not to say that such a favourable position is automatically translated into policy choices. It all depends upon domestic conditions, where personal leadership, political cohesion, technical ability, and social responsiveness undoubtedly play key roles. There is no single structural adjustment rule valid for all countries. Domestic reforms can be implemented either swiftly or gradually. Most authors would agree that a flexible approach is preferable to brutal intervention. Third, Mexico and Brazil evidence the difficulty new democracies experience in extricating themselves from their previous economic strategies and from the dark ground of clientelist practices, to which the central authoritarian bureaucracy had, until the recent past, relegated local politics. Fourth, Brazil features more political mobilization than any other new Latin American democracy. Brazil is living intensely the paradox between liberal reforms, in the sense of state reduction and business *laissez-faire*, on the one hand, and the increasing and unrestrained social demands of the people, on the other. Opposition voices its concerns inside as well as outside the walls of state institutions, questioning the behaviour of politicians, scrutinizing every corner of public service, opposing privatization, and fostering social pacts between industry and workers. To use a paradoxical term for a tropical country where there are no real seasons, the 'Brazilian spring' is well under way and full of lessons for the understanding of the dynamics behind democratic transitions.

Our three case studies also show that, in the process of reconciling capital and labour to build a majority consensus around reform policies, new democratic regimes are poorly equipped to design practical methods. In Brazil, political parties remain anaemic. They desperately seek coalitions to build a majority in their own ranks. To enjoy a majority electoral base, the PSDB, with Cardosa as candidate for the presidency, had to make a surprising coalition with the rightist PFL, particularly strong in the densely populated northeast region. There is no doubt that such an unlikely alliance weakened the president's capacity to pursue social reform, and especially agrarian reform, to which the PFL was adamantly opposed. Under these circumstances, daily political life became frantic in official circles. Decision makers resorted to every possible means to create the illusion of an united executive and a common front, and sought to hide from the public the innumerable concessions they had to make to uneasy, poorly disciplined political allies. The relationship between the new elites and the voter was likely to remain distant, as if two distinct worlds were living separate lives. This is all the more awkward since the costs of reforms should be explained to all, simply because they are shared by all.

As Przeworski has pointed out, transitional costs associated with drastic economic changes are the main threat to new democracies (Przeworski, 1991: 136ff). For such types of changes, the costs are unavoidable. However, alternatives are available to decision makers. They may decide to implement less drastic but also less effective heterodox policies; or they can seek to stimulate political participation and gather more support from the representatives of organized groups. The first choice leads to heterodoxy, while the second opens the road to broader public participation, within the logic of political or 'social pacts.' Heterodoxy may be the only practical way for some countries, such as Brazil. Mexico has usually relied on the second option. We are not suggesting that heterodox policies are desirable in themselves, but they certainly play an essential role in defusing extreme tensions within the political system and civil society. As for political pacts, many authors see them as mere manipulation of public opinion by state executives, through traditional inter-elite bargaining in the context of neo-corporatism.

What, then, about reform through communication channels? We expect that in consolidated democracies, governments must maintain a high level of dialogue with all social groups, which does not mean they must yield to every demand arising in the process. Nonetheless, they are bound to interact with society in a credible way. Less consolidated, transitional democracies desperately seek to establish such a dialogue and to replace corrupt traditional and clientelist networks by new institutions. The survival of reformers depends upon the success of communication strategies. A recent piece of research from Chile is highly suggestive in this regard. Through a public opinion survey, Halpern and Bousquet (1991) explore a path which should enable us to better understand the economic perceptions of the 'average citizen' concerning governmental action on issues such as monetary stabilization, the fight against inflation, unemployment, and training programs. Data from this survey indicate that authoritarian regimes, by interrupting communications with the people for decades and concealing relevant information about the goals and the impact of public policies, have fostered anti-government attitudes, cynicism with regard to government actions, and subjective perceptions of the results. Public opinion became private opinion and centred around highly individual values related to personal achievement and visible wealth in the family environment. 'As a worker (or a trader, or a businessman), am I doing better now, under such and such a policy, than I was before?' is the only question with which individuals concern themselves after seventeen years of military rule. By re-establishing channels of communication, releasing credible information, and welcoming dialogue with institutionalized social groups that will act as 'public-opinion makers,' democratic regimes can eventually win public acceptance for their strategies. This might be the only means by which transitional costs can be democratically dealt with; yet such costs must also remain within acceptable limits. To be credible, public policy has to integrate minimal concerns for equity.

On the Effects of Regional Integration

One policy that shifts decisively away from the authoritarian and nationalistic tradition is the enduring commitment of the new Latin American democracies to regional integration. They appear to share a common diagnosis of the previous state of crisis, based upon the patterns which led to impoverishment. They recognize that industrial strategies based on tight protectionism and discrimination against foreign (especially neighbouring) countries are no longer feasible. For the first time in Latin American history, national elites are accepting the plain fact that, in the medium term, their respective economies will be at least partly regulated through conflict-solving institutions. It is becoming clear that they will engage in economic specialization and create competitive niches for their national products on the wider regional market. They will deregulate transactions between producers and consumers across boundaries. Patterns of investment and of labour-to-capital relationships will thereby be deeply transformed and internationalized. Further, constitutional reforms and legal arrangements in the domestic arena will foster economic interdependence and the free circulation of capital, manpower, and technology throughout the continent in the near future. New Latin American democracies will become prime actors in free trade, from which they expect a better positioning of their economies in a highly competitive world market. This ambitious program will take some time. Hence, the question: what, in the short term, do new democracies seek from regional integration that leads them to hasten the process?

Is free trade a manifestation of globalization of a world market, led by First World countries? Is it related to the liberal reforms undertaken in several Latin American countries – a reward offered by leading countries such as the United States to local champions of reform such as Mexico? The North America Free Trade Agreement initiative fits quite nicely with such a hypothesis. Is regional integration, in Foxley's terms, related to a general tendency towards liberalism, quite independently from structural reform, that is, more as a consequence of an already sophisticated strategy of export diversification, as in Brazil? Or is it, rather, a reaction to globalization, aimed at protecting what is left of the international position of less-developed Southern economies, much in the way Brazilians seem to envision MERCOSUR? What is at stake here is the commitment of new democracies to create a sense of solidarity with their immediate partners.

All formally share common values and goals; however, given their distinct domestic political environments, they might not behave in the same way when faced with economic and social issues. Therein lies the interest of relating regional integration with specific paths to structural change in their respective contexts. We have attempted to show that these individual paths are at times complementary and at times contradictory.

In our view, the problem is far more complex than simply relating reform policies to regime variation, or to the emergence of new political parties, strong leadership, the presence of the military, and cultural values. Our objective has been to relate liberal reforms, possibly structural change conducted by new democracies in their respective domestic arenas, to regional integration experiments, with the example of MERCOSUR in mind. How far can democracies go in creating a sound regional basis for their new realm? How do they manage to seek support from their democratizing neighbours in times of economic hardship, of mounting local opposition, and of threat from the ever-present military? What is likely to serve as such a support? How does a free-trade agreement fit into an already successful and diversified export strategy, as in Brazil and Chile? How feasible is the prospect of developing a thriving regional economy from trade with long-neglected neighbouring countries, which possibly are endowed with few comparative advantages?

The reader notices that there are still more questions than answers for this agenda. There is little literature on such recent issues. We are left with the task of building a bridge over rough seas of unknown depth. With some help from game theory, we have suggested that the motivations of public as well as corporate actors could be a starting point for the understanding of some of the phenomena under scrutiny. We came to see regional integration as an expression of changing attitudes. Obviously, motivations differ among governments pursuing distinct reform strategies indicative of different domestic conditions, which give them either more or less authority to shape the new situation according to their plans. Large economies such as that of Brazil will obviously behave in a different manner from middle-sized economies such as those of Argentina or Chile. There is no question either that less-industrialized Paraguay and Uruguay will be happy with only a few of the trickle-down effects of those measures needed to stimulate an economy the size of Brazil's.

There is a long and thorny road ahead for corporate actors before they come to perceive regional integration as an alternative to the kind of special position they enjoyed within the nest of the authoritarian regime. They will have to overcome structural problems and forge complementary projects from scraps. Data indicate that, given their new freedom of action, entrepreneurs in all MERCOSUR countries are nevertheless engaging in significant joint ventures and demonstrating interest in the regional project. We are probably not dealing here with support from the traditional oligarchy; possibly, it comes from a thriving class of new entrepreneurs. If regional integration as a common project is to be pursued any further, there needs to be a common language shared across boundaries by state and corporate partners. As for any reform in the implementation phase, although the initial impetus must come from the political executives of new democracies, entrepreneurs are the only ones who can make it happen.

The issue of regional integration is more than strictly political. Its outcome depends upon common projects, on the performance of the entrepreneurs themselves, and on a hoped-for common prosperity. Wealth is the only sound basis upon which new democracies can build their hopes of consolidation: not the wealth of a thriving elite with a strong appetite for sophisticated patterns of consumerism; but, rather, a reasonable degree of wealth for the Latin American majority.

On the Scope of Socially Oriented Policies

There is no question that social reforms, not only market adjustment programs, represent the threshold of a democratic consolidation. We have repeatedly stated that democracy is not just a new label for the traditional order (either populist or semi-authoritarian) but the cradle of a sound institutional framework mediating mutually independent social forces. More than formal democratic institutions, new public policies are the true indicators of the profound changes now fully under way in Latin America.

The more they distance themselves from earlier practices, the more these policies foster the hypothesis that democracy is extricating itself from military protectors and the coveted traditional networks of influence suggested by the continuity thesis. Political parties are becoming stronger and more autonomous from interest groups; they respond more effectively to the demands of a wide range of public opinion, where the vote counts; they are able to obtain political benefits from economic recovery and minimize the adverse effects of transition costs and recession. Non-partisan and non-governmental organizations are also thriving all over the sub-hemisphere. They consistently issue demands, which are more or less formally met. Moreover, the realm of the politically possible expands. Under such conditions, the future prospects for democracy in Latin America are more encouraging than we had expected at the outset of this project.

We conclude that the Chilean and Brazilian democracies are at this point moderately consolidated. Chile is gradually turning away from a drastic ortho-dox model and is introducing social concerns not incompatible with the policies of the previous period. Brazil, because it has been unable to pursue an orthodox adjustment program and probably never will, is searching for a genuine model of its own, which sooner or later will have to integrate social concerns not readily discernible at this point. Mexico has adopted and pursued quite consistently and at its own pace a strategy of change that included a preoccupation for containing transition costs, and therefore socially targeted public spending. Semi-authoritarian rules of government will not likely survive the adjustment experiment. The dominant, although much weakened, one-party system is now successfully challenged by opposition forces, which display stronger organizational capacities. Our survey substantiates the hypothesis that the more the reforms proceed (which they have done quite swiftly since the late-1994 peso crisis), the more the PRI loses its traditional dominance over the political arena. Since the stabilization package in the aftermath of the peso crisis involved the termination of PRONASOL, it is probable that the PRI-dominated traditional system will give way to a political alternative in the next election, although it remains unclear whether the right-wing PAN or the centre-left PRD will then gain dominance. Given the respective programs of the two contenders, particularly on social issues, it is predictable that the succession will be marked by increased polarization.

The path of the Brazilian New Republic towards democracy is a more puzzling one. It is this puzzlement which has forced so many scholars into forming a precipitate and unfavourable judgment on its behaviour in times of adjustment. Brazilian presidents from Collor de Mello to Fernando Henrique Cardoso have challenged all accepted views on the way leaders ought to act as reformers, either as market advocates or social democrats. In matters of policy, liberal reformers expect that a straightforward rationality will be consistently followed to its end. Political scientists commit themselves to more modest expectations. To us, it is far more stimulating to envision the comparative analysis of public policies as an empirical exercise that makes it possible to acknowledge the emergence of features related to the rise of democracy in a very complex, rapidly changing environment, where, in the daily practice of politics, the advocates of change come face to face with the deeply entrenched forces of continuity.

Notwithstanding the preliminary stage of this field research, we are firmly convinced that the Brazilian New Republic, Chile under the Concertación, and the alternative political forces now rising in Mexico, while following their comparable although distinct paths, shed some revealing light on the manner in which the democratic debate on economic and social policy has unfolded since the withering away of authoritarianism. Throughout the period under study, we have met individuals and social groups who hold doggedly to an obscure intuition with which they grapple in a language not yet formalized. In a poignant search for practical yet still inaccessible answers, they make it plain that what the military, corrupt technocrats, and political opportunists have marred, only true democrats can now put right.

Appendix: Tables

TABLE 1
Gross Domestic Product (Average Annual Per Cent Growth)

	1973–80	1980–5	1985–90	1990–5	1994	1995[a]	1996[b]
Brazil	6.8	0.7	1.9	2.7	5.8	4.2	3.0
Chile	3.7	0.1	6.4	7.5	4.2	8.5	7.2
Mexico	6.2	1.2	1.6	1.1	3.5	6.9	5.1

Source: World Bank, *Trends in Developing Economies* (various years)
[a]Data from World Bank, *World Development Indicators* (1997)
[b]Selected data from *L'État du monde* (1998)

TABLE 2
Inflation Rates at Consumer Prices (Average Annual Per Cent Growth)

	1973–80	1980–90	1990–5	1994	1995[a]	1996[b]
Brazil	42.9	314.9	1044.8	2668.6	66	11.3
Chile	128.5	20.6	13.6	8.9	8.2	6.6
Mexico	20.3	73.8	15.5	7.1	34.9	27.7

Source: World Bank, *Trends in Developing Economies* (various years)
[a]Data from World Bank, *World Development Indicators* (1997)
[b]Selected data from *L'État du monde* (1998)

TABLE 3
Gross Domestic Investment / GDP

	1981	1985	1986	1987	1988	1989
Brazil	23.1	19.2	19.1	22.3	22.8	22.3
Chile	22.7	13.7	14.6	16.9	17.0	23.6
Mexico	27.4	21.2	18.3	19.3	20.5	21.7

	1990	1991	1992	1993	1994	1995
Brazil	21.5	18.9	17.5	19.2	20.8	21.9
Chile	20.2	21.6	21.3	28.8	26.8	27.4
Mexico	21.9	23.7	24.4	22.8	23.5	19.4

Sources: World Bank, *Trends in Developing Economies*; *World Bank Book*

TABLE 4
Total External Debt (U.S.$ Billions)

	1980	1985	1990	1993	1995
Brazil	71.5	106.7	116.1	132.7	159.1
Chile	12.1	20.2	19.1	20.6	25.6
Mexico	57.4	97.4	96.8	118	165.7

Source: World Bank, *World Development Report* (various years)

TABLE 5
Debt Indicators

	1980	1985	1990	1992	1993	1994
Brazil						
EDT/XGS	313.3	362.1	334.5	318.4	330.9	298.2
EDT/GNP	31.8	50.3	26.0	35.5	34.2	27.9
INT/XGS	34	31.5	6.1	9.3	9.9	12.9
INT/GNP	3.5	4.4	0.5	1.0	1.0	1.2
TDS/XGS	63.5	38.6	22.4	20.7	25.3	31.8
Chile						
EDT/XGS	192.5	434	183	148.9	167.4	151.8
EDT/GNP	45.5	141.7	67.4	46.9	46.8	45.5
INT/XGS	19.0	41.3	17.1	10.4	9.1	8.0
INT/GNP	4.5	13.5	6.3	3.3	2.5	2.4
TDS/XGS	43.1	48.4	26.4	21.0	23.1	19.2
Mexico						
EDT/XGS	250.1	326	238.8	238.6	236.7	228.1
EDT/GNP	30.5	55.2	43.8	34.6	33.2	35.2
INT/XGS	26.5	34.4	16.7	16.0	14.0	14.2
INT/GNP	3.2	5.8	3.1	2.3	2.0	2.2
TDS/XGS	47.8	51.5	25.9	44.3	42.3	33.9

Source: World Bank, *World Debt Tables* (various years)
ETD: Total debt stocks
GNP: Gross national product
INT: Interest payments
TDS: Total debt service
XGS: Exports of goods and services

TABLE 6
IMF Credit / Exports (Ratio in Per Cent)

	1980	1985	1990	1991	1992	1993	1994
Brazil	0.0	15.8	5.0	3.5	1.9	0.7	0.4
Chile	2.0	23.3	11.0	8.2	5.6	3.9	1.9
Mexico	0.0	9.8	15.0	11.9	12.6	9.6	6.6

Source: World Bank, *Trends in Developing Economies* (various years)

TABLE 7
IMF Credit / GDP

	1980	1985	1990	1991	1992	1993	1994
Brazil	0.0	2.1	0.4	0.3	0.2	0.1	0.0
Chile	0.4	6.6	3.8	2.8	1.7	1.0	0.5
Mexico	0.0	1.6	2.7	2.4	1.8	1.3	1.0

Source: World Bank, *Trends in Developing Economies* (various years)

TABLE 8
Official (Government) Creditors / Long-Term Debt

	1980	1985	1990	1991	1992	1993	1994
Brazil	12.3	16.9	29.7	29.0	26.7	24.9	23.6
Chile	14.5	11.9	35.9	35.7	34.2	31.8	33.1
Mexico	10.9	10.0	27.3	29.0	30.5	30.4	27.9

Source: World Bank, *Trends in Developing Economies* (various years)

TABLE 9
Hard Currency Reserves (U.S.$ Billions)

	1980	1985	1990	1992	1993	1994	1995
Brazil							
Reserves excl. gold	5.7	10.6	7.4	22.5	30.6	35.0	
Reserves includ. gold	6.8	11.6	9.2	23.2	31.7	39.5	53.7
Chile							
Reserves excl. gold	3.1	2.4	6.0	9.1	9.6	13.1	
Reserves includ. gold	4.1	2.9	6.7	9.7	10.4	13.8	14.8
Mexico							
Reserves excl. gold	2.9	4.9	9.8	18.9	25.1	6.3[a]	
Reserves includ. gold	4.1	5.6	10.2	19.1	25.3	6.4[a]	16.9

Source: World Bank, *Trends in Developing Economies* (1996)
[a]as a result of the 1994 peso crisis

TABLE 10
Trade Balance (U.S.$ Millions)

	1980	1985	1990	1994	1995
Brazil					
Total exports (FOB)	20.1	25.6	31.4	43.6	46.1
Total imports (CIF)	23.0	13.2	20.7	33.1	49.7
Balance	2.9	12.4	10.7	10.5	3.6
Export price index (1987 = 100)	107	97	111	116	121
Import price index (1987 = 100)	120	79	113	139	148
Terms of trade (1987 = 100)	89	123	98	84	82
Chile					
Total exports (FOB)	4.7	3.8	8.3	11.6	16
Total imports (CIF)	5.5	3.2	7.7	11.8	15.9
Balance	0.8	0.6	0.6	0.2	0.1
Export price index (1987 = 100)	137	85	129	125	161
Import price index (1987 = 100)	104	99	121	113	122
Terms of trade (1987 = 100)	132	86	107	111	132
Mexico					
Total exports (FOB)	15.5	22.9	26.8	40.4	53.4
Total imports (CIF)	18.9	14.5	31.3	58.9	46.3
Balance	3.4	8.4	4.5	18.5	7.1
Export price index (1987 = 100)	145	125	111	110	122
Import price index (1987 = 100)	83	99	113	119	123
Terms of trade (1987 = 100)	175	127	98	93	99

Source: World Bank, *Trends in Developing Economies* (various years)
FOB: free on board
CIF: cost, insurance, and freight

TABLE 11
World Trading Partners (Exports as Percentage of World Total)

	1986	1988	1990	1992	1993	1994	1995
Brazil							
North America	27.6	27.4	26.3	20.8	21.9	21.7	19.8
EEC	25.1	28.3	31.4	29.6	25.7	27.1	27.9
Latin America	12.9	11.1	10.2	21.1	23.6	22.5	21.6
Asia (excl. f. USSR)	16.7	17.5	19.3	18.3	18.0	18.2	20.1
Rest of the world	17.7	15.7	12.8	10.2	10.8	10.5	10.6
Chile							
North America	20.2	18.9	16.9	15.8	16.5	16.2	13.2
EEC	35.8	37.6	36.9	28.5	25.3	22.0	26.1
Latin America	16.9	13.0	12.3	16.7	19.8	21.1	19.2
Asia (excl. f. USSR)	18.9	19.5	24.5	26.0	28.0	29.5	31.5
Rest of the world	8.2	11.0	9.4	13.0	10.4	11.2	10.0
Mexico							
North America	73.0	67.3	71.3	83.2	86.1	87.0	86.3
EEC	11.4	14.6	12.7	7.2	5.0	4.6	4.2
Latin America	3.3	3.9	3.3	3.0	3.1	3.0	3.5
Asia (excl. f. USSR)	8.2	9.4	7.7	3.1	2.5	2.6	2.5
Rest of the world	4.1	4.8	5.0	3.5	3.3	2.8	3.5

Source: United Nations, *International Trade Statistics Yearbook*, Vol. 1 (various years)

TABLE 12
Privatizations in Brazil, 1990–7 (U.S.$ Millions)

	Sales value	Transferred debt	Total
1. Results for 1997			
a) Privatizations monitored by the federal government			
CVRD – auction	3,132	3,559	6,691
CVRD – employees' offer	167	–	167
Light – employees' offer	153	–	153
Escelsa	119	–	119
Tecon 1 – Santos	251	–	251
Meridional	239	–	239
RFFSA (northeast networks)	15	–	15
Subtotal of controlled firms	4,076	3,559	7,635
Minority participation	190	–	190
Total results	4,266	3,559	7,825
b) Privatizations monitored by local states			
Coelba	1,598	213	1,811
CEEE – Norte-Ne	1,486	149	1,635
CEEE – Centro-Oeste	372	64	1,436
Banerj	289	n/a	289
CPFL	2,731	102	2,833
Enersul	565	218	783
Energipe	520	40	560
Cosern	606	112	718
Metrô	262	n/a	262
Others	1,800	601	2,401
Subtotal of privatized firms	11,229	1,499	12,728
Minority participation	2,388	–	2,388
Total results	13,617	1,499	15,116
c) Telecommunications			
	4,639	–	4,639
Total results for 1997 (a + b + c)	22,522	5,058	27,580

TABLE 12 (*Concluded*)
Privatizations in Brazil, 1990–7 (U.S.$ Millions)

	Sales value	Transferred debt	Total
2. Privatization program results from 1990 to 1997			
a) Privatizations monitored by the federal government			
	17,955	8,119	2,074
b) Privatizations monitored by local states			
	15,023	1,863	16,886
c) Telecommunications			
	4,639	–	4,639
Total 1990–7 results	37,617	9,982	47,599

Source: *O Estado de São Paulo*, 12.21.1997: B12

TABLE 13
Balance of Payments (U.S.$ Millions)

	1975	1980	1985	1990	1992	1994	1995
Brazil							
Exports of goods and nfs[a]	9,418	21,857	27,713	33,282	37,674	44,966	47,846
Imports of goods and nfs	14,323	27,788	16,928	23,808	24,983	36,187	53,516
Resource balance	−4,905	−5,931	10,785	9,475	12,691	8,779	−5,670
Net factor income	−2,106	−7,044	−11,213	−13,316	−8,696	−12,58	−15,246
Net current transfers	0	0	0	834	100	2,597	3,513
Current account balance (before official transfers)	−7,011	−12,975	−428	−3,007	4,095	−1,203	−14,404
Financing items (net)	5,946	8,990	1,842	4,000	10,792	8,203	30,450
Changes in net reserve	1,065	3,706	−1,414	−1,119	−14,887	−7,000	−13,046
Chile							
Exports of goods and nfs	1,832	5,968	4,497	10,152	12,539	14,451	19,194
Imports of goods and nfs	2,049	7,023	4,013	9,364	11,694	13,704	17,959
Resource balance	−217	−1,055	484	788	846	747	1,235
Net factor income	−284	−1,029	−2,043	−1,811	−1,860	−1,735	−1,430
Net current transfers	10	0	147	54	111	358	355
Current account balance (before official transfers)	−491	−2,02	−1,413	−969	−903	−630	160
Financing items (net)	206	3,216	1,314	3,192	2,952	3,824	901
Changes in net reserve	285	−1,321	99	−2,368	−2,369	−3,194	−1,061

TABLE 13 (*Concluded*)
Balance of Payments (U.S.$ Millions)

	1975	1980	1985	1990	1992	1994	1995
Mexico							
Exports of goods and nfs	6,066	20,844	27,726	38,351	41,363	50,717	63,532
Imports of goods and nfs	8,466	25,189	19,915	41,214	59,680	71,136	55,203
Resource balance	−2,400	−4,345	7,811	−2,862	−18,317	−20,419	8,329
Net factor income	−1,783	−6,669	−8,996	−7,716	−6,876	−13,012	−12,948
Net current transfers	59	275	1,986	3,465	2,385	4,011	3,965
Current account balance (before official transfers)	−4,124	−10,739	801	7,114	−22,808	−29,419	−655
Financing items (net)	4,327	9,962	−3,222	7,065	24,842	11,028	11,505
Changes in net reserve	−204	738	2,421	49	−2,034	18,391	−10,850

Source: World Bank, *Trends in Developing Economies* (various years)
[a]nfs: non-factor services

TABLE 14
Ownership in 1993 of the 500 Largest Firms in Brazil (by Volume of Sales)

Nationality of ownership	Number of firms	Percentage	Number of the 50 largest firms with same nationality of ownership
Brazilian	353	70	25
American	56	11	9
German	22	4	3
German-American*	1	.02	1
English-Dutch**	1	.02	1
French	10	2	2
English	10	2	2
Italian	10	2	2
Swiss	10	2	1
Dutch	5	1	3
Japanese	6	.09	0
Canadian	1	.02	0
Others	15	3	0

Source: *Exame 20 Anos: Os Melhores e os Maiores*, São Paulo, August 1993: 66–85
*Autolatina, the largest firm of the 500, with Volkswagen and Ford as partners.
The consortium was terminated in 1996.
**Shell

TABLE 15
Real Interest Rates (Annualized)

	1990	1991	1992	1993	1994[a]
Brazil					
On deposits	3.3	34.7	31.9	23	26
On loans	405.8	89.6	196.8	229.1	301
Equiv. in foreign currency	16.4	30.2	40.8	27	54.6
Chile					
On deposits	10.4	3.1	5	5.3	5.7
On loans	17.1	8.4	10	10.8	10.4
Equiv. in foreign currency	24	10.2	16.5	5.9	22.2
Mexico					
On deposits (30 days)	1	1.3	3.4	6.9	5.8
Equiv. in foreign currency	17.2	12.2	14	15.9	8.5

Source: World Bank, *Economic Survey of Latin America and the Caribbean* (1994–5)
[a]preliminary figures

TABLE 16
Countries of Destination for Brazilian Exports, with a List of the Six Main Products of Trade*
(in U.S.$ millions and per cent)

Country	1993	Percentage	1992	Percentage
United States	6,506	20.21	5,745	19.75
Footwear and components	1,171	3.46	802	2.76
Piston engines and parts	268	0.83	233	0.80
Radio systems	248	0.77	221	0.76
Gasoline	221	0.69	118	0.41
Vehicle parts	216	0.67	176	0.61
Orange juice	195	0.61	315	1.09
Argentina	2,928	9.10	2,463	8.47
Vehicle parts	280	0.87	194	0.67
Cars	239	0.74	344	1.19
Piston engines and parts	98	0.31	73	0.25
Steel/iron sheets	96	0.30	183	0.63
Trucks	87	0.27	134	0.46
Iron concentrates	76	0.24	65	0.22
Netherlands	2,108	6.55	2.011	6.91
Soya bran	493	1.53	428	1.47
Ground soya	432	1.34	260	0.90
Orange juice	278	0.86	321	1.11
Aluminum	66	0.21	146	0.50
Copper cathodes	51	0.16	37	0.13
Tobacco leaves	41	0.13	47	0.16
Japan	2,003	6.23	1,867	6.42
Iron concentrates	437	1.36	399	1.37
Aluminum	379	1.18	365	1.25
Ships	136	0.42	133	0.46
Iron binders	100	0.31	97	0.34
Steel/iron sheets	99	0.31	51	0.18
Chicken meat	87	0.27	87	0.30
Germany	1,494	4.64	1,657	5.69
Iron concentrates	282	0.88	347	1.20
Piston engines and parts	90	0.28	107	0.37
Footwear and components	86	0.27	58	0.20
Coffee beans	77	0.24	97	0.33
Tobacco leaves	68	0.21	61	0.20
Furniture and parts	61	0.19	23	0.08

TABLE 16 *(Continued)*
Countries of Destination for Brazilian Exports, with a List of the Six Main Products of Trade*
(in U.S.$ millions and per cent)

Country	1993	Percentage	1992	Percentage
Italy	1,078	3.35	1,223	4.20
Soya bran	158	0.49	102	0.35
Iron concentrates	117	0.36	120	0.41
Coffee beans	110	0.34	96	0.33
Ground soya	60	0.19	50	0.17
Trucks	53	0.17	106	0.31
Cars	43	0.13	52	0.18
Belgium-Lux.	955	2.97	953	3.28
Aluminum	182	0.57	69	0.24
Paper pulp	128	0.40	167	0.58
Orange juice	89	0.28	137	0.47
Iron concentrates	75	0.24	107	0.37
Cigarettes and cigars	66	0.21	62	0.22
Tobacco leaves	43	0.14	24	0.08
United Kingdom	954	2.97	1,011	3.48
Transformed beef meat	109	0.34	117	0.40
Footwear and components	100	0.31	78	0.27
Tobacco leaves	79	0.5	70	0.24
Plywood / pressed wood	38	0.12	29	0.10
Iron concentrates	37	0.12	58	0.20
Piston engines and parts	37	0.12	58	0.20
Chile	938	2.92	733	2.52
Trucks	82	0.26	74	0.26
Vehicle parts	79	0.25	49	0.17
Iron/steel bars	53	0.17	37	0.12
Iron/steel sheets	50	0.16	52	0.18
Cars	36	0.11	58	0.20
Buses	34	0.11	11	0.04
Mexico	835	2.60	920	3.16
Buses	126	0.39	101	0.35
Vehicle parts	89	0.28	95	0.34
Piston engines and parts	69	0.21	90	0.31
Auto bodies	51	0.16	81	0.28
Iron/steel sheets	42	0.13	3	0.15
Gasoline	26	0.08	26	0.09

TABLE 16 (*Concluded*)
Countries of Destination for Brazilian Exports, with a List of the Six Main Products of Trade* (in U.S.$ millions and per cent)

Country	1993	Percentage	1992	Percentage
Paraguay	816	2.54	450	1.55
Cigarettes and cigars	59	0.19	27	0.09
Tires	57	0.18	30	0.10
Bedclothes / table linen	28	0.09	18	0.06
Footwear and components	26	0.08	8	0.03
Refrigerators / freezers	22	0.07	10	0.04
Beer	21	0.07	18	0.07
China	713	2.22	371	1.28
Iron/steel sheets	225	0.31	22	0.08
Iron/steel semi-transformed	130	0.18	14	0.05
Iron/steel bars	123	0.17	2	0.01
Iron concentrates	92	0.12	86	0.30
Copper cathodes/components	23	0.03	23	0.08
Wrapping materials	12	0.04	7	0.03
Other countries	10,850	33.71	9,687	33.29

Source: 'Exportação & Importação,' *Relatorio da Gazeta Mercantil*, 21.12.93
*January to October of respective years

TABLE 17
Trade between Brazil and MERCOSUR Partners (in 1993 U.S.$ Thousands)

	January to June 1993			January to June 1992
	Exports	Imports	Surplus	Surplus
Argentina	1,556,146	1,172,437	383,709	584,587
Paraguay	484,619	110,552	374,097	115,478
Uruguay	336,217	187,926	148,291	22,351
MERCOSUR (A)	2,376,982	1,470,895	906,097	722,416
Total Brazil (B)	18,575,398	11,249,554	7,325,844	7,113,746
Per cent or (A/B)	12.8	13.08		

Sources: Secretaria de Comercio Exterior (for exports); Secrataria da Receita Federal (for imports)

TABLE 18
Trade among MERCOSUR Partners, January to June (U.S.$ Millions)

	1993	1994	% variation
Argentina			
Exports	6,465	7,613	+10.0
Imports	7,130	10,036	+40.8
Trade balance	−665	−2,923	+339.5
Brazil			
Exports	18,503	20,127	+8.8
Imports	11,231	13,682	+21.8
Trade balance	+7,272	+6,445	−11.4
MERCOSUR[a]			
Exports	26,222	28,523	+8.8
Imports	20,145	26,242	+30.3
Trade balance	+6,077	+2,281	−62.5

Source: *Bulletin TIPS* [Sistema de Promoción y de Información
Tecnologica, Gobierno de Argentina] 1/1 (Sept. 1994): 5
[a]Data include regional and outside MERCOSUR trade.

TABLE 19
Brazilian Foreign Investment, by Country of Destination (Cumulative in U.S.$ Millions)

Country	1988	1989	1990	1991	1992[a]
Caiman Islands	212	428	576	1,987	1,988
United States	797	821	874	1,055	1,064
United Kingdom	91	96	198	234	234
Portugal	7	96	110	140	136
Argentina	74	76	77	85	87
Dutch Antilles	79	79	79	79	79
Paraguay	56	56	56	58	58
Chile	57	57	57	50	50
Germany	18	18	18	48	48
Bermuda	39	39	39	39	38
Uruguay	36	36	36	36	36
Other countries	226	239	343	269	278
Total	1,735	2,059	2,506	4,123	4,139

Source: Central Bank of Brazil, in *Gazeta Mercantil*, 13.10.93
[a]from January to June

TABLE 20
Poverty and Social Indicators (Annual Growth Rates)

	1980–90	1990–5	1995–2010[a]
Brazil			
Population	2.0	1.5	1.2
Labour force	3.2	1.6	1.3
Chile			
Population	1.7	1.5	1.1
Labour force	2.7	2.1	2.0
Mexico			
Population	2.3	1.9	1.5
Labour force	3.5	2.8	2.5

Sources: World Bank, *World Development Indicators* (various years)
[a]forecast from World Bank, *World Development Report* (1997)

TABLE 21
Access to Safe Water (Percentage of Population)

	1970–5	1980–5	1988–93	1994–5
Brazil	55.0	75.3	96.1	92.0
Chile	70.0	86.8	86.0	96.0
Mexico	62.0	80.0	77.5	87.0

Sources: World Bank, *Anuario estadistico de América Latina y el Caribe* (1992); *World Development Indicators* (1997) (for 1994–5 data)

TABLE 22
Percentage of Illiterates in the Population Aged Fifteen Years and Over

	1970	1980	1985	1990
Brazil	33.8	25.5	21.5[a]	18.9[a]
Chile	11.0	8.9	7.8[a]	5.7[b]
Mexico	25.8	16	15.3[a]	12.4[b]

Source: ECLAC, *Statistical Yearbook for Latin America and the Caribbean* (1995)
[a]UNESCO estimates
[b]information from 1990 census

TABLE 23
Education: Secondary Enrolment
(Percentage of School-Age Population)

	1970–5	1980–5	1988–93
Brazil	26	36	39
Chile	48	67	72
Mexico	34	53	55

Source: World Bank, *Social Indicators of
Development* (1995)

TABLE 24
Urban Unemployment Rate (Annual Average)

	1970	1980	1985	1990	1991	1992	1993	1994
Brazil[a]	6.5	6.3	5.3	4.3	4.8	5.8	5.4	5.1
Chile[b]	4.1	11.7	17.0	6.5	7.3	5.0	4.1	6.3
Mexico[a]	7.0	4.5	4.4	2.7	2.7	2.8	3.4	3.7

Source: ECLAC, *Statistical Yearbook for Latin America and the Caribbean* (1995)
[a]main urban areas
[b]capital city

TABLE 25
Infant Mortality (per 1,000 Live Births)

	1970	1980	1985	1990	1992	1994	1995
Brazil	95.0	74.2	66.2	59.4	57.0	56.5	54.0
Chile	77.0	33.2	20.4	17.4	17.0	16.9	12.0
Mexico	72.0	52.6	44.2	37.4	35.0	35.2	33.0

Sources: World Bank, *Emerging Capital Markets* (1993), Vol. 2 of *Trends in Developing
Economies* (data extracted from various tables); *Anuario estadístico de América Latina y
el Caribe* (1992); *World Development Indicators* (1997) (for 1970 and 1995 data)

TABLE 26
Life Expectancy at Birth (in Years)

	1970–5	1975–80	1980–5	1985–90	1990–5
Brazil	59.8	61.8	63.3	64.8	66.3
Female advantage	4.6	4.6	4.6	4.7	4.7
Chile	63.6	67.2	70.7	72.7	74.7
Female advantage	6.3	6.3	6.8	7.0	7.0
Mexico	62.6	65.3	67.7	69.8	71.5
Female advantage	4.7	5.4	6.1	6.1	6.1

Sources: ECLAC, *Statistical Yearbook for Latin America and the Caribbean* (1995); World Bank, *Social Indicators of Development* (1995)

TABLE 27
Central Government Expenditure, by Function
(Percentage of Total Expenditure)

	1981–90	1991–5
Brazil		
Health	7.1	5.9
Education	3.9	3.5
Social security and welfare	26.8	30.6
Defence	3.9	2.8
Chile		
Health	7.5	11.4
Education	13.2	13.5
Social security and welfare	37.7	33.5
Defence	11.4	9.2
Mexico		
Health	1.4	3
Education	11.9	23.7
Social security and welfare	10	21
Defence	2.2	3.8

Source: World Bank, *World Development Report* (1997)

TABLE 28
Tax Composition (as Percentage of GDP)

	Direct taxes (on income)	Indirect taxes (on consumption)
Brazil		
1980	3.2	10.8
1993	3.4	5.1
Chile		
1980	5.5	13
1993	6.2	13.3
Mexico		
1980	5.7	4.8
1993	6	7

Source: ECLAC, *Tendencias Econômicas e Sociais na America Latina e no Caribe em Gráficos*, p. 58

TABLE 29
Distribution of Expropriated Land in Chile from 1974 to 1979
(in Per Cent)

Allocations:	38.2
To co-operatives	10.9
To UAFs[a]	20.4
Sold to co-operatives per DL 2.247[b]	6.7
Converted to house lots	0.1
Adjustments[c]	30.1
Transfers:	
To non-profit institutions	17.5
Auctioned per DL 2.247[b]	6.3
Unsolved cases	7.9

Source: Jarvis 1985, table 2.2, p. 12
[a]UAF: agricultural family unit
[b]Decree 2.247
[c]Includes revocations (23.1%) and partial restitutions (7.0%)

References

Agosin, Manuel R. 1993. 'Exportaciones chilenas en la encrucijada.' *Economía y Administración* [Santiago, University of Chile] 115: 23–5.

Armijo, Leslie E., ed. 1995. *Conversations on Democratization and Economic Reform*. Working Papers of the Southern California Seminar, Center for International Studies. Los Angeles: University of Southern California.

Arnaud-Ameller, P. 1989. 'Bilan de l'ALADI (1970–1986).' *Problèmes d'Amérique Latine* 91: 67–87.

Aspe Amella, P., and M. Aguayo Mancera. 1989. 'Convenio del gobierno de México con el Fondo Monetario International.' *Comercio Exterior* 39/4: 355–9.

Balmaceda, Felipe, and Carlos Olguín. 1993. 'Crecimiento y equidad.' *Economía y Administración* [Santiago, University of Chile] 115: 25–46.

Bank of Mexico. 1992. *The Mexican Economy 1992*. Mexico City: Official Documents.

Barthélémy, F. 1991. *Un continent en quête d'unité*. Paris: Éditions ouvrières.

Birdsall, Nancy. 1993. *Social Development Is Economic Development*. Washington, DC: World Bank.

Brazil, Instituto Brasileiro de Geografía e Estatística (IBGE). 1997. *Anuario Estatístico 1996*. Brasília: Fundação Instituto Brasileiro de Geografía e Estatística.

Bresser Pereira, L.C. 1993a. 'Economic Reforms and Economic Growth: Efficiency and Politics in Latin America.' In *Economic Reforms in New Democracies: A Social-Democratic Approach*, ed. L.C. Bresser Pereira, J.M. Maravall, and A. Przeworski, 15–76. Cambridge: Cambridge University Press.

– 1993b. 'Economic Reforms and Cycles of State Intervention.' *World Development* 21/8: 1337–53.

– 1989. 'Expériences d'un gouvernement: Le Ministère des Finances au Brésil.' *Problèmes d'Amérique latine* 93: 49–67.

Bresser Pereira, L.C., J.M. Maravall, and A. Przeworski, eds. 1993. *Economic Reforms in New Democracies: A Social-Democratic Approach*. Cambridge: Cambridge University Press.

Buchanan, P.G. 1989a. 'Plus ça change? A Administração Nacional do Trabalho e a Democracia no Brasil: 1985–1987.' *Dados: Revista de Ciências Sociais* 32/1: 75–123.
– 1986b. 'La crisis del corporatismo mexicano.' *Foro Internacional* 304: 695–735.
Business International Corporation (BIC). 1991. *Privatization in Latin America: New Competitive Opportunities and Challenges.* Washington, DC: BIC.
Camargo, S. de. 1989. 'Brasil-Argentina: A Integração em Questão.' *Contexto Internacional* 9: 45–62.
Carvalho Nunes, José A. 1993. 'A Descentralização das Políticas Públicas de Ciência e Tecnologia: O Caso da Bahia (1983–92).' M.A. Thesis, COPPE/UFRJ, Rio de Janeiro.
Castañeda, Jorge G. 1993. *Utopia Unarmed: The Latin American Left After the Cold War.* New York: Alfred A. Knopf.
Castro Escudero, A. 1991. 'MERCOSUR: El nuevo modelo de integración.' *Comercio Exterior* 41/11: 1041–8.
Chile, Comité Interministerial de Desarrollo Productivo (CIDP). 1992. *Modernización productiva: Instrumentos de fomento y servicio de apoyo.* Santiago: CIDP.
Chile, Corporación de Fomento (CORFO). 1992. *Chile Economic Report (CER).* Santiago and New York: CORFO.
Chudnovsky, D., and F. Porta. 1989. 'En torno a la integracion econômica argentino-brasileña.' *Revista de la CEPAL* 39: 125–45.
Collier, D., ed. 1980. *The New Authoritarianism in Latin America.* Princeton: Princeton University Press.
Comercio Exterior. Monthly review published by the Banco Nacional de Comercio Exterior, Mexico City. 1950–
Costa Vaz, A. 1992. 'The Enterprise for the Americas Initiative Under the Brazilian Perspective.' A Presentation at the 17th Annual Congress of the Latin American Studies Association (LASA).
Couffignal, G. 1990. 'La Grande Faiblesse du syndicalisme mexicain.' *Revue de PIRES* 2: 161–79.
Cox Edwards, A., and S. Edwards. 1992. 'Markets and Democracy, Lessons from Chile.' *World Economy* 15/3: 203–19.
Davila-Villers, D.A. 1992. 'Competition and Co-operation in the River Plate: The Democratic Transition and MERCOSUR.' *Bulletin of Latin American Research* 11/3: 261–77.
Delaunay Maculán, A.M. 1993. 'New Definitions of the Brazilian R and D Policy in the 1980s.' Working Paper of the COPPE/UFRJ, Rio de Janeiro.
De Melo, Marcus André B.C. 1993. 'Anatomia do Fracasso: Intermediação de Interesses e a Reforma das Políticas Sociais na Nova República.' *Dados: Revista de Ciências Sociais* 36/1: 119–62.
Diamond, L., and M.F. Plattner, eds. 1995. *Economic Reform and Democracy.* Balti-

more and London: Johns Hopkins University Press. The papers collected in this book were previously published in *Journal of Democracy* 5/4 (October 1994).

Dos Reis Velloso, J.P. 1990. *A Dívida Externa tem Solução*. São Paulo: Editora Campus.

Drake, Paul. 1989. *The Money Doctor in the Andes: US Advisers, Investors, and Dependent Development in Latin America from World War I to the Great Depression*. Durham, NC: United Kingdom University Press.

Dresser, D. 1991. *Neopopulist Solutions to Liberal Problems: Mexico's National Solidarity Program*. Center for U.S.–Mexican Studies. Current Issue Brief number 3. San Diego: University of California.

Duquette, Michel. 1989. *Grands Seigneurs et Multinationales: L'économie politique de l'éthanol au Brésil*. Montreal: Presses de l'Université de Montréal.

Duquette, M., S. Turcotte, C. Soldevila, and M. Ancelovici. 1994. 'L'intégration régionale dans un contexte néolibéral: les cas du Chili, du Mexique et du Brésil.' In *L'Amérique du Nord et l'Europe communautaire: Intégration économique, intégration sociale?* ed. D. Brunelle et C. Deblock, 113–34. Quebec: Presses de l'Université du Québec.

Echenique, L. Jorge. 1989. 'Les Deux Faces du boom agricole.' *Problèmes d'Amérique Latine* 94: 66–85.

Evans, P. 1992. 'The State as Problem and Solution: Predation, Embedded Autonomy, and Structural Change.' In *The Politics of Economic Adjustment: International Constraints, Distributive Conflicts, and the State*, ed. S. Haggard, and R.P. Kaufman, 139–81. Princeton: Princeton University Press.

Ferrer, A. 1991. 'Argentina y Brasil: Ajuste, crecimiento y integración.' *Comercio Exterior* 41/2: 135–44.

Ffrench-Davis, R., and P. Meller. 1990. *Structural Adjustment and World Bank Conditionality: A Latin American Perspective*. Santiago: Notas técnicas CIEPLAN 137.

Fishlow, Albert. 1995. 'Inequality, Poverty and Growth: Where Do We Stand?' Paper presented at the World Bank Conference on Development Economics, Washington, DC.

Flaño, Nicolas. 1991. 'El fondo de la solidaridad e inversión social: En que estamos pensando?' In *Estado, política social y equilibrio macroeconómico*, 153–64. Santiago: Colección Estudios CIEPLAN.

Fox, J. 1994. 'The Difficult Transition from Clientelism to Citizenship: Lessons from Mexico.' *World Politics* 46/2: 151–84.

Foxley, A. 1983. *Latin American Experiments in Neoconservative Economics*. Berkeley and Los Angeles: University of California Press.

Fritsch, W., and G. Franco. 1992. 'Los avances de la reforma de la politica comercial e industrial en Brasil.' In *Adonde va América Latina? Balance de las Reformas Económicas*, ed. J. Vial, 135–58. Santiago: Editores CIEPLAN.

Gaete, E. 1991. 'El trote hacia el siglo XXI.' *APSI* 400: 51–3.

Gana, E., and A. Bermúdez. 1989. 'Options for Regional Integration.' *UN Economic Commission for Latin America and the Caribbean Review* 37: 79–93.

Garreton, M.A. 1990. 'The Feasibility of Democracy in Chile: Conditions and Challenges.' *Canadian Journal of Latin American and Caribbean Studies* 15/30: 67–84.

Gazeta Mercantil. Rio de Janeiro, São Paulo, and Brasília. Daily financial newspaper.

Grayson, P. 1988. *Oil and the Mexican Foreign Policy.* Princeton: Princeton University Press.

Guzman Organ, C. 1993. 'Sócios para exportar.' *Progreso: La Revista de la Libre Empresa* [Santiago]: (October): 28–9.

Haggard, S. 1990. 'The Political Economy of the Philippine Debt Crisis.' In *Economic Crisis and Policy Choice: The Politics of Adjustment in the Third World*, ed. Joan M. Nelson, 215–56. Princeton: Princeton University Press.

Haggard, S., and S.B. Webb. 1994. 'Building Coalitions for Reform.' In *Voting for Reform: Democracy, Political Liberalization, and Economic Adjusment*, ed. S. Haggard and S.B. Webb, 16–24. Oxford and New York: Oxford University Press and the World Bank.

Haggard, S., and R.P. Kaufman, eds. 1995. *The Political Economy of Democratic Transitions.* Princeton: Princeton University Press.

– 1992. *The Politics of Economic Adjustment: International Constraints, Distributive Conflicts, and the State.* Princeton: Princeton University Press.

Halpern, P., and E. Bousquet. 1991. 'Opiníon pública y política económica: Hacia un modelo de formació de percepciones económicas en transición democrática.' *Colección Estudios CIEPLAN* 33: 123–46.

Hausman, Ricardo. 1984. *Sustaining Reform: What Role for Social Policy?* Washington, DC: Inter-American Development Bank (IDB) 1994.

Hayek, Friedrich A. von. 1943. *The Road to Serfdom.* Chicago: University of Chicago Press.

Helleiner, G.K. 1986. 'Policy-based Program Lending: A Look at the Bank's New Role.' In *Between Two Worlds: The World Bank's Next Decade*, ed. R.E. Feinberg, 47–64. Washington, DC: Overseas Development Counc.

Heredia, Blanca. 1993. 'Making Economic Reform Politically Viable: The Mexican Experience.' In *Democracy, Markets, and Structural Reform in Latin America: Argentina, Bolivia, Brazil, Chile, and Mexico*, ed. W. Smith, C.H. Acuña, and E.A. Gamarra, 265–96. New Brunswick and London: Transaction Publishers.

Hirschman, A. 1992. 'The Case against [One Thing at a Time].' In *Towards a New Development Strategy for Latin America*, ed. Simon Teitel, 13–19. Washington, DC: Inter-American Development Bank.

Hirst, Mónica. 1992. 'Condiciones y motivaciones del proceso de integración en América Latina.' *Integración latinoamericana* (Jan.–Feb.): 19–31.

– 1988. 'Contexto e Estratégia do Programa de Integração Argentina-Brasil.' *Revista de Economia Política* 25/8: 55–71.

Hojman, D.E. 1990. 'Chile after Pinochet: Aylwin's Christian Democrat Economic Policies for the 1990s.' *Bulletin of Latin American Studies* 9/1: 25–47.

Horton, S., R. Ranbar, and D. Mazundar. 1994. *Labor Markets in an Era of Adjustment.* Vol. 2. EDI Development Studies. Washington, DC: Economic Development Institute of the World Bank.

Hufbauer, G.C., and J.J. Scott. 1992. *North American Free Trade: Issues and Recommendations.* Washington, DC: Institute for International Economics.

Hunter, Wendy. 1997. 'Civil-Military Relations in Argentina, Chile, and Peru.' *Political Science Quarterly* 112/3: 453–75.

Hurtado, Alvaro G. 1991. 'Las orientaciones de la política social.' In *Estado, política social, y equilibrio macroeconómico*, 131–40. Santiago: Colección Estudios CIEPLAN.

Infobrazil [Department of External Affairs]. Weekly report on Brazilian affairs. Brasília, São Paulo, and Rio de Janeiro.

International Bank for Reconstruction and Development (The World Bank). *Annual Reports; Anuario estadístico de América Latina y el Caribe; Economic Survey of Latin America and the Caribbean; External Finance for Developing Countries; Trends in Developing Economies; World Debt Tables; World Development Indicators.* Washington, DC: Publications of the World Bank, various years.

Jarvis, L. 1985. *Chilean Agriculture under Military Rule: From Reform to Reaction, 1973–1980.* Berkeley: Institute of International Studies, University of California.

Kahler, M. 1992. 'External Influence, Conditionality, and the Politics of Adjustment.' In *The Politics of Economic Adjustment: International Constraints, Distributive Conflicts, and the State*, ed. S. Haggard and R.R. Kaufman, 89–138. Princeton: Princeton University Press.

– 1990. 'Orthodoxy and Its Alternatives: Explaining Approaches to Stabilization and Adjustment.' In *Economic Crisis and Policy Choice: The Politics of Adjustment in the Third World*, ed. Joan M. Nelson, 33–62. Princeton: Princeton University Press.

Kaufman, Robert R. 1990. 'Stabilization and Adjustment in Argentina, Brazil, and Mexico.' In *Economic Crisis and Policy Choice: The Politics of Adjustment in the Third World*, ed. Joan M. Nelson, 63–112. Princeton: Princeton University Press.

Köves, A., and P. Marer., eds. 1991. *Foreign Economic Liberalization. Transformations in Socialist Countries.* Boulder: Westview Press.

Latin American Data Bank. *Notisur – Latin American Affairs; SourceMex.* Albuquerque: University of New Mexico, various years.

Latin American Weekly Report (LAWR). London, England. Latin American Newsletter, 1986–

Luders, R.J. 1991. 'Massive Disenvesture and Privatization: Lessons from Chile.' *Contemporary Policy Issues* 9: 1–18.

Mammana, Guilherme P. 1994. 'O Financiamento do Setor Elétrico e as Políticas de Meio Ambiente e de Conservação de Energia no Brasil.' Master's Thesis. UNICAMP, Faculty of Mechanical Engineering, Campinas.

Manzetti, L. 1990. 'Argentine-Brazilian Economic Integration: An Early Appraisal.' *Latin American Research Review* 25/3: 109–40.

Maravall, J.M. 1993. 'Politics and Policy: Economic Reforms in Southern Europe.' In *Economic Reforms in New Democracies: A Social-Democratic Approach*, ed. L.C. Bresser Pereira, J.M. Maravall, and A. Przeworski, 77–131. Cambridge: Cambridge University Press.

Maravall, J.M., and J. Santamaria. 1989. 'El cambio político en España y las perspectivas de la democracia.' In *Transiciones desde un gobierno autoritario. 1. Europa Meridional*, ed. G. O'Donnell, P. Schmitter, and L. Whitehead, 112–64. Buenos Aires: Editorial Paidós SAICF.

Marcel, M. 1989. 'La privatización de empresas públicas en Chile, 1985–1988.' In *Privatización: Alcance e implicaciones*, ed. P. Bazdresch and V.L. Urquidi, 93–208. Mexico City: Documento de trabajo CIDE and Centro Tepoztlan.

Mármora, L., and D. Mesner. 1991. 'La integración de Argentina, Brasil y Uruguay: Concepciones, objectivos, resultados.' *Comercio Exterior* 41/2: 155–66.

Marquez Diaz, M. 1993. 'Towards a New R and D Policy in Chile.' Unpublished paper, Programa de Investigaciones en Energia (PRIEN) / University of Chile, Santiago.

Massad, C. 1989. 'A New Integration Strategy.' *United Nations Economic Commission for Latin America and the Caribbean (ECLAC) Review* 37: 95–103.

MERCOSUR, 1991a. 'Acuerdo relativo a un consejo sobre comercio y inversión entre los gobiernos de la República Argentina, la República Federativa del Brasil, la República de Paraguay, la República Oriental de Uruguay, y el gobierno de los Estados Unidos de América.' *Integración Latinoamericana* 7 (July).

– 1991b. 'Argentina-Brazil-Paraguay-Uruguay: Treaty Establishing a Common Market.' *International Legal Materials* 30/4.

Michalopoulos, C. 1987. 'World Bank Programs for Adjustment and Growth.' Paper presented at the Symposium on Growth-Oriented Adjustment Programs, Washington, DC.

Middlebrook, K.J. 1989. 'The Sounds of Silence: Organized Labour's Response to Economic Crisis in Mexico.' *Journal of Latin American Studies* 21/2: 195–220.

– 1986. 'Political Liberalization in an Authoritarian Regime: The Case of Mexico.' In *Transitions from Authoritarian Rule. 3. Latin America*, ed. G. O'Donnell, P. Schmitter, and L. Whitehead, 123–47. Baltimore: Johns Hopkins University Press.

Moneta, C.J. 1992. 'L'Intégration latino-américaine dans le contexte international des années 1990.' *Problèmes d'Amérique Latine* 7: 27–37.

Moniz Bandeira, L.A. 1989. *Brasil / Estados Unidos: A Rivalidade Emergente (1950–1988)*. Rio de Janeiro: Civilização Brasileira.

Montero, Cecilia C. 1992. 'Chili: Les Nouveaux Entrepreneurs.' *Problèmes d'Amérique Latine* 4: 117–35.

Moore, Barrington. 1966. *Social and Economic Origins of Dictatorship and Democracy: Lord and Peasant in the Making of the Modern World*. Boston: Beacon Press.

Mota Menezes, A. Da. 1990. *Do sonho à Realidade: A Integração Latino-Americana*. São Paulo: Alfa Omega.

Muñoz, Oscar, ed. 1993. *Después de las privatizaciones: Hacia el estado regulador*. Santiago: CIEPLAN.

Nelson, Joan M. 1990. 'Introduction: The Politics of Economic Adjustment in Developing Nations.' In *Economic Crisis and Policy Choice: The Politics of Adjustment in the Third World*, ed. Joan M. Nelson, 3–32. Princeton: Princeton University Press.

– ed. 1994a. *A Precarious Balance: Democracy and Economic Reforms in Latin America and Eastern Europe*. Washington, DC: International Center for Economic Growth and Overseas Development Council.

– ed. 1994b. *Intricate Links: Democratization and Market Reforms in Latin America and Eastern Europe*. Washington, DC: Transaction Publishers and Overseas Development Council.

O'Donnell, Guillermo. 1994. 'Delegative Democracy?' *Journal of Democracy* 5/1: 55–69.

– 1993. 'On the State, Democratization, and Some Conceptual Problems: A Latin American View.' *World Development* 21/8: 1355–69.

O'Donnell, G., L. Whitehead, and P. Schmitter. 1986. *Transitions from Authoritarian Rule*. Vol. 1: *Prospects for Democracy*. Vol. 2: *Southern Europe*. Vol. 3: *Latin America*. Vol. 4: *Comparative Perspectives*. Vol. 5: *Tentative Conclusions about Uncertain Democracies*. Baltimore and London: Johns Hopkin University Press 1986.

Ominami, C., and R. Madrid. 1989. 'Le Développement du secteur exportateur: Éléments d'évaluation.' *Problèmes d'Amérique Latine* 94: 85–101.

Peña, F. 1989. 'L'Intégration économique et les défis actuels de l'Amérique latine.' *Problèmes d'Amérique Latine* 91: 47–65.

Perroux, F. 1991. *L'économie du XXe siècle*. Grenoble: Presses de l'Université de Grenoble.

Petras, J., and S. Vieux. 1992. 'Twentieth-Century Liberals, Inheritors of the Exploits of Columbus.' *Latin American Perspectives* 19/3: 25–46.

Prévot Shapira, M.F. 1989. 'Le Mexique après les élections: La Chute d'un cacique syndical.' *Problèmes d'Amérique Latine* 92: 67–74.

Proença, Jr., D., ed. 1993. *Uma Avaliação da Indústria Bélica Brasileira: Defesa, Indústria e Tecnologia*. Rio de Janeiro: UFRJ / Grupo de Estudios Estratégicos / Forum de Ciência e Cultura.

Przeworski, Adam. 1991. *Democracy and the Market: Political and Economic Reforms in Eastern Europe and Latin America.* Cambridge: Cambridge University Press.
– ed. 1995. *Sustainable Democracy.* Cambridge: Cambridge University Press.
Psacharopoulos, George, ed. 1993. *Poverty and Income Distribution in Latin America: The Story of the 1980s.* Washington, DC: World Bank, Technical Department of the Latin American Commission.
Ramos, J. 1986. *Neoconservative Economics in the Southern Cone of Latin America, 1973–1983.* Baltimore and London: Johns Hopkin University Press.
Remmer, Karen L. 1993. 'The Political Economy of Election in Latin America.' *American Political Science Review* 87/3: 393–407.
– 1992–3. 'The Process of Democratization in Latin America.' *Studies in Comparative International Development* 27/4: 3–24.
– 1990. 'Democracy and Economic Crisis: The Latin American Experience.' *World Politics* 42/3: 315–35.
Ritter, A.R.M. 1990. 'Developement Strategy and Structural Adjusment in Chile, 1973–1990.' *Canadian Journal of Latin American and Caribbean Studies* 15/30: 159–92.
Rosenthal, G. 1990. *Un examen crítico a treinta años de integración en América latina.* Notas sobre la economía y el desarrollo 499. Santiago: United Nations Economic Commission for Latin America and the Caribbean (ECLAC).
Ross, John. 1996. 'Amid Poor Prospects for Peace in 1997, Zapatista National Liberation Army Observes Third Anniversary of Uprising.' In *Latin American Data Bank – SourceMex* 7/47. Albuquerque: University of New Mexico.
Sáez, Raúl E. 1993. 'Las privatizaciones de empresas in Chile.' In *Después de las privatizaciones: Hacia el estado regulador,* ed. Oscar, Muñoz, 75–110. Santiago: Editores CIEPLAN.
Salman, Paulina T. 1992. 'Chile invadiendo: El conquistador de mercados.' *Engenieros: Revista del Colegio de Engenieros de Chile* 125: 31–6.
Scheuer, Luiz A. 1993. 'El Brasil como en sus mejores días.' *Progreso: La Revista de la Libre Empresa* [Santiago] 39: 3–5.
Schneider, B.R. 1992. 'A privatização no Governo Collor: Triunfo do Liberalismo o Colapso do Estado Desenvolvimentista?' *Revista de Economía Política* 12/1: 5–18.
– 1988. 'Partly for Sale: Privatization and State Strength in Brazil and Mexico.' *Journal of Interamerican Studies and World Affairs* 30/4: 89–116.
Schwartz, G. 1990. 'Stabilization Policies under Political Transition: Reform versus Adjustment in Brazil, 1985–89.' *The Developing Economics* 28/1: 16–41.
Silva, E. 1992. 'The Political Economy of Chile's Transition to Democracy: From Radicals to Pragmatic Neoliberal Policies.' In *The Struggle for Democracy in Chile, 1982–88,* ed. Paul Drake and Ivan Jaksic, 98–127. Lincoln: University of Nebraska Press.

Simonen Ass. Mercosul. 1992. *O Desafio do Marketing de Integração*. São Paulo: Makron Books do Brasil.

Smith, William C., Carlos H. Acuña, and Eduardo A.Gamarra. *Democracy, Markets, and Structural Reform in Latin America: Argentina, Bolivia, Brazil, Chile and Mexico*. New Brunswick and London: Transaction Publishers / North-South Center.

Spencer, Erich R. 1991. 'Segunda étapa exportadora: Hacia los negocios internacionales.' *Economía y administración* [Santiago, University of Chile] 98: 15–8.

Stallings, B. 1992. 'International Influence on Economic Policy: Debt, Stabilization, and Structural Reform.' In *The Politics of Economic Adjustment: International Constraints, Distributive Conflicts, and the State*, ed. S. Haggard, and R.P. Kaufman, 41–88. Princeton: Princeton University Press.

Stallings, B., and R. Kaufman. 1989. *Debt and Democracy in Latin America*. London: Westview Press.

Streeten, Paul. 1993. 'Markets and States: Against Minimalism.' *World Development* 21/8: 1281–8.

Tavares de Almeida, M.H. 1987. 'Pacto Social na Nova República.' *Presença* 3: 10–23.

Tavares de Araujo, J. 1990a. 'Integración económica en América del Norte y en el Cono Sur.' *Comercio Exterior* 40/8: 739–44.

– 1990b. *A Política Comercial Brasileira e a Integração Latino-Americana*. Texto para Discussão 233. Rio de Janeiro: UFRJ / Instituto de Economia Industrial.

– 1988. *O Programa de Integração Argentina-Brasil e as Tendencias Atuais da Economia Mundial*. Texto para Discussão 181. Rio de Janeiro: UFRJ / Instituto de Economia Industrial.

Teichman, J. 1992. 'The Mexican State and the Political Implications of Economic Restructuring.' *Latin American Perspectives* 19/2: 88–104.

Thorp, Rosemary, and Laurence Whitehead, eds. 1987. *Latin American Debt and the Adjustment Crisis*. Pittsburgh: University of Pittsburgh Press.

Tironi, E.B. 1982. *El modelo liberal chileno y su implantación*. Santiago: CED Documento de Trabajo 1.

United Nations, Economic Commission for Latin America and the Caribbean (ECLAC). 1997. *The Equity Gap*. 1997.

– 1996. *Tendencias Econômicas e Sociais na America Latina e no Caribe em Gráficos*. Rio de Janeiro: ECLAC/CEPAL-IBGE – Corecon Rio.

– 1991a. 'La iniciativa para las Américas: un examen inicial.' *Comercio Exterior* 41/2: 206–13.

– 1991b. 'La evolución reciente de los procesos de integración en América latina y el Caribe.' In *Notas sobre la economía y el desarrollo*, 509–10.

Urías Brambila, H. 1991. 'Iberoamérica hacia el nuevo milénio.' *Comercio Exterior* 41/8: 68–75.

Vial, Joaquin, ed. 1992. *Adonde va América Latina? Balance de las reformas económicas.* Santiago: Editores CIEPLAN.

Weintraub, S. 1990. *A Marriage of Convenience: Relations between Mexico and the United States.* New York and Oxford: Oxford University Press.

Werneck, R.F. 1992. 'El primer ano del programa brasileño de privatizacion.' In *Adonde va América Latina?* ed. J. Vial, 263–76. Santiago: Editores CIEPLAN.

– 1989. 'Aspectos Macroeconómicos da Privatização no Brasil.' *Pesquisa e Planejamento Económico* 19/2: 277–308.

Whitehead, Lawrence. 1993. 'On Reform of the State and Regulation of the Market.' *World Development* 21/8: 1371–93.

– 1992. 'The Alternatives to Liberal Democracy: A Latin American Perspective.' *Political Studies* 40/2: 146–59.

– 1986. 'Bolivia's Failed Democratization, 1977–1980.' In *Transitions from Authoritarian Rule. 3. Latin America,* ed. G. O'Donnell, P. Schmitter, and L. Whitehead, 49–71. Baltimore: Johns Hopkin University Press.

Williamson, John, ed. 1994. *The Political Economy of Policy Reform.* Washington, DC: Institute for International Economics.

– 1993. 'Democracy and the Washington Consensus.' *World Development* 21/8: 1329–36.

Williamson, John, and S. Haggard. 'The Political Conditions for Economic Reform.' In *The Political Economy of Policy Reform,* ed. John Williamson, 527–96. Washington, DC: Institute for International Economics.

Wonnacott, R.J. 1991. *The Economics of Overlapping Free Trade Areas and the Mexican Challenge.* Toronto: C.D. Howe Institute and National Planning Association of the United States.

Yañez, José. 1993. 'Precisiones numéricas sobre la reforma tributária.' *Economia y Administración* [Santiago, University of Chile] 115: 13–6.

Yotopoulos, P.A. 1989. 'The Rip Tide of Privatization: Lessons from Chile.' *World Development* 17/5: 663–702.

Zantman, A. 1990. 'Le Plan Collor dans l'oeil du cyclone: De l'hyperinflation à l'hyperstagflation.' *Problèmes d'Amérique Latine* 97: 73–97.

Index